DATE DUE

THE CENTER HOLDS

The Power Struggle Inside the Rehnquist Court

JAMES F. SIMON

SIMON & SCHUSTER

New York   London   Toronto
Sydney   Tokyo   Singapore

SCHUSTER
Rockefeller Center
1230 Avenue of the Americas
New York, NY 10020

Designed by Levavi & Levavi

Manufactured in the United States of America

1 3 5 7 9 10 8 6 4 2

Library of Congress Cataloging-in-Publication Data
Simon, James F.
The center holds : the power struggle inside the Rehnquist Court /
James F. Simon
p.   cm.
Includes bibliographical references and index.
1. United States. Supreme Court—History. 2. Civil rights—United
States—History. 3. Political questions and judicial power—United States—
History. I. Title.
KF8742.S55 1995
347.73'26—dc20
[347.30735]   95-11729
                                                                      CIP

ISBN 0-684-80293-7

For Marcia,
Sara, Lauren, Tom, Elyse, David,
and for my mother, Natalie Simon

CONTENTS

PART IV
THE FIRST AMENDMENT   235

EPILOGUE   295

**Justice William
O. Douglas**
Court Term:
1939–1975

**Justice William
J. Brennan, Jr.**
Court Term:
1956–1990

**Justice Potter
Stewart**
Court Term:
1958–1981

**Justice Byron
R. White**
Court Term:
1962–1993

**Justice
Thurgood
Marshall**
Court Term:
1967–1991

**Chief Justice
Warren E.
Burger**
Court Term:
1969–1986

**Justice Harry A.
Blackmun**
Court Term:
1970–1994

**Justice Lewis F.
Powell, Jr.**
Court Term:
1972–1987

JUSTICES

**Chief Justice
William H.
Rehnquist**
Court Term:
1972–1986
(Associate Justice)
1986–present
(Chief Justice)

**Justice John
Paul Stevens**
Court Term:
1975–present

**Justice Sandra
Day O'Connor**
Court Term:
1981–present

**Justice Antonin
E. Scalia**
Court Term:
1986–present

**Justice Anthony
M. Kennedy**
Court Term:
1988–present

**Justice David H.
Souter**
Court Term:
1990–present

**Justice Clarence
Thomas**
Court Term:
1991–present

**Justice Ruth
Bader Ginsburg**
Court Term:
1993–present

**Justice Stephen
G. Breyer**
Court Term:
1994–present

PREFACE

This is the story of a conservative judicial revolution that failed. It was led by the chief justice of the United States, William H. Rehnquist, and actively encouraged by two conservative Republican presidents, Ronald Reagan and George Bush. They hoped to reverse the liberal legacy of the Warren Court and its successor, the Burger Court, which had given the broadest scope in the nation's history to the civil rights and civil liberties protections of the Bill of Rights and the Fourteenth Amendment. With five Court appointments, and an aggressive litigation strategy developed by their Justice Department attorneys, Reagan and Bush had good reason to think they would succeed.

The numbers alone strongly suggested that the Supreme Court of the United States of the late 1980s and early '90s would take a radical turn to the right in all crucial areas of civil rights and liberties. By 1988, after the confirmation of Reagan's third appointee, Anthony M. Kennedy, Chief Justice Rehnquist operated with a working conservative majority: Rehnquist himself, the three Reagan appointees—Sandra Day O'Connor, Antonin E. Scalia, and Kennedy—and Byron R. White, a conservative holdover from the Warren and Burger Courts. Bush's appointments of David H. Souter and Clarence Thomas put the finishing touches on what conservatives inside, and outside, the Administration expected to be a solid majority that would steer the Court safely to the right into the next century.

But predicting the Court's direction has always been a hazardous business. In part, this is because the life-tenured justices often find a voice independent of their presidential sponsors once they are securely ensconced on the Court. That independence is encouraged by the Court's internal decision-making process itself, which is the central focus of this book. A justice's firm vote in private conference may change as a result of a colleague's argument put forward in conversation, internal memorandum or draft opinion. That happened many times in the cases discussed in this book. In most instances, the center held largely because liberal justices were able to attract support from their more moderate brethren who refused to join the ideologically committed conservatives on the right wing of the Court.

The cases discussed in this book reveal the justices' intense internal struggles during some of the most critical moments of the Rehnquist Court. They were selected in four crucial areas of civil rights and civil liberties—racial discrimination, abortion, criminal law and First Amendment freedoms. The book is not meant to be a definitive study of the Rehnquist Court. Instead, it focuses on key decisions that, to a significant degree, have determined the Court's philosophical direction. In most, but not all, of the cases, there is a clear-cut confrontation between the old liberal order and the emerging conservative majority. Although the cases are divided by topic into separate sections, the justices' deliberations take place concurrently over the same time period, primarily from the Court's October 1986 term, the first in which Rehnquist presided as chief justice, through the October 1991 term, the first in which Clarence Thomas sat on the Court.

Part One is devoted to a single case, in which a black woman, Brenda Patterson, charged that she had been harassed and ultimately fired from her job because of her race. The Court's conservatives, led by Chief Justice Rehnquist, not only rejected Patterson's racial harassment claim, but threatened to overturn two key civil rights precedents of the Warren and Burger Court eras that had provided broad legal remedies for racial minorities. The Patterson case, then, represented a threshold opportunity for the conservatives to take the Court in an entirely new constitutional direction in the civil rights field.

Part Two begins with the most controversial decision of the modern Court era, *Roe v. Wade,* and the efforts of the conservatives on the Rehnquist Court to overrule it. The issue was furiously joined by *Roe*'s author, Harry A. Blackmun, but was ultimately decided by three appointees of Reagan and Bush: Kennedy, O'Connor and Souter. Their secret collaboration, unknown to any of their colleagues, produced a joint opinion in the 1992 case of *Planned Parenthood of Southeastern Pennsylvania v. Casey,* which preserved *Roe*—and stunned Rehnquist and Scalia.

In Part Three, Justice Thurgood Marshall pleads for the life of a death row inmate, Warren McCleskey, whose case came before the Rehnquist Court three times between 1986 and 1991. This part, which follows the conservative turn of the Court in criminal cases, also reveals the private deliberations and many changes in the positions of the justices in the case of convicted murderer Oreste Fulminante. Fulminante's case raised serious constitutional issues about the admissibility of a coerced confession into evidence and gave the chief justice his long-awaited chance to overturn a venerable Court doctrine mandating the reversal of any conviction in which a coerced confession had been introduced at trial.

Part Four focuses on First Amendment issues in which the Reagan and Bush Administrations made a major effort to convert their political successes into constitutional victories. Both Reagan and Bush had encouraged the increased use of religious symbols and traditions in public life; their Justice Department attorneys, in turn, attempted to persuade the Court to abandon an important series of modern Court precedents that drew a clear constitutional line between church and state. As occurred in the *Casey* decision, the three conservative centrists—Kennedy, O'Connor and Souter—clung to the center and frustrated the plans of the chief justice and his colleagues, Scalia and Thomas. The other First Amendment cases covered in the section deal with the emotional issue of whether the Constitution's protection of speech extends to flag-burning, which was defended as symbolic political expression. President Bush, who had made patriotism a major issue in his 1988 presidential campaign, offered his view, backed by a proposed constitutional amendment—flag-burning should be punished. But the justices did not take positions as predictable on the issue as did the president.

Leading the conservative charge in all of the cases was Chief Justice Rehnquist, who was appointed to the Court by President Richard M. Nixon in 1971 and quickly earned the reputation as the most outspoken conservative on the Court in more than a quarter of a century. As associate justice and later as chief justice, he consistently supported government regulations of individual liberties and rejected the civil rights claims of racial minorities.

His most reliable supporter among pre-Reagan appointees was Byron White, who had been named to the Court by President John F. Kennedy in 1962. White owed his appointment, in part, to his effectiveness as Robert Kennedy's deputy attorney general in enforcing the nation's civil rights laws with stern, understated authority. On the Court, White retained his sternness but little of the Kennedy Administration's liberal spirit. Instead, he wrote sharp dissents to many of the Warren and Burger Courts' most expansive libertarian decisions.

President Reagan's first appointee, Sandra Day O'Connor, had been a law school classmate of Rehnquist's at Stanford. Although not as rigidly conservative in her ideology as Rehnquist, O'Connor frequently supported government regulation of civil liberties, was openly critical of *Roe v. Wade* and opposed liberal interpretations of federal laws and the Fourteenth Amendment that provided broad legal remedies to racial minorities.

Antonin Scalia, appointed to the Court by Reagan the same day in 1986 that Rehnquist was elevated to the chief justiceship, championed a strong conservative ideology that matched well with Rehnquist's. With supreme confidence in his ability to defend his views, Scalia was eager to take on all comers in the privacy of the justices' conferences, in open court and in his uncompromising judicial opinions.

The Reagan Administration was confident that it had provided Chief Justice Rehnquist with the crucial fifth vote for his conservative majority with the appointment of Judge Anthony Kennedy of the U.S. Court of Appeals for the Ninth Circuit. Kennedy's name had surfaced after the bruising, unsuccessful confirmation fight over Judge Robert Bork. Although he was no ideologue, Kennedy exhibited a steady, cautious conservative record as a federal appeals judge.

The challenge to the Court's diminishing liberal wing after Kennedy's confirmation was daunting. But led by one of the modern Supreme Court's most influential liberals,* Justice William J. Brennan, Jr., it was by no means a lost cause. Through the 1970s and most of the '80s, Brennan had, improbably, continued to mold and preserve

---

* The term "liberal" is used to describe a justice who gives the political branches a wide latitude to effect social and economic reform while insisting that those political branches do not interfere with individual rights. Conceding the deficiencies in such one-word descriptions of judicial

majorities for his expansive constitutional vision of civil rights and liberties on an increasingly conservative Court.

Steadfastly supporting Brennan was the Court's first African-American, Thurgood Marshall. A legendary civil rights attorney before his Court appointment by President Lyndon B. Johnson in 1967, Marshall continued to argue on the Court that the justices were obligated to provide broad constitutional protections to racial and other minorities in American society.

The third member of what became the liberal opposition to the Rehnquist Court's conservatives was Harry Blackmun. Appointed by President Nixon in 1970, Blackmun came to the Court with a fine legal reputation as a trusts and estates attorney in his native Minnesota and later as a moderately conservative judge on the U.S. Court of Appeals for the Eighth Circuit. But Blackmun shocked the nation, and his sponsors, by writing the Court's opinion in *Roe v. Wade*. After *Roe*, Blackmun gradually shifted to the liberal side of the Court; by 1994, his last year on the Court, Blackmun frequently articulated the most liberal position of any justice on a wide range of civil rights and liberties issues.

The final member of the group opposing the Rehnquist Court conservatives, John Paul Stevens, had confounded a media eager to place the justices into neatly defined categories since his appointment by President Gerald R. Ford in 1975. Stevens's approach to constitutional law defied judicial labels. But the more assertive conservatives on the Rehnquist Court became, the more Stevens reacted with his own spirited opinions, usually aligned with those of his liberal colleagues.

After Brennan's retirement in 1990 and Marshall's a year later, President Bush appeared to solidify the conservative majority with two appointments. Little was known about his first appointee, David

---

philosophies, Chief Justice Rehnquist, nonetheless, distinguished "liberal" from "conservative" in describing the justices of the Court in the early 1950s this way: "[Justice] Black was regarded as a member of the Court's 'liberal' wing—a wing that conceded to the government great authority under the Constitution to regulate economic matters, but which sharply circumscribed that power when it was pitted against claims of individual rights. The 'conservative' wing, on the other hand, was inclined to sustain governmental action pretty much across the board."

Souter, who had toiled quietly on the trial and state appellate courts in New Hampshire. The same could not be said for Bush's second appointee, Clarence Thomas, whose aggressively conservative political pronouncements while chairman of the Equal Employment Opportunity Commission in the 1980s had endeared him to both Reagan and Bush.

Three other justices are important to this story. The first is Justice William O. Douglas, appointed to the Court by President Franklin D. Roosevelt in 1939, whose lobbying among his colleagues during their deliberations in *Roe v. Wade* influenced the outcome. Finally, Justices Ruth Bader Ginsburg and Stephen G. Breyer, named to the Court by President Bill Clinton, became the first appointees by a Democratic president in a quarter century, interrupting a succession of ten Republican-appointed justices. Although it is too early to predict exactly where Ginsburg and Breyer will fit in ideologically, their prior records of moderation as federal appeals court judges virtually assure the denouement of the conservatives' revolution.

What follows is an in-depth account of the justices on the Rehnquist Court as they fight for majorities in the privacy of their conference room and in their chambers, in their confidential internal memoranda, notes and letters, and in unpublished draft opinions. It is not always a tidy process, nor do the individual justices always act wisely or with good humor. But the justices' intensity as they argue— sometimes diplomatically, other times with bare-knuckled determination—underscores the importance of their work. For the outcome of their struggles, as they well knew, would profoundly affect the future of the Court and the nation.

PART I

RACE

What the Court declines to snatch with one hand, it
steals with the other. . . . The Court's fine phrases about
our commitment to the eradication of racial
discrimination seem to count for little in practice. When
it comes to deciding whether a civil rights statute should
be construed to further that commitment, the fine
phrases disappear, replaced by a formalistic method of
interpretation antithetical to Congress' vision of a
society in which contractual opportunities are equal.

From the unpublished dissent of
JUSTICE WILLIAM J. BRENNAN, JR.,
in *Patterson v. McLean Credit Union* (1989)

CHAPTER ONE

A DREAM
DESTROYED

The case of Brenda Patterson, a black woman who charged that she had been harassed and subsequently fired from her job with a North Carolina credit union because of her race, was argued before the Rehnquist Court in February 1988 and reargued eight months later. The fact that the justices selected the case for oral argument in the first place, from more than five thousand petitions, suggests that Brenda Patterson had raised an important legal question that the Court wanted to resolve. After reading the thick legal briefs from the opposing sides in the case and hearing a full hour's oral argument, the justices requested a second set of briefs and arguments.

As is true of most important decisions of the Supreme Court of the United States, the case of *Patterson v. McLean Credit Union* began quietly, when Brenda Patterson went to a lawyer after she was dismissed from her clerical job at the McLean Credit Union in Winston-Salem, North Carolina. Patterson told attorney Harvey Kennedy that her white supervisor had continually harassed her during her ten-year employment at the credit union, had given her demeaning tasks (dusting, for example) not assigned to white workers, and had denied her training and promotion opportunities that were offered to white employees with Patterson's skills.

Kennedy brought a lawsuit on behalf of Patterson against the credit union in federal district court in North Carolina, charging racial harassment, failure to promote and, finally, the illegal discharge of Brenda Patterson in violation of the nation's first civil rights statute, the Civil Rights Act of 1866. That post–Civil War statute gave blacks the same rights "to make and enforce contracts . . . as is enjoyed by white citizens."

There were several pragmatic reasons for Harvey Kennedy to bring the Patterson suit under the 1866 law rather than Title VII of the Civil Rights Act of 1964. Procedurally, the older statute offered Patterson advantages, including a jury trial. Most importantly, the 1866 law provided Patterson with a substantially greater monetary remedy; she could sue the McLean Credit Union for back pay beyond the two-year limitation of Title VII as well as for punitive damages, which were barred by the 1964 statute.

The federal district court judge rejected Patterson's argument that racial harassment could be the basis for a claim under the 1866 statute, and a jury then ruled against Patterson on her promotion and discharge claims. Patterson later lost her appeal in the U.S. Court of Appeals for the Fourth Circuit, setting the stage for the first Supreme Court argument on February 29, 1988.

Two months after the Court first heard arguments in the Patterson case, a narrow Court majority made up of its five most conservative members (Rehnquist, White, O'Connor, Scalia and Kennedy) created panic among civil rights attorneys by requesting reargument in *Patterson* to focus on the issue of whether a critical twelve-year-old civil rights precedent, *Runyon v. McCrary*, should be overruled. *Runyon* had held that the 1866 civil rights statute applied to racial discrimination by a private employer as well as to official acts of racial discrimination by state governments. If the Court's conservatives carried through on their threat to reverse *Runyon*, private employment discrimination could be cut off from the statute's coverage.

The Rehnquist Court announcement was perceived by the civil rights community as not only a threat to Brenda Patterson's case, which was bad enough, but to one of the foundation decisions in civil rights in which the Warren and Burger Courts had provided broad legal protection for racial minorities over three decades. Most of the amicus curiae (friend of the court) legal briefs filed by interested parties that flooded into the justices' chambers during the summer of 1988—not just from civil rights organizations, but also from Reconstruction-era historians, constitutional scholars, congressmen and state attorneys general—urged the Court to preserve *Runyon*.

When the justices heard the second argument in *Patterson* on October 12, 1988, the case was already being heralded by the media as the most important of the term. *Patterson* not only presented an unusual claim of racial harassment in the workplace, but, more broadly, offered the Rehnquist Court its first serious opportunity to chart a new course in civil rights law.

The tension among observers and lawyers in the courtroom was palpable during the second *Patterson* oral argument, and that tension later carried over to the justices, who fought over the resolution of the *Patterson* case for the next eight months. For *Patterson* presented the Court's conservatives with the chance to exploit their majority and pursue a very different civil rights path from the one that had been taken by the Court for more than three decades. Civil rights progress during that period was often measured by decisions of the modern Supreme Court, which had become the crucial American institution in the civil rights revolution, inspiring, nurturing and finally demanding the elimination of racial discrimination in the United States.

Many of those civil rights decisions had been written by the Court's liberal leader, Justice William Brennan. But with the *Patterson* challenge, it appeared that the Court's leadership, and Brennan's, might be relegated to no more than a historic relic. By the late 1980s, the nation's political mood had turned decidedly more conservative, and so had the Supreme Court, led by Chief Justice Rehnquist. The struggle within the Court over *Patterson*, therefore, assumed large political, as well as judicial, overtones. If the chief justice succeeded in achieving his conservative goals, the Court would no longer offer the broad-based legal remedies that had been crucial to modern civil rights reform.

•   •   •

In 1972, the year that Brenda Patterson was hired by the McLean Credit Union, her new job had been a cause of celebration for Brenda and her husband, Marshall Patterson. Marshall then worked as a driver for the United Parcel Service in Winston-Salem, North Carolina, and Brenda had come home with the exciting news that she had just been offered the position of accounting clerk by McLean. The second income was important to the Pattersons, but working for the credit union of the McLean Trucking Company was a source of particular pride to Brenda. She and her husband had often driven by the McLean building on Waughtown Street in Winston-Salem, and Brenda had told Marshall that she wanted to work there someday.

A graduate of Winston-Salem State University and a former part-time elementary school teacher, Brenda Patterson accepted the job as an accounting clerk with the expectation that she would advance to more interesting and lucrative positions within the company. One of only ten general employees, Brenda was confident that she would make a satisfying career at McLean. "It was a happy time for her," Marshall Patterson remembered, "because a dream had come true."

When she was hired, Brenda Patterson was the only black working at the credit union. At her initial interview with her supervisor, Robert Stevenson, she had been warned that she "was going to be working with all white women . . . and that probably they wouldn't like me because they weren't used to working with blacks." Stevenson himself had had no experience working with blacks.

After only a few months at McLean, Brenda Patterson's initial joy dissipated. With increasing regularity, she came home to tell her husband that her supervisor was piling work on her but not on his white employees. She also told Marshall that her supervisor would stare at her for several minutes at a time, and this made her nervous and unable to concentrate on her work. Brenda said that she was singled out for criticism in staff meetings while white employees were criticized in private.

It seemed to Brenda Patterson that she was regularly asked to help white clerical workers but that nobody helped her. Patterson noticed that she alone among McLean's credit union employees was asked to sweep and dust the office. After she complained about the amount of work she was given, Brenda was told by Robert Stevenson that "blacks are known to work slower than whites by nature." Later she remembered that Stevenson made the same point by telling her that "some animals [are] faster than other animals."

As the work piled up and criticism by her supervisor intensified, Brenda Patterson's health began to deteriorate. Marshall Patterson watched his wife, whom he described as a pleasant, happy person, transformed into a nervous and depressed spouse who frequently burst into tears when she told him about her difficulties at work. "She felt humiliated, downgraded, because she didn't feel that she was being treated as the other girls were treated," Marshall recalled. Despite her difficulties, Brenda continued to work at McLean, hoping that conditions would change.

One Monday in July 1982, Brenda reported to work as usual. She received written notice during the day that she had been laid off, after ten years of service.

"Well, is this it? You're just laid off like that?" Marshall asked when his wife came home.

"Yes," she replied.

"Well, maybe they'll call you back in a week or so," Marshall said, reassuringly.

The callback never came.

In 1984, Brenda Patterson's lawsuit was heard in federal district court in North Carolina, but her best hope for success was quickly dispelled by the trial judge, even before her case went to the jury. The judge rejected Patterson's argument that her claim of racial harassment was covered by the 1866 civil rights law, ruling that such harassment on the job, even if proven, was not prohibited by the language of the statute. The judge, having thrown out Patterson's racial harassment charge, instructed the jury that Patterson was required to show that she was better qualified than the white employee who was promoted to the job that Patterson believed she deserved. The jury then ruled against Patterson on both her promotion and discharge claims, and the U.S. Court of Appeals for the Fourth Circuit affirmed the lower court decision.

Harvey Kennedy, who had argued Patterson's case in both the trial and appeals courts, turned the case over to attorney Penda Hair of the NAACP Legal Defense Fund,* who petitioned the Supreme Court to hear Patterson's appeal. The justices granted the petition, and the case of *Patterson v. McLean Credit Union* was placed on the Court's docket for the October 1987 term.†

On his fourth day as an associate justice of the Supreme Court of the United States, Anthony Kennedy (who had been nominated to the Court by President Reagan soon after Judge Robert Bork, Reagan's first choice to replace Justice Lewis F. Powell, Jr., failed to be confirmed by the Senate) listened with his brethren to attorney Penda Hair present the first argument to the justices on behalf of Brenda Patterson. "Mr. Chief Justice, and may it please the Court," Hair began at 10:57 A.M. on February 29, 1988. For the next twenty-seven minutes (she reserved three minutes for rebuttal), Hair attempted to persuade the justices that the McLean Credit Union had violated Brenda Patterson's rights under the Civil Rights Act of 1866 by subjecting her to racial harassment during her ten years at the company, as well as passing over her for promotion because of her race in favor of a white employee and later discharging her.

Hair spent virtually her entire thirty minutes of oral argument attacking the notion that the 1866 civil rights statute's contract provisions, which prohibited racial discrimination in the "making" of a contract, failed to cover the harassment that Brenda Patterson claimed in her lawsuit. "Under that rule of law," Hair asserted, "a black worker can get a job but the black worker can be forced to pay a very high price for that job in loss of dignity. The employer can say to that worker, 'We'll hire you, but only if you submit to conditions of employment in which you are humiliated and demeaned because of your race.' It is our position that that type of condition of employment is exactly the badge of inferiority that the Thirteenth Amendment and

---

* The organization is formally known as the NAACP Legal Defense and Educational Fund, Inc.

† Each Court term officially begins on the first Monday in October and usually extends through the following June when the justices announce their final decisions of the term.

Section 1981 [the designation of the relevant provisions of the 1866 statute in the United States Code] were designed to prohibit."

Hair continued, "It seems obvious that a black worker who is forced to pay the price of stigma and humiliation in order to be able to perform the contract that she has a right to enter into, has not been afforded the same right to make and enforce a contract. The black worker's exercise of her right to make and enforce a contract has been burdened because of her race."

Chief Justice Rehnquist was the first to interrupt Hair's argument, questioning the attorney's assertion that racial harassment on the job was covered by the statute. "Well, I don't think that's crystal clear, Ms. Hair," said Rehnquist, "that the consequences like you're talking about, bad as they may be, necessarily implicate the right to make or enforce a contract. That certainly isn't an inclusive term."

"I would submit," Hair responded, "that the right to make and enforce a contract has to include the right to perform that contract free from racial discrimination. If the right to make and enforce a contract is going to have any meaning, it must include the right not to be burdened in the exercise of your right to make and enforce a contract free of racial discrimination."

Again, Rehnquist challenged Hair. "Well, supposing, Ms. Hair," he said, "that an employer hires a black person for $50,000 and the black person later comes in and says, well, if I'd been white, they would have paid me $55,000, so they violated 1981. Do you think if the black employee can prove that, that's a cause of action under 1981?"

"Yes, I do," Hair replied without hesitation. "It's racial discrimination in pay."

Later in her oral argument, Hair was closely questioned by Justices Scalia, White, O'Connor and Kennedy. Did the language in the 1866 statute—"to make and enforce contracts"—specifically cover Patterson's situation? Instead of seeking redress in the federal courts, should Brenda Patterson have sued for breach of contract in the state courts of North Carolina? Or in federal court under Title VII of the Civil Rights Act of 1964?

Throughout the interrogation, Hair held to her argument that the racial harassment charged by Patterson was exactly the kind of conduct that the Reconstructionist Congress in 1866 intended to reach by its civil rights statute and, further, that her interpretation was consistent with modern Court decisions interpreting the legislative history and intention of the statute's framers.

When it was his turn to speak to the justices, H. Lee Davis, Jr., attorney for the McLean Credit Union, argued that Brenda Patterson's claims were unsubstantiated in fact but, in any case, could not succeed under the precise contract language of Section 1981. If Brenda Patterson had a legitimate grievance, Davis maintained, she should have sought redress under Title VII of the 1964 Civil Rights Act or, alternatively, under North Carolina contract law.

During Davis's argument, Kennedy asked the question whose answer would prove crucial to his initial vote, at the justices' conference, in support of Brenda Patterson's claim—and to his later reversal. Assume, Kennedy told Davis, "that a contract is made in good faith and in non-discriminatory terms, but once its performance begins, highly onerous conditions are imposed. Are there no conditions that are so onerous that 1981 would not be implicated?" With his question, Kennedy suggested that racial harassment on the job might be so egregious and pervasive (as Patterson had claimed) that it effectively undercut the "making" of an employment contract, even if the employer had originally entered into the contract in good faith.

Davis responded to Kennedy's question by arguing that the language of the statute barred *any* coverage of conditions, such as racial harassment on the job, that were separate and independent of the initial "making" of the contract.

Throughout his argument, the McLean Credit Union's attorney concentrated on technical distinctions in the law which, finally, was too much for Thurgood Marshall. After Davis contended that no evidence had been submitted to the jury that proved his client had failed to promote Brenda Patterson because of her race, Marshall interrupted.

"Mr. Davis, you talk of no evidence," said Marshall. "What about this flat statement [in the trial record] that negroes are just slower than everybody else? What do you do with that?"

"Justice Marshall," Davis responded, "I dare say that there are few of us in the world who have not had a prejudiced thought or made a prejudiced comment, whether the prejudice may be racial, sexual or religious or some other basis."

Marshall persisted. "What do you do?" he asked. "Just ignore it [the evidence]?"

"No, sir, I don't think you ignore it," Davis said. But the attorney noted that the statement that "negroes are just slower" was challenged by the defense at trial, and in any case, it was only a single piece of evidence.

"Well, you've taken 87 other pieces," said Marshall. "I'm going to take one piece. And I still haven't gotten an answer to it."

Pressed on the point, Davis stuck to his position that there was not sufficient evidence, including the statement that Marshall had quoted, to conclude that McLean's failure to promote Patterson was racially motivated.

As was his custom, the senior justice on the Court, William J. Brennan, Jr., asked no questions during oral argument. He would have much to say to his colleagues in the privacy of their conference room three days after the oral argument, when the justices argued and first voted in the case of *Patterson v. McLean Credit Union*. A memorandum of law, which had been prepared by a Brennan law clerk for the *Patterson* case, argued that the appellate court's ruling against Brenda Patterson should be reversed. Support for that position, it was pointed out in the memorandum, came from the Court's decision in *Runyon v. McCrary*, the 1976 Court decision that had held that Section 1981 prohibited racial discrimination by a private employer in making a contract, even though the plain language of the statute appeared to be directed exclusively against discriminatory state laws. The clerk's memorandum emphasized that the Court in both *Runyon* and *Jones v. Mayer*, a 1968 Warren Court decision ruling that the 1866 law applied to racial discrimination in the sale of private property, had declared that the language of the post–Civil War statute should be construed broadly in light of the legislative history. Brennan had voted with the majority in *Runyon* and *Jones* and had long contended that historical documents revealed the post–Civil War Congress's intention to cover private as well as public acts of racial discrimination.

The memorandum argued that Brenda Patterson was entitled to bring a legal action even if there was, in a strict technical sense, no direct interference with a contract right. So long as racially motivated conduct reduced the enjoyment of the contract relationship, and Patterson's harassment charge certainly qualified, the memorandum concluded that she had a claim under Section 1981.

Chief Justice Rehnquist presided over the conference on March 2.* His views on what he considered the correct interpretation of the Civil Rights Act of 1866 were a matter of public record and well known to his colleagues before he entered the justices' conference room to discuss *Patterson*. He had been an associate justice on the Court when *Runyon v. McCrary* was decided in 1976 and had joined the dissenting opinion, written by Justice White. Rehnquist believed that the statute applied only to the official actions of state governments. It was a narrow interpretation that in the modern day, when state governments rarely were found guilty of official racial discrimination, would have effectively rendered the statute meaningless. Rehnquist had shown no inclination to change his original *Runyon* position and, indeed, had told his colleagues in a conference discussion of a civil rights case during his first year as chief justice that he still believed that *Runyon* and the earlier Warren Court decision, *Jones v. Mayer*, which also applied the 1866 statute to private conduct, were wrongly decided.

Patterson presented the chief justice with his first realistic opportunity to reverse *Runyon*, since he now counted four other conservative members of the Court who might agree with him. At the judicial conference on March 2, 1988, in which the justices considered the *Patterson* case, Rehnquist began by discussing the facts and legal issues in *Patterson*. But then he raised the issue of whether *Runyon* should

---

* As chief justice, Rehnquist is entitled to preside at the justices' conferences, present the facts and legal issues in each case and assign the majority opinion if he is a member of the majority. If the chief justice is in dissent, the senior justice in the majority assigns the majority opinion.

be overruled, even though the issue had not been briefed or argued by either counsel in the *Patterson* case. Having raised the issue on his own, Rehnquist reiterated his view that *Runyon* was wrong and Justice White's dissent, which he had joined, was correct. The chief left no doubt where he stood; Justice Marshall, who took notes at the conference, recorded Rehnquist's position as "overrule *Runyon*."

At the *Patterson* conference, Justice White, who had dissented in both *Runyon* and the earlier *Jones* decision, reminded his colleagues that both decisions "still live." He then discussed the issue that the chief justice had raised: should *Runyon* be overruled? Justice Marshall put "Etc. . . Etc. . . Etc. . . Etc." next to the initials of Justice White. White voted to reconsider *Runyon*.

Since Brennan and Marshall had been members of the Court majorities in both *Runyon* and *Jones*, it was hardly surprising that they opposed reconsideration of either precedent. Indeed, Brennan had prepared for the *Patterson* conference on the assumption that *Runyon* and *Jones* were good law, and stood as important precedents in support of Brennan's argument that Brenda Patterson had properly brought her claim of racial harassment under the 1866 statute.

Justice Harry Blackmun injected a personal note into the *Patterson* conference discussion. While a member of the U.S. Court of Appeals for the Eighth Circuit in the 1960s, Blackmun had written the appellate court's decision in *Jones v. Mayer*, rejecting the argument that the Civil Rights Act of 1866 reached private acts of racial discrimination. The Supreme Court "reversed me," Blackmun told his colleagues in the *Patterson* conference, "but I'm a good soldier." He opposed reconsideration of either *Jones* or *Runyon*.

Justice John Paul Stevens strongly opposed reconsideration of *Runyon*, telling his colleagues at the *Patterson* conference that Section 1981 was applicable to the private discrimination charged in *Patterson*, as it had been held by the Court in *Runyon v. McCrary*. Stevens believed that it was institutionally important for the Court to honor a prior Court decision interpreting a congressional statute, particularly one that had not later been challenged by Congress. Stevens's point was underscored by his own position when *Runyon* was decided in 1976. At that time, Stevens had expressed reservations about the Court majority's interpretation of the 1866 act. But Stevens had noted then that *Jones v. Mayer* had been decided eight years earlier, and the Court's interpretation of the post–Civil War statute in *Jones* "accords with the prevailing sense of justice today." Since Congress, through legislation, could have sent a clear signal to the Court after *Jones* and *Runyon* that the justices had erred in their statutory interpretations—and had not done so—Stevens urged the Court not to tamper with the *Jones* or *Runyon* precedents.

At this point in the discussion, the chief justice could count only two votes, his own and Justice White's, for reconsideration of *Runyon* (and *Jones*, which almost certainly would have followed *Runyon's* reversal). But the three Reagan-appointed justices—O'Connor, Scalia and Kennedy—had not yet expressed their opinions.

When it was her turn to speak, O'Connor criticized both the *Runyon* and *Jones* decisions, suggesting that she might be prepared to overrule the civil rights precedents. After expressing her views, O'Connor voted with the chief justice to reconsider *Runyon*.

With characteristic verve and certainty, Justice Scalia enthusiastically joined the incipient movement to review the 1976 precedent. "*Runyon* looks like it ought to be reconsidered," Scalia told his colleagues; he added that he thought the 1968 *Jones* decision should be reconsidered as well. Scalia's critical views of *Runyon* and *Jones*, reflected in his comments and vote, were consistent with the views on statutory interpretation that he had expressed in his judicial opinions on the Court of Appeals for the District of Columbia, and, later, on the Supreme Court. In his opinions, Scalia had advocated a narrow approach to statutory interpretation: the Court was obligated only to look at the actual language of a statute for its meaning, and should not engage in speculation about Congress's purpose (which was frequently unclear). In *Runyon* and *Jones*, as the dissents had pointed out, the Court had looked beyond the text for the 1866 statute's meaning.

That left the final vote for reargument in *Patterson* to the junior justice, Anthony Kennedy, who had served on the Court for only a week. Less assertive than Scalia, Kennedy nonetheless supported the conservatives' initiative. That made five votes—a majority—for reargument and reconsideration of *Runyon*.

There was irony in the timing and result: this newly minted conser-

vative majority, presumed philosophically bound to be especially so-
licitous of the institution's link with past decisions, appeared at the
first opportunity poised to uproot two of the most important civil
rights precedents of the modern Supreme Court era. But the daring
action, initiated by the chief justice, was characteristic of William
Hubbs Rehnquist, who throughout his professional life had missed
few opportunities to try to advance his own conservative goals.

"I'm going to change the government," Bill Rehnquist told his
Atwater Elementary School class during the Depression. The change
the precocious young man had in mind did not include the social and
economic experimentation of Franklin Roosevelt's New Deal. In the
household of his parents—William Benjamin Rehnquist, a wholesale
paper salesman, and his wife, Margery, a college-educated linguist—
the family's heroes were Republicans Herbert Hoover, Alf Landon
and Wendell Willkie.

"We learned early on how bad Roosevelt was," recalled Jerry
Oberembt, one of Rehnquist's high school classmates and close
friends. "Our parents would listen to FDR on the radio, gnash their
teeth and then turn the dial to Father Coughlin" (the demagogic "radio
priest" who commanded a vast radio audience during the Depression).

Bill Rehnquist grew up in a tan stucco house in the neatly mani-
cured Milwaukee suburb of Shorewood and attended the all-white
Shorewood High School. Tall and conspicuously uncoordinated in
movement and dress, Rehnquist won acceptance among his peers
with his relaxed affability and wry sense of humor. He quoted Win-
ston Churchill, dazzled his classmates with feats of memory in world
history class, and graduated eighth in his high school class without, it
seemed to his friends, really trying.

After only a few months as a freshman at Kenyon College, a small
liberal arts college in Ohio, Rehnquist joined the Army Air Corps and
spent three years as a weather observer, ending his World War II tour
of duty in North Africa. When he returned to the United States, he enrolled at Stanford University on the GI Bill and earned a Phi Beta
Kappa key and both bachelor's and master's degrees in political science.

At Stanford, Rehnquist had already begun to draw the attention of his classmates with his uncompromising political conservatism. He was, by then, greatly influenced by Frederick Hayek's *The Road to Serfdom*, described as "a classic warning against the dangers to freedom inherent in social planning." As if to test his conservative resolve, Rehnquist plunged into the intellectual center of the liberal world, Harvard University. There he completed his studies for a second master's degree in political science, despite being rankled by "Harvard liberalism." Uncertain of his future career, Rehnquist registered for the law school aptitude test, scored in the ninety-ninth percentile, and headed, once again, for Stanford to study law.

On the balmy Palo Alto campus, political debate was muted, which may have been the reason that Rehnquist's conservatism was so conspicuous. "Bill was so far out politically," one law school classmate recalled, "that he was something of a joke." Rehnquist graduated first in his class at law school and was invited by Supreme Court Justice Robert H. Jackson to be one of his law clerks.

He arrived in Washington in the winter of 1952 to be Justice Jackson's clerk and picked up where he had left off at Stanford. "He could give you all the good conservative arguments on any issue," said Donald Trautman, then a clerk to Justice Felix Frankfurter. "When you talked about the problem of the cities or the poor or blacks, it was clear he had no understanding," Trautman recalled. "It was a universe he didn't comprehend."

Rehnquist's memoranda to Justice Jackson discussing whether legal questions presented in petitions to the Court merited the justices' review contained outspoken conservative views. He vigorously advocated a severely limited role for government in eliminating racial discrimination, for example, and his views were revealed in vivid detail. The tone and substance of Rehnquist's memos to Justice Jackson were illustrated in *Terry v. Adams,* a case in which black residents of Fort Bend County, Texas, challenged a system that effectively prevented them from exercising their right to vote. For sixty-three years the all-white Jaybird Democratic Association of Fort Bend County had picked candidates for the official Democratic primary and, without exception, the Jaybirds' candidates had been elected to county office. Since the black petitioners could not become members of the Jaybird

Association, they argued that they were disenfranchised because of their race in violation of the Constitution's Fifteenth Amendment.

"I have a hard time being detached about this case," Rehnquist wrote Jackson, "because several of the Rodell school of thought [his reference was to liberal Professor Fred Rodell of the Yale Law School] among the clerks began screaming as soon as they saw this, 'Now we can show those damn southerners,' etc. I take a dim view of this pathological search for discrimination à la Walter White [then a leader of the NAACP], Black, Douglas, Rodell, etc., and as a result, I now have something of a mental block against the case."

After the justices agreed to hear the case, Rehnquist again put forward very strong views (although two decades later, at the time of his Senate confirmation hearings for a seat on the Court, he suggested that he was merely paraphrasing Jackson's own position). "It is about time the Court faced the fact that the white people in the south don't like the colored people," Rehnquist wrote. "The constitution restrains them from effecting this dislike through state action, but it most assuredly did not appoint the Court as a sociological watchdog to rear up every time private discrimination raises its admittedly ugly head. To the extent that this decision advances the frontier of state action and 'social gain,' it pushes back the frontier of freedom of association and majority rule."

Justice Jackson did not adhere to the position laid out by his clerk. Instead, he voted with an 8-to-1 Court majority that declared that the all-white Jaybird preprimary was state action that violated the Fifteenth Amendment.

No member of the Senate Judiciary Committee was aware of the Rehnquist memoranda in *Terry v. Adams* when Rehnquist appeared before the committee in December 1971 as President Richard Nixon's Supreme Court nominee. However, one Rehnquist memorandum, also written when he was a clerk to Justice Jackson, did come to the committee's attention, and it seriously jeopardized his nomination. As in *Terry v. Adams*, the issue was racial discrimination. In anticipation of the challenge to public school segregation, Rehnquist had been asked to write a memo discussing whether *Plessy v. Ferguson*, the decision by the Supreme Court in 1896 that had established the constitutionality of the separate-but-equal doctrine, should be overruled.

Attacking the argument made by the NAACP Legal Defense Fund's attorney, Thurgood Marshall, that *Plessy* was wrong and that the Fourteenth Amendment forbade racial segregation in the public schools, Rehnquist expounded on a philosophy that asserted that minority rights were only as secure as the majority wished them to be. "To the argument made by Marshall, Thurgood not John, that a majority may not deprive a minority of its constitutional right," Rehnquist wrote, "the answer must be made that while this is sound in theory, in the long run it is the majority who will determine what the constitutional rights of the minority are. One hundred and fifty years of attempts on the part of this Court to protect minority rights of any kind—whether those of business, slaveholders or Jehovah's Witnesses—have all met the same fate. One by one the cases establishing such rights have been sloughed off, and crept silently to rest. If the present Court is unable to profit by this example, it must be prepared to see its work fade in time, too, as embodying only the sentiments of a transient majority of nine men." The memo concluded, "I realize that it is an unpopular and unhumanitarian position, for which I have been excoriated by 'liberal' colleagues, but I think *Plessy v. Ferguson* was right and should be re-affirmed."

After Rehnquist's *Plessy* memorandum was made public in 1971, the Court nominee sent a letter to the chairman of the Senate Judiciary Committee, James Eastland, denying that the memorandum expressed his views. "The particular memorandum in question differs sharply from the normal sort of clerk's memorandum that was submitted to Justice Jackson during my tenure as a clerk," Rehnquist wrote. "While he [Justice Jackson] did expect his clerks to make recommendations based on their memorandum as to whether certiorari [review] should be granted or denied, he very definitely did not either expect or welcome the incorporation by a clerk of his own philosophical view of how a case should be decided." Rehnquist concluded that he prepared the memorandum for the justices' conference as a statement of Justice Jackson's tentative views, not his own.

In 1971 and again in 1986, after Rehnquist was nominated to be chief justice, Rehnquist's 1971 statement to the Senate Judiciary

Committee was discussed and greeted with great skepticism. Justice Jackson's longtime secretary, Elsie Douglas, said, "Justice Jackson did not ask law clerks to express his [Jackson's] views." Professor Dennis Hutchinson of the University of Chicago Law School, who was writing a biography of Jackson, also challenged Rehnquist, declaring that Rehnquist's contention that the memorandum on *Plessy* represented Jackson's views was "absurd." Justice Jackson always instructed his clerks to express their own views, not his, said Hutchinson.

The written record provides further reasons to question whether Rehnquist's memoranda represented Jackson's views, and not his own. In his unpublished memoranda on the case of *Brown v. Board of Education of Topeka,* Justice Jackson expressed doubts about the constitutional justification for overruling *Plessy*, but on moral and political grounds he was certain that *Plessy* was wrong. Furthermore, Jackson, in an unpublished twenty-three-page memorandum written two months before Chief Justice Warren announced the unanimous decision in *Brown* (and not available to the Senate Judiciary Committee in 1971), concluded that *Plessy* should be overruled because the changed conditions of blacks and public education demanded it.

When he was asked about *Brown* (which overruled *Plessy*) years later, Rehnquist said that he supported the decision but that there was "a perfectly reasonable argument the other way" based on the doctrine of stare decisis, the Latin term which means that the Court should respect precedent. Asked at his 1986 confirmation hearings how he would have voted in *Brown*, Rehnquist replied, "I thought the stare decisis argument in *Plessy* was a strong one."

If the dispute over whose views were expressed in Rehnquist's memoranda to Justice Jackson was never resolved, there was no such problem in identifying the source of the outspoken conservative views later expressed by Rehnquist as a young Phoenix attorney—views for which Rehnquist took full credit. Attracted by the warm weather and small-firm law practice, Bill Rehnquist had moved with his bride, Natalie, from Washington to Phoenix, Arizona, in 1953, where he joined one of the old-line Phoenix law firms that, with only nine lawyers, nevertheless ranked as one of the largest in the city. He also offered his services to the Goldwater wing of the newly invigorated Republican Party, helping to organize local elections and give free legal advice.

By 1957, with his law practice and family prospering (the Rehnquists raised three children in Arizona), Rehnquist initiated a bold political attack on what he considered the left-leaning Supreme Court. In a speech to the local bar association, he denounced the "left-wing" philosophers of the Warren Court (he mentioned by name Chief Justice Warren and Justices Black and Douglas) for "making the Constitution say what they wanted it to say." That same year, he wrote an article published in *U.S. News & World Report* complaining that the justices were unduly influenced by liberal law clerks devoted to a political philosophy that he characterized as "extreme solicitude for the claims of Communists and other criminal defendants, expansion of federal power at the expense of state power, great sympathy toward any government regulation of business."

On the issue of the government's role in eliminating racial discrimination—the subject of Rehnquist's controversial memoranda to Justice Jackson—Rehnquist took a position similar to that expressed in his *Terry v. Adams* memoranda. The government, according to Rehnquist, had an extremely limited obligation to eliminate racial discrimination, particularly when it intruded on personal preferences of private citizens. In 1964, for example, Rehnquist was one of three private citizens who spoke against a Phoenix public accommodations ordinance that prohibited racial discrimination in private restaurants opened to the public (thirty Phoenix residents spoke in favor of the ordinance). The ordinance passed unanimously, but Rehnquist, undaunted, wrote one of the Phoenix newspapers that the law was "a mistake." The ordinance would not eliminate indignities to blacks, Rehnquist argued, but would leave the "unwanted customer and the disliked proprietor . . . glowering at one another across the lunch counter. It is, I believe, impossible to justify the sacrifice of even a portion of our historic individual freedom for a purpose such as this."

After Rehnquist joined the Nixon Administration in 1969 as assistant attorney general, Office of Legal Counsel, he drafted a proposed constitutional amendment that would have had the effect of reversing many of the liberal decisions of the Supreme Court in the late 1960s that had promoted desegregation in the public schools. In a memo accompanying the proposal, Rehnquist wrote that the amendment would stop federal court intervention, even if local officials set up school attendance boundaries "with a motive or partial motive of separating the races in the schools." The amendment, which was never publicly proposed, would also have prohibited busing as a tool to implement federal desegregation decrees.

When Rehnquist was nominated as associate justice of the Supreme Court in 1971, civil rights leaders denounced the nomination as "an insult to Americans who support civil rights." Roy Wilkins, then the president of the NAACP, went further. Referring to Rehnquist's informal charm and genuine friendliness, Wilkins said that the nominee "may accept you as a buddy, but his philosophy will kill you."

For civil rights advocates, Wilkins's bitter observation became prophesy. Associate Justice Rehnquist, more than any other member of the Court, voted against civil rights petitioners who came to the Court for relief. The NAACP Legal Defense and Educational Fund reported that in eighty-three cases in which members of the Court had disagreed on the application of a twentieth-century civil rights statute, Rehnquist had voted on eighty occasions for the application least favorable to racial minorities, women, the elderly and the disabled. In the same report, the NAACP noted that in fourteen racial discrimination cases brought on behalf of a black complainant between 1971 and 1986 that were decided against the plaintiff, 5 to 4, Rehnquist always cast his vote with the narrow majority. Rehnquist held tenaciously to his views even when his positions left him alone at the far right of the Court. Rehnquist filed the single dissent, for example, when the other eight members of the Court rejected a private segregated school's claim that it should enjoy tax-exempt status.

After the justices' conference on *Patterson v. McLean Credit Union*, Chief Justice Rehnquist assigned himself the task of drafting a brief opinion announcing the Court's request for reargument in *Patterson* focusing on the issue of whether *Runyon v. McCrary*, the Court's 1976 decision extending the 1866 civil rights statute to private contracts, should be overruled. Rehnquist attempted to present the request for reargument in *Patterson* as little more than routine, listing a series of decisions by the Court within the previous two decades in which the justices had asked for reargument of the merits of an existing precedent. The chief justice further noted that the Court had explicitly overruled precedents in a number of cases in which the Court had interpreted federal statutes. But the chief's attempt to whistle casually through the controversy failed miserably.

The first reaction to the circulation of his draft erupted, naturally, in the privacy of the chambers of the Court's dissenting justices. Harry Blackmun read the majority's decision to reconsider *Runyon* as tantamount to the conservatives overruling *Runyon*.

For Blackmun, Rehnquist's draft opinion was a formal declaration of war, and he launched a fierce counterattack. In his dissent, Blackmun asked aloud why the Court had reached out to decide an issue that was never touched on by the parties to the controversy either in their legal briefs or their oral arguments before the justices. This was not, Blackmun wrote, an instance of the Court revisiting "some neglected subtlety" or "overlooked jurisdictional detail." Blackmun accused the majority of attempting to unravel the entire fabric of the modern Court's interpretation of the 1866 Civil Rights Act. Such an action by the Court, Blackmun asserted, was "neither restrained, nor judicious, nor consistent with the accepted doctrine of *stare decisis*."

In the final paragraph of Blackmun's dissent, his finger-pointing criticism became personal. "I am at a loss to understand the motivation of five Members of this Court to reconsider an interpretation of a civil rights statute that so clearly reflects our society's earnest commitment to ending racial discrimination, and in which Congress so evidently has acquiesced."

Blackmun's dissent was followed by an equally acerbic dissent from Justice Stevens (both dissents were joined by Justices Brennan and Marshall). For Stevens, the majority's action sent a devastating signal to racial minorities that the new conservative Court majority felt free to rewrite any decision of the modern Court that had benefited civil rights litigants. The Court's decision would, Stevens suggested, be perceived by the public as an exercise of pure political power by an institution that was assumed to decide cases on judicial grounds, with due respect for precedent. "If the Court decides to cast itself adrift from the constraints imposed by the adversary process and to fashion its own agenda, the consequences for the Nation—and for the future of this Court as an institution—will be even more serious than any temporary encouragement of previously rejected forms of racial discrimination," Stevens concluded. "The Court has inflicted a serious—and unwise—wound upon itself today."

The extraordinary accusatory bite of the dissenting opinions of Blackmun and Stevens angered Rehnquist, who, in his redraft of the unsigned majority opinion, responded to the dissenters with a huffy rebuttal. "One might think from the dissents of our colleagues that our decision to hear argument as to whether decision in *Runyon v. McCrary* should be reconsidered is a 'first' in the history of the Court," the chief wrote. "One would also think from the language of the dissents that we have decided to overrule *Runyon v. McCrary*." But to ask for reargument was "no affront" to settled jurisprudence, Rehnquist assured, and did not mean that the Court would necessarily overrule the precedent at issue.

If Blackmun's and Stevens's dissents raised the banner of civil rights progress, the chief justice would counter with the lofty principle of the Court's obligation to treat *all* litigants fairly. "Both of the dissents intimate that the statutory question involved in *Runyon v. McCrary* should not be subject to the same principles of *stare decisis* as other decisions because it benefitted civil rights plaintiffs by expanding liability under the statute," Rehnquist wrote in the last paragraph of the redrafted per curiam (a brief, unsigned Court opinion). The Court, Rehnquist reminded his brethren in dissent, could not be influenced in applying jurisdictional rules by "the worthiness of the litigant in terms of extralegal criteria [such as moral grounds]." The Court opinion concluded that "we think this is what Congress meant when it required each Justice or judge of the United States to swear to 'administer justice without respect to persons, and do equal right to the poor and the rich.' "

The rumor making the rounds among clerks at the Court had it that the newest justice, Anthony Kennedy, had drafted the last paragraph of the reworked Court opinion. But in a private note to the chief, Justice Kennedy suggested that it was Rehnquist's handiwork, though Kennedy, for one, was pleased with the result. In his note to Rehnquist (with copies to other members of the majority), Kennedy applauded the chief's redraft. "I am in full agreement with your recirculated Per Curiam opinion," Kennedy wrote Rehnquist. "I might add the dissents do not sit well with me, and are most disappointing."

When the Court publicly announced its request for reargument, civil rights attorneys as well as larger segments of the bar and legal academic communities expressed their outrage. Picking up on the fervor and alarm of the dissenters, they denounced a new, radical conservative majority that seemed prepared to undo any liberal modern Court precedent that met with their disapproval. If *Runyon* was about to be leveled, could *Jones* be far behind? And once the conservatives gained momentum, the Court's affirmative action decisions, such as *Regents of University of California v. Bakke* (which held that race could be taken into consideration in a state medical school's admissions policies without violating the Fourteenth Amendment's Equal Protection Clause), would be in danger as well.

Reams of newspaper and law-journal copy were devoted to possible explanations of the Court's action in *Patterson*. Almost no one accepted the idea that this was ordinary Court business. The Court's action was widely read as a bold warning that an activist conservative majority had prepared a civil rights agenda unlike that of any majority for the previous fifty years. Those civil rights groups still reveling in the defeat of President Reagan's nomination of Judge Robert Bork to the Court stopped their celebration. This Court, with the more cautious Anthony Kennedy in residence, would make certain that liberals paid dearly for their Pyrrhic victory.

Briefs opposing the Court's overruling of *Runyon v. McCrary* inundated the justices. One of the most notable was signed by seven of the nation's most distinguished American historians, including Louis R. Harlan, Leon F. Litwack and C. Vann Woodward, all recipients of the Pulitzer Prize. Their brief unequivocally supported the Court's interpretation of the 1866 Civil Rights Act that was expressed in *Runyon*—and strongly supported by Justice Brennan. A comprehensive study of Reconstruction history must necessarily conclude, they asserted, that the intention of the 1866 statute was to reach private, as well as state-imposed, racial discrimination.

In their effort to persuade the justices, the historians elaborated on the point that the NAACP Legal Defense Fund's Penda Hair had made briefly in her oral argument in *Patterson*—that extensive documentation that preceded the passage of the Civil Rights Act of 1866 strongly suggested that the statute's framers intended to reach private racial discrimination. When emancipated blacks attempted to enforce their private contractual rights or acquire property, the historians wrote, their so-called "rights" were more often than not imposed on white employers' terms—and those terms included violence and torture as a means of contract negotiations. In Virginia, the historians' brief noted, blacks were tied up by their thumbs if they refused to work for the price set by white landowners. In addition to physical violence, white landowners also extracted concessions by using a range of improper economic tactics, including price-fixing, lifetime contracts, exorbitant rent, and food charges equivalent to the freedmen's wages.

The historians wrote that the man who drafted the Civil Rights Act of 1866, Senator Lyman Trumbull, made clear in his speeches on the Senate floor and in his private correspondence that the purpose of the 1866 statute was to extend the Thirteenth Amendment's negative prohibitions of slavery to an affirmative guarantee of liberty to all Americans. "This measure," Trumbull told his Senate colleagues, "is intended to give effect to that declaration [the Thirteenth Amendment] and secure to all persons within the United States practical freedom."

The historians rejected Chief Justice Rehnquist's position that the intention of the 1866 statute was to limit its application to official acts of racial discrimination by state governments. They cited Senator Trumbull's private correspondence in 1866 in which he recognized that the primary need of southern blacks and whites loyal to the Union was the protection from violence and harassment of private

41

individuals, not the removal of formal legal barriers of racial discrimination erected by state governments.

"In sum," the historians wrote in their *Patterson* amicus brief, "the framers of the Act understood that they were enforcing broad constitutionally secured rights of all American citizens. They left no question that they intended to apply federal authority over civil rights to private individuals." The brief concluded that the holding in *Runyon v. McCrary* was in accord with the framers' intent, "and reconsideration by this Court of that holding is unwarranted and unwise."

A second amicus brief, signed by 66 members of the U.S. Senate and 118 members of the U.S. House of Representatives, maintained that Section 1981, as interpreted in *Runyon*, "is an essential component of the statutory framework barring discrimination by private parties." Reinforcing the point that Justice John Paul Stevens had made in the justices' conference and in his dissent, the members of Congress assured the Court that the legislators had purposely *not* passed legislative amendments that would have undercut the Court's interpretations of the 1866 Civil Rights Act in *Jones* and *Runyon*. On the contrary, Congress's intention was to support those decisions.

The congressmen's brief noted that in 1972, four years after *Jones*, Congress discussed and rejected proposed amendments to Title VII of the Civil Rights Act of 1964 that would have eliminated recourse to Section 1981 in the area of employment discrimination. In 1976, Congress enacted the Civil Rights Attorney's Fees Award Act, which extended to prevailing parties the right to recover attorney's fees in actions brought under Section 1981, including actions brought for discrimination by private parties. Congress's rejection of an amendment in 1972 and its passage of the 1976 statute, the legislators' brief concluded, "give rise to a virtually conclusive presumption that the Congress has approved *Runyon*."

And if the justices were concerned that the states disapproved of the Court's interpretation of the 1866 statute in *Runyon*, a third amicus brief put that idea to rest. It was signed by forty-seven of the fifty state attorneys general and urged the Court to honor the *Runyon* precedent.

CHAPTER TWO

"FIVE VOTES CAN DO ANYTHING AROUND HERE"

After the Rehnquist Court majority had raised the stakes in *Patterson*, the director-counsel of the NAACP Legal Defense Fund, Julius L. Chambers, was brought in to reargue the case on behalf of Brenda Patterson. The reargument, as the justices had requested, would focus primarily on whether the Court was justified in overruling *Runyon*. Chambers nonetheless considered it important to learn more about the factual background of the case from Brenda Patterson, and to link her experience (and legal charges) with the history and language of the post–Civil War statute.

In an interview with Patterson, Chambers asked his client to describe the McLean Credit Union's work environment. It was a description Chambers said that he knew all too well: "Brenda had a college degree and had gone to work with this company hoping that she would be able to move up in this division of the company. But while there, the company continued to bring in younger whites with less education and, in fact, less experience and moved them up above Brenda. Brenda was relegated to a demeaning role as a minority employee. And in that sense, it's part of a pattern that other blacks with experience and qualifications were experiencing, not just in the credit or banking industry but in practically every other area of employment."

When Chambers addressed the Court on behalf of Brenda Patterson the morning of October 12, 1988, he was convinced that his client had been mistreated at the McLean Credit Union in a manner punishable under the 1866 statute. But he also knew that his primary task was considerably more complicated than simply arguing the justness of Patterson's legal cause. He would first have to fend off the threat of the Rehnquist Court to overrule *Runyon*.

The amicus briefs had made the justices well aware of the wide range of opposition to their overruling *Runyon*. Chambers therefore needed no histrionics to make his major points. Congress by its actions in the 1970s had encouraged the use and enforcement of Section 1981 in cases of private racial discrimination, Chambers argued, and a Court decision overruling *Runyon* would not only flout Congress's intentions but also abandon the Court's venerated doctrine requiring respect for its precedents.

In his argument to the justices, Chambers compared the 1866 statute's application to racial discrimination suffered by freedmen after the Civil War with application of the same statute to his client, Brenda Patterson. "And as we look at the legislative history [of the 1866 statute]," Chambers told the justices, "we see a Congress that saw blacks, freed blacks, harassed in the workplace, denied pay, and that's the kind of conduct this Congress was trying to reach. We're not working the farms now. We're working in the credit union. So, the type of discrimination may differ, but the conduct—the discrimination, the enslavement, the badges of slavery are the things we are trying to reach. And that's what Congress meant to reach in 1866. . . . We're talking about a black person trying to work at a bank who was subjected to harassment and working in conditions that make it unbearable for a black to survive."

Chambers's adversary at oral argument, New York attorney Roger Kaplan, who had been hired by the McLean Credit Union to reargue its case, attempted to persuade the justices that the Court's *Runyon* decision impeded the natural, orderly flow of civil rights legislation.

Specifically, Kaplan argued that Congress had intended to attack private racial discrimination exclusively through the enforcement provisions of Title VII of the Civil Rights Act of 1964. By permitting lawsuits charging private employment discrimination to be brought under the 1866 law, instead of Title VII, the Court, Kaplan contended, was interfering with Congress's purpose.

But even Kaplan's most sympathetic listener, Justice Antonin Scalia, quickly grew impatient with the argument.

"Why should we go back and change a decision that we've made?" asked Scalia. "What is special about this statute?"

"The problem is that it intrudes on the operation of Congress," responded Kaplan. "That's basically where the fundamental problem lies."

"If that's all you have, Mr. Kaplan," said an exasperated Scalia, "I'm afraid it's nothing, because that's always the case when we interpret a statute incorrectly."

In Brennan's chambers before the second *Patterson* argument and justices' conference, Brennan's law clerk who had been assigned to write a memorandum of law in the case developed a cautious strategy for Brennan's defense of *Runyon*. In his *Patterson* memorandum, the clerk did not emphasize the table-pounding argument that *Runyon* was correct on the merits. Instead, he advocated the more modest position that the Court majority in *Runyon* had presented a "plausible" interpretation that the 1866 statute reached private conduct. Such a "plausible" interpretation in *Runyon*, the memo argued, should not be disturbed—particularly since Congress, which had the authority to correct any erroneous statutory interpretation by the Court, had not acted (a point that had been made at length in the congressional amicus brief).

For Brennan's supporters outside the Court who admired the justice as the uncompromising champion of civil rights, the clerk's cautious *Runyon* strategy might have been disappointing. But Brennan's clerks, who were familiar with Brennan's modus operandi, knew that the justice's willingness to seek a common ground among five justices, a majority, on an increasingly conservative Court was necessary for success. And Brennan, against increasingly long odds, continued to succeed in forging liberal majorities. Brennan preferred victory to some abstract declaration of principle, and his best hope to preserve *Runyon* was to appeal to the *conservative* instincts of his more conservative brethren.

The memorandum prepared for the second *Patterson* conference in Brennan's chambers stressed the need for the Court to respect precedent which, as the memo argued, "must surely mean that we will not revisit a close question of statutory interpretation that has been settled in a carefully considered and detailed opinion [*Runyon*] joined by seven members of the Court, and that has been reaffirmed many times since." The memorandum then offered substantive reasons why *Runyon*, in particular, should be preserved. "Our decision in *Runyon* has become an important part of the fabric of civil rights protections," the memo continued. "*Runyon* has become the basis for the hopes—and conduct—of members of racial minorities, who see our interpretation of Section 1981 as both a powerful symbol and an essential practical tool for combating discrimination."

At the judicial conference on October 14, 1988, following the reargument in *Patterson*, Chief Justice Rehnquist opened the discussion by stating that no legal brief and no point made at oral argument had persuaded him to change his opinion about *Runyon*. Justice White's dissent in *Runyon* was right, he told his colleagues. The only issue for the chief was whether a decision that was wrongfully decided should be overruled. Rehnquist cited two Court decisions that supported the position that a wrongly decided Court decision, such as he considered *Runyon*, need not stand. But then Rehnquist left the door open to the possibility of defeating Brenda Patterson's claim without overruling *Runyon*. *Patterson* and *Runyon* were very different cases in terms of their facts and applications of Section 1981, he said. The justices could decide that the language in Section 1981 did not apply to the harassment charged in *Patterson*, and distinguish their decision from *Runyon*, eliminating the necessity of overruling the 1976 precedent. Either way, Brenda Patterson lost. The Court could rule against her and overrule *Runyon*, or it could leave *Runyon* alone and still say that Section 1981 did not apply to her racial harassment claim.

After the chief justice had spoken, Brennan, as expected, made the argument that *Runyon* should be preserved. He was later supported in his position by the three other dissenters to the Court's order for reconsideration of *Runyon*—Justices Marshall, Blackmun and Stevens.

Justice Byron White reiterated his view that *Runyon* and *Jones* were wrongly decided. But that didn't settle the issue of whether those precedents should be overruled, White continued. He then declared that *Runyon* should not be reversed, adopting the position taken by Justice Stevens in the first *Patterson* conference: Congress, by its actions since *Runyon*, had indicated that it accepted the *Runyon* majority's interpretation of Section 1981, i.e., that it applied to private employment discrimination.

Brennan had found his majority on the *Runyon* issue, but before the conference was over, he could claim much more. Justice O'Connor, the third member of the Court majority (after the chief justice and White) who had voted to reconsider *Runyon*, also accepted the argument that the Court did not have sufficient reason to overrule *Runyon*, even though it was a flawed decision.

"*Runyon* was wrong," Justice Scalia declared anew, speaking after O'Connor, "but public reaction [to the threat of overruling it] is appropriate and I would not overrule [*Runyon*]."

The final member of the majority who had requested reargument, Justice Kennedy, took a different position from his four conservative brethren. Kennedy had done considerable reading on the history of Reconstruction during the summer. He told his colleagues that he thought *Runyon* was correctly decided and, had he been on the Court in 1976, he would have voted with the *Runyon* majority. According to Kennedy, the 1866 Civil Rights Act was intended to reach both private and state-imposed racial discrimination in contractual agreements. *Runyon* should stand.

When the final votes were tallied, even the chief justice had backed away from insisting on an outright reversal of *Runyon*. A unanimous Court—including the chief justice and the four associate justices who had voted for reargument (as well as the four liberals who had opposed it)—reaffirmed the Court's holding in *Runyon v. McCrary*.

47

But that decision on *Runyon*, of course, did not spell victory for Brenda Patterson. And on the merits of Brenda Patterson's racial harassment claim, the chief justice, for one, was undeterred by the *Runyon* precedent. With or without *Runyon*, Rehnquist told his colleagues, the language of the 1866 statute on the making and enforcing of contracts did not apply to on-the-job racial harassment.

Brennan had already taken the opposing position at the first *Patterson* conference and he held to that position in the second. Acceptance of the chief justice's narrow interpretation of the post–Civil War statute would reduce Brenda Patterson's right to a meaningless abstraction, Brennan believed. Under such a restricted statutory interpretation, a racist employer could sign a contract with a black woman, then proceed to harass her at will. The employer would, arguably, have complied with the narrowest requirement of "making" a contract. But could that possibly have been what the Reconstructionist Congress in 1866 had in mind? Brennan's answer was a firm no. There was powerful evidence that the Reconstructionist Congress in 1866, and a modern-day Congress more than a century later, intended that the Court interpret the contract provisions more broadly.

Justices Marshall, Blackmun and Stevens joined Brennan. But Justice White, who had voted with Brennan to preserve the *Runyon* precedent, disagreed with his senior colleague that Patterson's racial harassment charge was properly brought under Section 1981. Instead, he supported the chief justice in his position that Section 1981 did not apply to Patterson's claim. Justices O'Connor and Scalia also voted to reject Patterson's argument. The vote was deadlocked 4 to 4.

Whether Brenda Patterson would succeed in her claim that her charges of racial harassment were covered by Section 1981 depended on the vote of Justice Anthony Kennedy. By tradition, the Court's junior justice spoke last at conference. When it was his turn to state his position on the merits of Patterson's racial harassment claim, Kennedy took an unexpectedly strong position in support of Brenda Patterson. Kennedy told his new colleagues that there was "abundant evidence" of racial harassment, as Patterson charged. The contract between the McLean Credit Union and the black woman, Kennedy continued, had not been made in good faith. It was not, Kennedy concluded, a valid contract under Section 1981 of the post–Civil War statute. Following his statement, Kennedy contributed the fifth vote necessary to create Justice Brennan's fragile majority.

As the senior justice in the majority (on both the *Runyon* and *Patterson* issues), Brennan was entitled to assign the majority opinion. He decided to give the assignment to himself, drawing on his vast experience to try, once again, to produce a majority opinion that would support his expansive vision of civil rights and liberties protections under the Constitution and federal statutes.

The eighty-two-year-old Brennan was serving his thirty-second Court term, one of the longest tenures of any justice, and his place in the institution's history was secure. During his Court years, Brennan's immense contributions to the Court's civil rights and liberties jurisprudence had established his reputation as one of the most influential justices of all time.

That judgment would have astonished everyone, including Brennan himself, when he was appointed to the Court by President Dwight D. Eisenhower in 1956. Meeting reporters after his nomination was announced, Brennan, with modesty and good humor, analogized his appointment to the mule entered in the Kentucky Derby. "I don't expect to distinguish myself," Brennan told reporters, "but I do expect to benefit from the association."

How had Brennan, thirty-two years later, reached such a revered status among all of the justices who had served on the Court? The story of Brennan's rise to an eminent place in constitutional history began in the city of Newark, New Jersey, where William J. Brennan, Sr., an Irish immigrant, and his wife, Agnes, raised the future justice, his three brothers and four sisters. Brennan Sr. stoked the boiler in a factory, heaved coal in the Ballantine brewery and later became a labor leader and elected local official. His son Bill Jr. contributed to the family's meager income by making change for passengers waiting for trolley cars and delivering milk in a horse-drawn wagon. There was no time, nor reason, for self-pity since the Brennans' neighbors were much worse off. "What got me interested in people's rights and liberties was the kind of neighborhood I was brought up in," Justice Brennan later recalled. "I saw all kinds of suffering—people had to struggle."

Those early memories inspired a lifelong philosophy—the need for government's protection of the worth and dignity of every human being—that Justice Brennan reiterated in opinion after liberal opinion for all of his years on the Court. During those years, Brennan never tired of retelling his favorite story of the Poor Old Woman in Yeats's play *Cathleen ni Hoolihan*. "Did you see an old woman going down the path?" asked Bridget. "I did not," replied Patrick, who had entered the house just after the old woman had departed. "But I saw a young girl and she had the walk of a queen."

A combination of brains, irrepressible personality and sheer energy propelled Brennan through a varied and uniformly successful professional career. An honors graduate of the Wharton School at the University of Pennsylvania, Brennan went on to finish in the top 10 percent of his class at the Harvard Law School and served as the president of the student legal aid society. After Harvard, Brennan returned to Newark to join one of the state's most prestigious law firms as a trial lawyer specializing in labor law.

In 1942, Brennan took a leave from his law firm to enlist in the armed forces, and spent his entire military career in the United States as a manpower troubleshooter, negotiating labor settlements in critical defense industries. To the trained eye, Brennan's skill during the war offered a blueprint for his later success on the Court. He impressed a War Department colleague as "the friendly Irish type . . . very convivial, easygoing. A great storyteller." But the jaunty charm did more than entertain. Without threat or bluster, Brennan got things done, his way. "He was a diplomat," a colleague recalled. "People liked to do what he wanted them to do." By war's end, Brennan had achieved the rank of colonel and had been awarded the Legion of Merit.

After the war, Brennan returned to his Newark law firm, which added his name to its official masthead. But in 1949, concerned about his health and diminishing time with his family (by then Brennan and his wife, Marjorie, were parents of three children), Brennan accepted an appointment by Governor Alfred Driscoll to the state trial court. Within three years, Brennan had been elevated first to the state appellate court and then to the New Jersey Supreme Court, where his proposals for court reform received national attention.

In 1956, President Eisenhower was well aware of the political advantage of naming an Irish Catholic to the Court in an election year. The enthusiasm with which Brennan's appointment was greeted, however, transcended partisan politics. Trial lawyers applauded the appointment because Brennan's own experience as a trial lawyer assured them that he, like them, knew "all the ins and outs of litigation" and had developed "a sixth sense that gets at the truth." Conservative political commentator Arthur Krock of the *New York Times* pointed to Brennan's unusual number of qualifications for the office, including his extensive experience as a lawyer and judge, and added that the appointment "is also proof of democracy when a Supreme Court Justice is representative of what America can, with honor and industry, achieve without birthright of social and economic privilege."

Brennan's moderation in politics—he was a registered Democrat but was not active in state politics—was viewed by the organized bar as an asset, particularly since the Court had become involved in such explosive subjects as desegregation and sedition. In contrast to Chief Justice Earl Warren, a former California governor, Brennan, members of the bar said, would bring to the Court a calm, moderating voice.

Brennan delighted in telling the story of his first meeting with Chief Justice Warren. After a hasty introduction in the chief's chambers, Warren escorted Brennan to Room 317 in the Supreme Court Building. Warren opened the door, and Brennan peered into total darkness. A light was turned on, and Brennan's new colleagues hurriedly shook his hand, then ordered the lights turned out again so that they could return to the serious business of watching the opening game of the 1956 World Series on television.

An avid sports fan, Brennan was not offended by the brusque introduction to the brethren. Indeed, his keen interest in baseball and football were matched by the chief justice's and the two immediately formed a close friendship, frequently attending sports events together and dining at each other's home. At the Court, they exchanged notes on pending cases. Later, the exchanges became more formalized, with weekly meetings on Thursdays in Brennan's chambers.

By Brennan's third term on the Court, Warren was relying on Brennan's judgment more than that of any of his colleagues. Early in that October 1958 term, the chief justice delegated to Brennan the responsibility for drafting the Court's opinion in the most important school desegregation case since *Brown v. Board of Education of Topeka*. In the case *Cooper v. Aaron*, the Court was faced with defiant opposition by Arkansas Governor Orville Faubus and other state officials to its *Brown* directive declaring that public schools in the southern states must be desegregated "with all deliberate speed." The state officials claimed that they were not bound by the Court's earlier desegregation ruling.

Following oral argument in *Cooper*, Warren marched into conference and declared to his colleagues that further delay by the State of Arkansas in implementing the *Brown* mandate was intolerable. "We knew the kind of opinion we wanted," Justice Brennan later recalled. Brennan's opinion in *Cooper* issued a stern warning to Arkansas's obstructionists, including its governor and the legislature. "The constitutional rights of respondents [black students attempting to attend the segregated Little Rock public schools] are not to be sacrificed or yielded to the violence and disorder which have followed upon the actions of the Governor and Legislature," Brennan wrote. *Brown* must be obeyed.

For the next eleven years, until the chief's retirement in 1969, Warren and Brennan maintained an uncommonly close bond, both philosophically and personally. The consequence of their intimate relationship for the protection of civil rights and liberties in this country was profound.

For Brennan, states with a history of official segregation incurred an affirmative duty to eliminate all vestiges of racism. Pronouncements of an end to official racial discrimination were not good enough. Writing for the Court in 1968, he told the New Kent County (Virginia) School Board that its desegregation plan was ineffective, and ordered the board to come forward with new steps, "which promise realistically to convert promptly to a system without a 'white' school and a 'Negro' school, but just schools."

Remarkably, the appointment by President Richard Nixon in 1969 of Judge Warren E. Burger of the U.S. Court of Appeals for the District of Columbia to succeed Earl Warren as chief justice did not diminish Brennan's liberal influence on the Court. He still managed to find five votes with regularity to support his ambitious concept of a Constitution that protects individual rights and liberties against a powerful government. Under Brennan's leadership, a Burger Court majority also cut through the familiar ruses and obfuscations to attack racial discrimination at its core and to offer meaningful and often controversial remedies. In civil rights decisions, Justice Brennan was the undeniable leader of the Court even when Chief Justice Burger's name appeared at the top of the Court's majority opinion. That was the case in the Court's first decision authorizing busing to public schools to implement a school desegregation decree.

Burger ostensibly wrote the majority opinion for the Court in *Swann v. Charlotte-Mecklenburg Board of Education* that affirmed a lower federal court's busing plan for a North Carolina school district. After receiving Burger's meandering draft opinion, Brennan wrote the chief a strongly worded ten-page memorandum suggesting critical changes to the chief justice's draft that were incorporated into Burger's final draft strengthening the Court's commitment to busing as a constitutional remedy to eliminate segregated public schools.

Throughout the 1970s and into the '80s, Brennan continued to press for broad remedies to eliminate racial discrimination, above as well as below the Mason-Dixon line. Brennan wrote the Court's opinion supporting a citywide school desegregation plan in Denver even though past racial discrimination had been proven in only one district of the city. "[C]ommon sense" suggested to Brennan that blatant segregationist policies promulgated by the school board in one section of the city had contaminated the entire system.

Brennan's commitment to making the Court an aggressive agent for the promotion of civil rights reforms extended beyond desegregation in the public schools. He wrote the Court opinion interpreting Title VII of the 1964 Civil Rights Act to permit voluntary affirmative action programs by private companies in their hiring practices. And he supported every decision of the Court that read the language of the post–Civil War statutes broadly enough to recapture, in his view, their original expansive meaning and spirit.

Brennan had for years taken mischievous pleasure in debunking theories of his great power and influence on the Supreme Court. Stories in the media claimed that Justice Brennan applied a vise-tight grip on his brethren, shrewdly camouflaged by an ingratiating charm and uncanny instinct for the possible. Brennan never denied that he worked tirelessly for his majorities, even enlisting his young law clerks in the hunt for the right result. But Brennan vigorously denied that he built his majorities in whispered corridor conversations with wavering colleagues.

Early in a Court term, usually after one of his new law clerks had raged over a hopelessly wrongheaded majority opinion by one of Brennan's more conservative colleagues, "the Boss," as Brennan was affectionately known, would treat his incensed clerk to his five-finger exercise. Raising his hand, Brennan would wiggle his five fingers and say, "Five votes. Five votes can do anything around here."

Brennan's five-finger exercise was never seen by the justice or his clerks as a cynical expression of judicial realpolitik. It was, rather, recognition of the fundamental truth that the Court functioned as a collegial body of nine independent-minded judges who must, by majority vote, make the most basic judgments about the direction of our constitutional democracy. For Brennan, the written word was his chosen tool of persuasion, and he used it with the skill of the patient craftsman in draft after laborious draft to find that common ground of agreement between himself and four of his colleagues.

In *Patterson v. McLean Credit Union*, Justice Brennan's vaunted powers of persuasion would be put to one of their severest tests.

Brennan's major challenge in *Patterson* was to hold the least-secure vote of his majority on the racial harassment issue, that of Justice Kennedy. Kennedy's wavering position became immediately clear in a note that he sent to Brennan (with copies to the other justices) five days after the October *Patterson* conference. While studying *Reconstruction*, a book written by Eric Foner, one of the signatories of the historians' amicus brief, Kennedy found a quote from the book that "the Civil Rights Bill [of 1866] was primarily directed against public, not private, acts of injustice." Kennedy then referred to the historians' amicus brief "in which they would seek to have us come to a contrary conclusion," noting that the quoted passage from Professor Foner's book was not included in the brief.

"I did not wish to raise this at oral argument," Kennedy continued, "but I do think that Foner's brief is highly misleading, especially when it purports to present an objective view of the Reconstruction period," Kennedy continued. "Since the historical materials have been reviewed in great detail by the majority and dissenting opinions in older cases, you may find it unnecessary to travel this road again. Nevertheless, I thought you should be aware of Foner's published views."

Brennan replied in writing to Kennedy the following day, first thanking his new colleague for bringing the passage to his attention. Brennan found nothing in the historians' brief "entirely inconsistent with Foner," but he added, "our reliance may be on the historical analyses our decided cases have followed over many years, and this is the approach I am taking in the proposed opinion I am preparing."

After he had completed a first draft of his *Patterson* opinion, Brennan took the unusual step of sending a copy to Justice Kennedy before he circulated it to other members of the Court. It was a gracious, and shrewd, gesture by Brennan, who did not want to circulate a draft that would be rejected outright by Kennedy—or encourage him to seek counsel from one of the *Patterson* dissenters.

Brennan devoted the first two-thirds of this draft opinion to the issue on which there was Court unanimity—the reaffirmation of *Runyon v. McCrary*. Brennan emphasized the established rule that the Court should not overrule precedents that interpret congressional statutes, since Congress had the power to correct interpretations that it did not approve of. Brennan laid out all of the exceptions to this rule, all of the times when the Court should overrule congressional statutes, and then demonstrated why the Court had reaffirmed, not overruled, *Runyon*.

He concluded the section on the conspicuously cautious note that his clerk had suggested in his *Patterson* memorandum: although the *Runyon* majority's interpretation of the 1866 Civil Rights Act was not the *only* acceptable interpretation of the statute, it was at the very least "plausible." And given the Court's respect for precedent, a "plausible" statutory interpretation by the Court, untouched by a later congressional amendment or statute, should be preserved.

Kennedy's response to that least-controversial section* of the draft opinion suggested that Brennan's skills as a draftsman and conciliator would be seriously tested in the months ahead. For even that section of Brennan's draft did not escape Kennedy's scrutiny and extensive criticism. In his four-page response of November 15, 1988, Kennedy suggested that Brennan devoted too much of his opinion to a discussion of legislative history showing that Congress intended to reach private acts of racial discrimination, which, Kennedy wrote, was not necessary to the Court's decision to preserve *Runyon* and was "unduly anticipatory of the merits of Patterson's harassment claim."

Kennedy also faulted Brennan for relying on congressional silence after *Runyon* to support the view that Congress had acquiesced in the Court's interpretation. "I am inclined to believe that Congressional silence, being inherently ambiguous, furnished no support for our decision to reaffirm *Runyon*," Kennedy wrote, and cited two Supreme Court decisions to support his point. He further recommended that Brennan drop a paragraph in a footnote that he considered unnecessary. Finally, he wrote that he was troubled by a statement in Brennan's draft that our society's commitment to the eradication of discrimination "is not bounded by legal concepts." Kennedy wrote, "I suppose this statement is true in the abstract, but it could be read as implying that our mandate is not limited by the law."

None of Kennedy's suggested changes in section one significantly altered the thrust of Brennan's opinion reaffirming *Runyon* or represented a threat to his majority on the issue. Brennan could concede points on section one, and he did. In response to Kennedy's memorandum, Brennan shortened two footnotes, eliminated one full paragraph of a third and deleted the offending sentence that spoke of society's commitment to eliminating racial discrimination that was

---

* Besides the *Runyon* and racial harassment issues, the Court dealt with Patterson's charge that she had been denied promotion because of her race. The lower courts had ruled that Patterson was required to show that she was better qualified for a position than the white who was promoted. The justices decided in *Patterson* that that was too heavy a burden of proof and returned the case on that issue to the lower court for further proceedings.

not "bounded by legal concepts." Brennan also reworked his draft so that it would be clear that Congress had not supported *Runyon* through silence but by the explicit rejection of an amendment that would have undercut it. So far, so good.

But Kennedy would not be so easily accommodated when it came to the next section of Brennan's precirculated draft majority opinion—on the crucial racial harassment issue. Here Kennedy, only a few weeks after the justices' conference on *Patterson*, appeared subtly—but, as it developed, decisively—to shift his position on the issue.

He wrote that an employee who was victimized by racial discrimination in the workplace after entering into a contract could make a claim under Section 1981 if it could be shown that the employer, by his discriminatory conduct, intended to evade the law's mandate "to make" contracts without regard to race. But in his next sentence Kennedy pointedly distinguished racial discrimination in the making of a contract from subsequent independent racial harassment on the job. In insisting that there was a clean, discernible line to be drawn between racial harassment in the making of the contract and later "unrelated" harassment, Kennedy distanced himself from the position he attributed to Brennan in the senior justice's precirculation draft. But in his criticism of the Brennan draft, Kennedy did not acknowledge that the Court majority at conference—and the other four members of the "majority" thought he was the fifth—had concluded that racial harassment *after* the contract did undercut the good faith *making* of the contract. And it was precisely that link in the *Patterson* case that Brennan had emphasized in his draft.

After Kennedy attributed a broader statutory interpretation to Brennan than to himself, his attack on the Brennan draft gathered momentum:

> I realize that the more expansive view reflected in your current draft finds some support in the legislative history of Section 1981. But in keeping with my usual approach to matters of statutory construction, I am unwilling to rely on legislative history to broaden significantly, as I firmly believe your draft does, the scope of the statute actually enacted by Congress. I am especially unwilling to

do so in this case, since an approach so divorced from the language of Section 1981 would perpetuate uncertainty among lower courts and litigants concerning the appropriate scope of the statute. . . . While we can reaffirm the holding in *Runyon* as plausible given the facts of that case, any attempt to construe the statute as a generalized proscription of racial discrimination in all aspects of contractual relationships would, in my view, carry the language of Section 1981 past the breaking point and lead to confusion among the lower courts.

When Kennedy's memorandum reached the Brennan chambers, there was, predictably, much gnashing of teeth and general grumbling among the clerks. They later speculated that, after the October judicial conference, Kennedy had changed his mind on the racial harassment issue and was attempting to find an honorable way to leave the Brennan majority. The Brennan clerks suspected that their counterparts in Justice Kennedy's chambers, whom they considered to be among the most zealous conservative thinkers in the building, had persuaded the justice to change his position.

There was also speculation that one of *Patterson*'s original dissenters, either Chief Justice Rehnquist, Justice White or Justice Scalia, may have belatedly caught the ear of the newest appointee. Rehnquist and White had, from the beginning of the justices' discussion of *Patterson*, opposed an interpretation of the 1866 statute that would have covered Brenda Patterson's racial harassment charges. As to the possible influence of Justice Scalia, the approach that Kennedy took in his memorandum—rejecting a broad, contextual reading of legislative history—was strikingly similar to Scalia's.

To "let off steam and to form a basis for discussion," one of Brennan's clerks drafted an answer to Kennedy that, without Brennan's diplomatic touches, responded to each of the objections that Kennedy had made in his November 15 memorandum. But Brennan put the clerk's draft aside for later discussion and wrote Kennedy a gracious note thanking his new colleague for taking so much time with his draft and expressing appreciation for "your most helpful comments." Brennan told Kennedy that he was sure that he would be able "to take account of nearly all of your concerns" in further revisions. "This may take a little time," Brennan wrote warmly, "but just bear with me and I'll have something for you as soon as possible."

During the next week Brennan discussed the Kennedy memorandum with his clerks and reviewed and reworked his clerk's draft response. The promised revisions were sent to Kennedy on November 22, with a covering letter from Brennan again thanking Kennedy for "your helpful comments" and expressing the hope that he had managed in his revised draft "to devise solutions that accommodate our differences."

Brennan met Kennedy's criticism of his treatment of the racial harassment issue head-on:

My difficulty with your comments on Part II [discussing the racial harassment issue] is not at all that I disagree with them, but that I thought the draft already stated that view of the scope of Section 1981. I can see now that some passages in Part II might have been misleading in this regard, and I have sought to remedy this. I certainly do not think that Section 1981 is a "generalized proscription of racial discrimination in all aspects of contractual relationships," and I have added a sentence to the opinion saying precisely that. See page 24. Rather, as I state on that same page, "the statutory language imposes a limit upon the type of harassment claims that are cognizable under Section 1981." I proposed in my last draft that the statutory language requires the plaintiff to prove harassment of a sort that "demonstrates that the employer has made the contract in issue in a racially discriminatory manner," and that the harassment was such "as effectively to belie any claim that the contract was made in a racially neutral manner" (page 33). In this draft, I have tried to make this position clearer, by adding that a plaintiff—using your phrase here—must show that the employer "has sought to evade the statute's strictures concerning contract formation" (page 25).

Despite Kennedy's criticism, Brennan refused to jettison his discussion of the legislative history of the statute, explaining his reasons:

I do believe that the discussion of legislative history in Part II is essential, for it shows that Congress had in mind that post-contractual behavior might be indicative of racial discrimination in entering into the contract. It is arguable that the language of the statute alone does *not* outlaw post-contractual behavior, *even* behavior that may be interpreted as evidencing an intent to evade the statute— and that is surely a point we may expect to be made in the dissent. I have endeavored to make plain that legislative history is being used only to counter such "an overly narrow" reading of the statutory language (page 22), and not to broaden the scope of the statute until it becomes a general bar to discrimination in contractual relationships. I have thus added the language indicated on pages 22–24.

Having insisted that his discussion of legislative history remain in his opinion, Brennan offered Kennedy a way to support his majority opinion on the racial harassment issue without subscribing to his views on the importance of the history in reaching his result in *Patterson*. Brennan simply reorganized the section of his opinion on racial harassment and discussed the history in a self-contained subsection. In this way, Brennan allowed Kennedy to reject his historical narrative and still support his conclusion on the racial harassment issue.

Ten days after receiving Brennan's proposed revisions, Kennedy responded to him in a cordial one-page letter thanking Brennan for "accommodating so many of my suggestions." In the three paragraphs that followed, Kennedy gave the strong impression that, despite his insistence that differences remained on the racial harassment issue, he would join Brennan's majority opinion.

Kennedy wrote that he continued "to believe that acts of harassment that occur after the parties enter into a contract should have only evidentiary value on the issue whether the contract was made in good faith, and should not give rise to an independent cause of action under Section 1981 if it is otherwise shown that the contract was made in good faith." But he added: "In light of the changes you have made to accommodate me, however, it seems unlikely that our differences would lead to divergent results in many cases. For the sake of having a Court on this important issue, I believe I can set aside my reservations and join your draft, though I wish to have the benefit of whatever comments and suggestions our colleagues will have after full circulation."

The next day, December 3, Brennan circulated the official first draft of his *Patterson* opinion to the other members of the Court, incorporating the agreed-upon changes suggested by Kennedy, using in several places Kennedy's phrasing (underlined):

> <u>Section 1981 cannot be construed as a general proscription of racial discrimination in all aspects of contractual relationships, for it expressly prohibits discrimination only in the making and enforcement of contracts.</u> Racial harassment severe enough to amount to a breach of contract as a matter of state law is certainly cognizable under Section 1981, for an employer's discriminatory failure to abide by the terms of a black employee's contract constitutes a denial of contractual opportunities as surely as does the initial offer of different employment terms to blacks and whites, or a race-based discharge. The term breached by the racial harassment may be an explicit one, or it may be the implied covenant of good faith and fair dealing often supplied and given content by state law. . . . Even if it does not breach an express or implied contract term, however, harassment is actionable under Section 1981 <u>if it demonstrates that the employer has sought to evade the statute's strictures concerning contract formation.</u> The question in each case in which an employee makes a Section 1981 claim alleging racial harassment and alleges no breach of contract is therefore whether in nature and extent the acts constituting harassment were sufficiently severe or pervasive as effectively to belie any claim that the contract was <u>entered into</u> in a racially neutral manner. . . .

Shortly after sending his draft to the Court printer, Brennan began to run a high fever and suffer chills. He was rushed by ambulance to the Bethesda Naval Hospital, where doctors, believing he had contracted pneumonia, treated the eighty-two-year-old justice with heavy doses of antibiotics. But Brennan's physicians soon changed their diagnosis and treatment, and removed his infected gallbladder. He remained in the hospital for a week of recuperation and then spent the December holiday period at home. All the while, Brennan kept in touch with his office, and Kennedy's, and continued to hope and work for his majority in *Patterson*.

CHAPTER THREE

FINE PHRASES

Justice Brennan's health improved during the winter months, but little else—at least as far as the Court's civil rights business was concerned—cheered him up. Justice Kennedy did not respond immediately to Brennan's revised December draft and continued to withhold his endorsement of Brennan's *Patterson* opinion (which had been formally joined by Blackmun, Marshall and Stevens in early December). And Justice Byron White circulated a strongly worded dissent on the racial harassment issue in *Patterson*, taking the position that the language of Section 1981 should not be interpreted to include conduct after the "making" of a contract, the very point that had concerned Kennedy as early as the first *Patterson* oral argument.

Meanwhile, the American public received strong evidence that a conservative majority had begun to wrest control of the Court on January 23, 1989, three days after George Bush was inaugurated as president of the United States. At that time, the Supreme Court announced in *City of Richmond v. J. A. Croson Co.* that a Richmond, Virginia, plan to set aside 30 percent of building subcontracts with the city for minority-owned businesses was unconstitutionally discriminating against white contractors. The Court majority, which included Justice Kennedy, insisted that a southern city trying to eliminate the effects of past racial discrimination be held to the same high standard of review that had been used by the Warren and Burger Courts for more than a quarter of a century to scrutinize efforts to protect official racial discrimination.

Justice O'Connor wrote the opinion for the Court, ruling that the Richmond city council's policy, modeled on an earlier federal "set aside" program that had been declared constitutional by the Burger Court, deprived nonminority businesses of equal protection under the Constitution's Fourteenth Amendment. The Rehnquist Court majority (which included Rehnquist, White, Stevens, O'Connor, Scalia and Kennedy) was not impressed by statistics showing that the building industry in Richmond had historically been controlled by whites. A consistent record of building contracts awarded to whites was not enough, wrote Justice O'Connor; there must be specific, documented evidence of past racial discrimination in Richmond's building industry to justify the city's remedial program.

In his *Croson* dissent, Justice Blackmun expressed astonishment at the majority's judgment. "I never thought I would live to see the day when the city of Richmond, Virginia, the cradle of the Old Confederacy, sought on its own, within a narrow confine, to lessen the stark impact of persistent discrimination. But Richmond, to its great credit, acted. Yet this Court, the supposed bastion of equality, strikes down Richmond's efforts as though discrimination had never existed or was not demonstrated in this particular litigation."

Spring arrived in Washington and still Brennan received no indication from Justice Kennedy that he was willing to sign on to Brennan's *Patterson* opinion. By April, Brennan and his clerks were braced for bad news. On April 27, Kennedy circulated an opinion that dissented from Brennan's on the crucial issue of racial harassment but still concurred in Brennan's result on the *Runyon* and promotion issues. Instead of supporting Brennan's position on the issue of Section 1981's application to racial harassment, Kennedy endorsed the views expressed by Justice White in his dissenting opinion. "I agree with Justice White's basic approach to interpreting the scope of Section

1981," Kennedy wrote. "That provision's most obvious feature is the restriction of its scope to forbidding discrimination in the 'making and enforcement' of contracts alone. . . ."

The same day that his draft was circulated, Kennedy wrote Brennan a courtesy note informing him of what Brennan had already learned from reading Kennedy's new draft:

> Dear Bill:
>
> As you must have surmised by now, my remaining doubts about your fine opinion in this case did not go away, though I had hoped to work through them.
>
> I feel quite strongly that since we read the language of Section 1981 literally to apply to private conduct (*Runyon*), we must also read those words precisely in delineating the reach of that statute. This is particularly so given the existence of Title VII.
>
> You are indeed a patient man.
>
> Sincerely,
Tony

When the Kennedy opinion arrived at the Brennan chambers, the clerks and Justice Brennan knew that they faced only difficult choices: either accept defeat on the racial harassment issue or find a respectable legal theory that would entice Kennedy to re-join Brennan's majority. "We could simply throw in the towel," one clerk concluded, but "we are right and AMK [Kennedy] et al are wrong."

One option suggested by a Brennan clerk was to retain Brennan's analysis on the racial harassment issue but rule against Patterson (since Kennedy was now on record among his colleagues as opposing her claim). To reach that conclusion, Brennan would have to perform a fancy technical retreat. Under this theory, Brenda Patterson would lose on the racial harassment issue since she claimed harassment, *by itself*, in her case constituted a violation of the statute; to succeed, she *should* have argued that harassment was *evidence* that her right to make a contract had been violated.

This option had the virtue of preserving Brennan's interpretation— that racial harassment could be reached under the terms of the 1866 statute—so that someone after Brenda Patterson (who would herself lose on the technicality) could successfully invoke Section 1981 in a future racial harassment suit. But that same strategy carried the risk of alienating one of the other three justices who had originally voted with Brennan—Blackmun, Marshall or Stevens.

Although it was not a perfect solution—there was none at this late stage—Brennan decided to float the clerk's hastily constructed theory in the Patterson case. Brennan wrote Blackmun, Marshall and Stevens a letter on May 1 explaining his new rationale:

> Tony's dissent leaves me without a Court on Part II of my opinion in this case, dealing with the harassment claim. In response, I have redrafted that part of the opinion. I retain my original reasoning in Parts II.A and II.B, making clear that Patterson might have stated a Section 1981 claim on these facts. But in Part II.C I now conclude that the dismissal of her harassment claim should nevertheless be affirmed.
>
> I reach this conclusion simply because Patterson failed ever to claim any link, evidentiary or otherwise, between the harassment she suffered and the making of the employment contract. Instead, she argued at the trial solely that harassment by itself violates Section 1981 (as her proposed jury instruction, now quoted in the opinion, demonstrates).

A day after Brennan had sent his proposed redraft to Blackmun, Marshall and Stevens, he circulated the revised draft to the other justices as the "opinion of the Court," declaring that the Supreme Court had affirmed the lower federal court's dismissal of Brenda Patterson's racial harassment claim. "We affirm the dismissal of Patterson's Section 1981 harassment claim," Brennan wrote, "because it is clear that petitioner at no point prior to or during trial sufficiently alleged that respondent's harassment *evidenced* a violation of Section 1981's strictures regarding contract formation."

Brennan had not earned his gigantic reputation as one of the most influential liberals of the modern era by making a habit of rejecting civil rights claims on legal technicalities. To the contrary, Brennan always seemed ready to overlook such technicalities when the broader

purposes of federal statutes and constitutional provisions (as he interpreted them) were served. But in *Patterson*, his only hope of salvaging
a majority on the racial harassment issue was to seize upon such a legal technicality, and reject Brenda Patterson's claim. If Brennan
could persuade Kennedy to join him—and hold his three liberal colleagues in the process—he would still be able to write an opinion for
a Court majority on the issue.

Brennan's strategy backfired. Kennedy not only refused to support
his latest circulated opinion, but he issued another draft of his own,
more determined than ever to advocate his new position that the
racial harassment charged by Patterson could not be a violation of
Section 1981. And now Kennedy attacked the Brennan opinion with a
vengeance, even criticizing language that had appeared in every
Brennan draft opinion since November.

In his new draft, Kennedy discovered numerous reasons to disdain
Brennan's opinion on the racial harassment issue. He quoted, for example, Brennan's statement that "racial harassment severe enough to
amount to a breach of contract as a matter of state law is *certainly* [the
italics are Kennedy's] cognizable under Section 1981." Kennedy retorted that "not one citation to any decision of this Court is offered for
this certainty" and added that "I think this proposition, which has
never been addressed directly by this Court, is far from clear." Later
he quoted disapprovingly from Brennan's opinion that "severe or pervasive racial harassment could belie any claim that the contract was
entered into in a racially neutral manner." The fact that racial harassment is severe or pervasive does not, Kennedy wrote, "magically
transform a challenge to the conditions of employment, not actionable
under Section 1981, into a viable challenge to the employer's refusal
to contract."

Besides Kennedy, Justice White took exception to Brennan's revised draft in his own revised dissent. White wrote that Brennan's new
position (that Patterson would lose her racial harassment claim on a
procedural defect) "will surely shock Mrs. Patterson, McLean Credit
Union, the Solicitor General, and 16 other amici who filed briefs
here—none of whom ever suggested any defect in Mrs. Patterson's
pleadings or in the presentation of her claim at trial or on appeal.

With all due respect," he continued, "Justice Brennan's proposed ending to this law suit is as unsatisfying as the conclusion of a bad mystery novel: we learn on the last page that the victim has been done-in by a suspect heretofore unknown, for reasons previously unrevealed."

If Brennan didn't have enough problems with Justices Kennedy and White, he was also confronted with the loss of one of his solid votes at judicial conference in *Patterson*, that of Justice Stevens. After reading Brennan's revisions on the racial harassment issue, Stevens had first considered supporting Brennan. But "reflecting further on the problem," Stevens wrote Brennan, "I have concluded that I will not be able to join a judgment affirming the dismissal of petitioner's racial harassment claim." Stevens was not, in other words, budging from his position that Brenda Patterson should be able to take her racial harassment claim to a jury under the 1866 statute.

In quick order the Court's *Patterson* lineup was turned upside down. Justice Kennedy, who had voted in October with Brennan in judicial conference and had represented the fifth member of Brennan's majority, was now assigned the opinion for the new majority (Rehnquist, White, O'Connor, Scalia and Kennedy) by Rehnquist, an unusual choice since Kennedy had not completed a full term on the Court. Ordinarily, such important opinions are given to more seasoned justices. But in *Patterson*, the chief needed Kennedy's vote to capture the Court for his conservative position and the assignment could help reinforce the junior justice's commitment. And if the chief had given the assignment to an outspoken conservative like Justice Scalia, he might risk losing the more moderate Kennedy once again.

Kennedy's reputation had been built on a long record of steady, cautious personal and professional achievement. But now Kennedy, the newly assigned author of the Court majority's *Patterson* opinion— which was sure to rankle large segments of the legal community—was placed squarely in the middle of a major controversy. He had rarely found himself in such a predicament.

Before his Court appointment, Anthony M. Kennedy had lived his entire life in the same white colonial house in Sacramento,

California, behind a camellia bush and a neat row of gardenias. He had followed his mother to Stanford University and had sent his three children to their alma mater. Kennedy's mother and father were practicing Irish Catholics and Kennedy himself bicycled to mass and continued to attend Sunday morning services throughout his adult life. Tony compiled a superb academic record at McClatchy High School, serving as valedictorian of his graduating class.

At Stanford, Kennedy assigned every minute of every day a careful purpose, even his prescribed nine hours of sleep. As an undergraduate, he signed up for eighteen credit hours and calculated that he would need thirty minutes of sleep for each credit. Nine hours of sleep every weekday and no exceptions.

Please, Tony, urged his father, Anthony "Bud" Kennedy, a raucous, cigar-chewing lobbyist in the state capital, do something naughty. Once, in desperation, Bud Kennedy offered his son a hundred dollars if he would join the other boys on just one daring escapade that would stimulate a call from the local police precinct. Bud Kennedy never heard from the police.

Tony Kennedy's pal John Hamlyn watched with anticipation as his friend unwrapped a full quart of hundred-proof Yellowstone whiskey after the two college students had set out by steamship for a summer tour of Europe. Alas, the moonshine was for gargling (in case of a sore throat), not drinking. Kennedy's most adventurous act of defiance was said to have occurred at the top of the Washington Monument when he was on a sightseeing trip with his high school class: it was said that he spit his wad of chewing gum over the ledge.

His greatest academic interest, even in pre–law school days, was constitutional law and history. After graduating from Stanford with a Phi Beta Kappa key, Kennedy enrolled at the Harvard Law School, where he emerged, three years later, with a law degree cum laude. Early in his career, Kennedy leapt at the opportunity to teach constitutional law at the McGeorge School of Law in Sacramento. His lecturing was not, it was observed, confined to the classroom; in court young Kennedy was known to have a penchant for lecturing judges on the fine points of law.

A short time after Kennedy joined a San Francisco law firm in the early sixties, his father died, and his career plans abruptly changed. He returned to Sacramento, settled his father's estate and took over Bud Kennedy's law practice with its heavy lobbying component. But where his father back-slapped his way from office to influential legislator's office, Tony Kennedy approached his lobbying job with clinical efficiency. He presented the case for favorable legislation for his clients, Schenley Industries, for example, with the precise analysis that had characterized his career in both classroom and courtroom. To be sure, he joined several private clubs and did his share of entertaining useful lawmakers, but the job was always done with tact, dutiful cheerfulness and seamless competence.

Kennedy's big professional break, which led to his oft-stated goal of becoming a judge, came in the early seventies, when California Governor Ronald Reagan's chief advisor, Ed Meese, was looking for a lawyer to draft a state referendum proposition that would limit state spending through taxation. Meese met Kennedy, was favorably impressed and asked the Sacramento lawyer to take on the assignment. Kennedy's drafting satisfied Meese, and when in 1975 an opening occurred on the U.S. Court of Appeals for the Ninth Circuit, Meese recommended Kennedy. At thirty-nine, he became one of the youngest federal appellate judges in the nation.

Over the next twelve years, Kennedy wrote more than four hundred judicial opinions, each reflective of Kennedy's cautious approach to the law. He rarely overturned judicial precedent. He interpreted federal statutes narrowly, never risking a construction that reached more than an arm's length from the explicit statutory language. And he chose not to decide constitutional issues that could be put over for another day or for a higher court. The resulting jurisprudence, naturally, favored the status quo.

Judge Kennedy was tough on criminal offenders and reluctant to support broad civil rights and liberties claims. On the controversial issues that mattered to the Reagan Administration—affirmative action, abortion, school prayer—Judge Kennedy's previous decisions gave little indication of where he stood. But his judicial pattern was unmistakably conservative, and the lack of a more definitive articulation of his philosophy was seen by the Reagan Administration as an asset, particularly after Judge Robert Bork had failed to be confirmed in one of the most controversial confirmation battles in history.

Judge Bork, a member of the U.S. Court of Appeals for the District of Columbia, had been President Reagan's first choice in the summer of 1987 to succeed the pivotal moderate, Justice Lewis F. Powell, Jr. As a law professor at Yale before his appointment to the federal appeals court, Bork had distinguished himself among conservative intellectuals—and outraged their liberal counterparts—with his attacks on the rulings of the Warren and Burger Courts. He had bluntly questioned both the wisdom and the constitutionality of the Civil Rights Act of 1964 (which the Warren Court upheld) and called *Roe v. Wade* "an unconstitutional decision, a serious and wholly unjustifiable judicial usurpation of state legislative authority."

In his opening statement at Bork's Senate confirmation hearings, Senator Edward Kennedy of Massachusetts declared, "In Robert Bork's America, there is no room in the inn for blacks and no place in the Constitution for women. And, in our America, there should be no seat on the Supreme Court for Robert Bork."

After Bork was turned down, President Reagan again picked a judge from the D.C. Court of Appeals, Douglas Ginsburg, as his second choice to replace Justice Powell. But almost immediately, the Ginsburg nomination ran into trouble amid charges of conflicts of interest and stories of pot-smoking as a law professor at Harvard. Judge Ginsburg abruptly withdrew his name from consideration and Reagan nominated Judge Kennedy, whose professional and personal backgrounds were controversy-proof.

On December 14, 1987, when Judge Kennedy entered the historic Senate Caucus Room, there were no long lines of visitors outside the hearing room, no live network television coverage and significantly fewer reporters inside than during the Bork hearings. The atmosphere among the senators was one of weary relief. Even the Democratic Huns of the Bork hearings—Joseph Biden and Edward Kennedy—seemed eager to praise Judge Kennedy. Chairman Biden told the nominee "[you] did not have any ideological briefs in your back pocket. You are an extremely honorable man." Unlike Bork, Kennedy had no ideological conservative tracts to defend. He could speak in expansive generalities about the Constitution, and he proved adept at the exercise. He provided articulate answers to every question posed, without committing himself to any specific, definable position. Asked if he possessed an overriding constitutional philosophy (as Judge Bork did), Kennedy replied, "I do not offer myself as someone with a complete cosmology of the Constitution."

Kennedy was asked by Senator Arlen Specter how he could reconcile *Brown v. Board of Education* with the "original intent" of the framers of the Fourteenth Amendment. "I do not think the Fourteenth Amendment was designed to freeze into society all of the inequities that then existed," Kennedy replied. He assured the committee that it was entirely appropriate for them to seek assurances that "a nominee to the Supreme Court is sensitive to civil rights. We simply do not have any real freedom if we have discrimination based on race, sex, religion or national origin."

On May 22, 1989, Justice Kennedy circulated the first draft of his majority opinion in *Patterson v. McLean Credit Union*. After briefly stating Brenda Patterson's legal claims and the lower court decisions, Kennedy carefully approached the first issue before the Court: should *Runyon v. McCrary* be overruled? "Some Members of this Court believe that *Runyon* was decided incorrectly, and others consider it correct on its own footing," Kennedy wrote, "but the question before us is whether it ought now to be overturned." It should not, and Kennedy proceeded to explain, with many of the reasons articulated in earlier Brennan drafts, why there was no special justification for overruling *Runyon*. There had been no Court decisions after *Runyon* or statutes enacted by Congress, Kennedy noted, that made *Runyon* an obstacle to a coherent development of the law. Kennedy made the further point, also made earlier by Brennan, that "*Runyon* is entirely consistent with our society's deep commitment to the eradication of discrimination based on a person's race or the color of his or her skin."

But a general commitment to fight racial discrimination did not, Kennedy quickly added, decide Brenda Patterson's racial harassment claim. At this point in his draft opinion, Kennedy focused on the issue

71

that had plagued him from the very beginning of the Court's consideration of the lawsuit: did Section 1981 prohibit the racial harassment that Brenda Patterson had charged? Kennedy announced his conclusion that the statutory language was meant to be interpreted narrowly and could not "be construed as a general proscription of racial discrimination in all aspects of contract relations" (a phrase that Kennedy had used to characterize, and criticize, Brennan's position—mistakenly, Brennan had insisted—in Brennan's first *Patterson* draft). The right to make a contract did not extend, Kennedy wrote, "as a matter of either logic or semantics to conduct by the employer after the contract relation has been established, including breach of the terms of the contract or imposition of discriminatory working conditions."

The conduct that Brenda Patterson labeled as "actionable racial harassment," Kennedy continued, occurred *after* the contract was made and, therefore, was not covered by Section 1981. Patterson should have pursued her claim under Title VII of the Civil Rights Act of 1964, which dealt with discriminatory working conditions after the employment contract had been made. By allowing Patterson's claim under Section 1981, the Court would "undermine" Title VII, Kennedy argued.

Kennedy then renewed his criticism of Brennan's *Patterson* opinion (now a dissent) in which Brennan had contended that racial harassment serious enough to be a breach of contract under state law was certainly severe enough to violate Section 1981. "Not one citation to any decision of this Court is offered for this certainty," Kennedy repeated. He added, "In fact, just the opposite is true." He also reiterated his charge that Brennan, "by magic," had attempted to force Patterson's claim under Section 1981 by fashioning his own definition of the statute's requirements ("where the nature and extent of the act constituting harassment are sufficiently severe or pervasive").

At the conclusion of his draft opinion, Kennedy offered conciliatory words toward those, like Justice Brennan, who would find his statutory analysis unfairly cramped and sure to result in many more defeats for civil rights plaintiffs in the future. "The law now reflects society's consensus that discrimination based on the color of one's skin is a profound wrong of tragic dimension," Kennedy wrote. "Neither our words nor our decisions should be interpreted as signaling one inch of retreat from the Congress' policy to forbid discrimination in the private as well as the public sphere."

Justice Stevens accepted the new *Patterson* order, and Kennedy opinion, philosophically. He wrote Brennan the day Kennedy's majority opinion was circulated:

Dear Bill:

On December 5, 1988, when I joined your proposed majority opinion, I thought your draft expressed a position on the racial harassment issue that had been adopted by four other Justices at Conference—indeed, the portion of your opinion discussing harassment that amounts to a breach of contract (under state law) was also endorsed by Byron, and possibly by the Chief as well. In the intervening months, further study has convinced at least three members of the present majority to modify their views—and, in one case, his vote. I have no quarrel with the process (having done so a number of times myself this Term as well as in the past) but thought I should let you know that since my vote is no longer necessary to produce a Court opinion, I shall probably end up writing separately. I would not want the fact that I signed on to your first draft (though not your third)* to inhibit what you might otherwise want to say in dissent. . . .

Justice Brennan would not likely consider the 1988 Court term one of his favorites. The year had brought serious illness and a stay in the hospital which, at the age of eighty-two, was not to be ignored. His extraordinary skills as a crafter of Court majorities (some said, prestidigitator) had not produced satisfactory results.

In the civil rights field alone, one in which Brennan had taken a leadership role for all of his years on the Court, the term had already been a wrenching disappointment. First, the Court had declared in January in *Croson* that Richmond's attempt to set aside 30 percent of its building subcontracts for minority contractors was a violation of

---

* Brennan's second draft, circulated in December, had contained only stylistic changes.

the constitutional rights of nonminority contractors. Four and a half months after the *Croson* decision was announced, two more block-buster Court decisions shocked the nation's civil rights advocates. Both decisions were squeezed out by a five-member conservative majority—Rehnquist, White, O'Connor, Scalia and Kennedy. In the first, the Court unceremoniously dismantled an eighteen-year-old Court precedent that employment discrimination lawyers had considered the key civil rights decision of the modern Court era. The Burger Court decision *Griggs v. Duke Power* had made it easier to prove racial discrimination in hiring.

In *Griggs*, the Court ruled that under Title VII of the Civil Rights Act of 1964, Congress intended to focus on the *consequences* of employment practices, not simply their motivation. If an employer hired a disproportionately large nonminority workforce, he had the burden under *Griggs* of showing that the job qualifications, a high school diploma, for example, were *necessary* to perform the job. Title VII, the Court declared, "proscribes not only overt discrimination but also practices that are fair in form, but discriminatory in operation."

But in June 1989, the Rehnquist Court majority declared in *Wards Cove Packing Co. v. Atonio* that the burden of showing discriminatory practices, once again, shifted to the employee. Justice Blackmun, a member of the *Griggs* majority, now in dissent, dispensed with legal technicalities in his conclusion: "One wonders whether the majority still believes that racial discrimination—or, more accurately, race discrimination against non-whites—is a problem in our society, or even remembers that it ever was."

In a second Court decision in early June, again by a 5-to-4 vote, the conservative majority ruled that white firefighters in Birmingham, Alabama, could sue to reopen an affirmative action settlement approved by a federal district court there eight years earlier to remedy discrimination that had kept blacks out of all senior positions in the city's fire department. The majority opinion in *Martin v. Wilks* was written by Chief Justice Rehnquist, who, in supporting the belated legal claim of the white firefighters, hearkened to "our deep-rooted historic tradition that everyone should have his own day in court."

Brennan had lost three important civil rights cases—*Croson*,

Wards Cove, and *Martin*—by narrow margins. And he faced the most excruciating defeat of all in *Patterson.* For in *Patterson,* unlike the others, he had had victory very much within his grasp. Had he been able to hold Kennedy's vote, the term would not have been the unmitigated civil rights disaster that it turned out to be.

But Brennan's extensive courting of his most junior colleague in *Patterson* had ended in abject failure. Justice Kennedy not only had rejected Brennan's opinion, but had also introduced language in his own majority opinion that appeared contemptuous of the senior justice's analysis. Finally, the likelihood that Brennan might persuade four other members of this Court in the future to take anything but a clenchingly narrow interpretation of a civil rights statute seemed remote.

There was, however, one consolation for Brennan in his new status in *Patterson.* He was no longer obligated to satisfy four justices with an accommodating majority opinion. Unencumbered by the demands of colleagues, he could write exactly what he thought about the legal issues—and the majority opinion of Justice Kennedy.

Brennan began his revised opinion with a wide-open endorsement of the Court's *Runyon* decision, shorn of the cautionary language of his now-defunct *Patterson* majority opinion. In his earlier draft, Brennan had termed the *Runyon* Court's interpretation of the 1866 statute "plausible." His opinion of June 8 emphatically endorsed the *Runyon* Court's interpretation of the 1866 statute as *correct,* not merely "plausible," and castigated the Rehnquist Court majority for ever requesting reargument:

> In the past, this Court has overruled decisions antagonistic to our Nation's commitment to the ideal of a society in which a person's opportunities do not depend on her race, e.g. *Brown v. Board of Education* (1954) overruling *Plessy v. Ferguson* (1896), and I find it disturbing that the Court has in this case chosen to reconsider, without any request from the parties, a statutory construction so in harmony with that ideal. Having decided, however, to reconsider *Runyon* and now to reaffirm it by appeal to *stare decisis,* the Court glosses over what are in my view two very obvious reasons for refusing to overrule this interpretation of Section 1981: that *Runyon*

was correctly decided and that in any event Congress has ratified our construction of the statute.

Turning to the racial harassment issue, Brennan accused Justice Kennedy in his majority opinion of "conducting an ahistorical analysis that ignores the circumstances and legislative history of Section 1981." He concluded that "the fact that Section 1981 provides a remedy for a type of racism that remains a serious social ill broader than that available under Title VII hardly provides a good reason to see it, as the Court seems to, as a disruptive blot on the legal landscape, a provision to be constructed as narrowly as possible."

Brennan's frontal attack on Kennedy's analysis set off a spiraling verbal brawl between the two justices. Kennedy answered Brennan in a revised draft, rejecting out-of-hand Brennan's statutory interpretation and reminding him that the Court need not decide whether *Runyon* was correct or not, but only whether it should adhere to the doctrine of stare decisis. Kennedy also dismissed Brennan's standard for determining racial harassment as "amorphous and manipulable."

It was now Brennan's turn, and in *his* revised opinion he inserted an introductory paragraph that sent Kennedy into a modulated rage. Brennan wrote:

> What the Court declines to snatch away with one hand, it steals with the other. Though the Court today reaffirms Section 1981's applicability to private conduct, it simultaneously gives this landmark civil rights statute a needlessly cramped interpretation. The Court has to strain hard to justify this choice to confine Section 1981 within the narrowest possible scope, selecting the most pinched reading of the phrase "the same right to make a contract," ignoring powerful historical evidence about the Reconstruction Congress' concerns, and bolstering its parsimonious rendering by reference to a statute enacted nearly a century after Section 1981, and plainly not intended to affect its reach. The Court's fine phrases about our commitment to the eradication of racial discrimination . . . seem to count for little in practice. cf. *Wards Cove Packing Co. v. Atonio* (1989); *City of Richmond v. J. A. Croson Co.* (1989). When it comes to deciding whether a civil rights statute

should be construed to further that commitment, the fine phrases disappear, replaced by a formalistic method of interpretation antithetical of Congress' vision of a society in which contractual opportunities are equal. . . .

When Brennan returned to his chambers from his granddaughter's graduation on June 13, 1989, he found a small manila envelope on his desk. The note inside, handwritten in ink on official Supreme Court stationery, had been sent to Brennan by Justice Kennedy. Kennedy's message consisted of only two sentences, but they delivered a tightly packaged warning, and a plea. "Dear Bill," Kennedy wrote. "The Patterson opinions match well and are ready to go, but the 1st, 3rd, and 4th sentences of your first paragraph ought not to go unanswered. If you wish them to stand, I'll send the enclosed to the printer; but do we really need to do this to each other? Yours, Tony."

Kennedy attached a one-page rebuttal to the opening paragraph of Brennan's dissent that would be inserted as a footnote if Brennan did not retreat:

> Once again this Term, a dissenter thinks it judicious to bolster his position by questioning the Court's understanding of the necessity to eradicate racial discrimination. See post. at 1. See also *Wards Cove Packing Co. v. Atonio* (1989) (Blackmun, J., dissenting); *City of Richmond v. J. A. Croson Co.* (1989) (Blackmun, J., dissenting). The commitment to equality, fairness, and compassion is not a treasured monopoly of our colleagues in dissent. Those ideals are shared by each member of the Court. We yield to no one in our own deep understanding both of these principles and of the obligations reposed in us by our oath. . . .
>
> Our point of disagreement with the dissenters in this case rests here: Although we loathe private discrimination as much as they, we do not believe this empowers us to construe congressional enactments beyond a fair reading of their terms. In interpreting the statutes before us we must remember that Equal Justice Under Law is not a promise made to just one of the parties in a suit. Neither analytic precision nor respect for this Court is advanced by barbs about our respective sensitivities.

A flurry of notes were exchanged among the justices on June 13, 1989. One was sent from Justice Brennan to Kennedy. A second was written by Chief Justice Rehnquist to Kennedy. Two more notes, which influenced the final opinions of both Brennan and Kennedy in *Patterson*, came from Justice Stevens, one addressed to Justices Brennan and Kennedy, and the other to Justice Brennan alone.

Brennan was not in much of a compromising mood. "Dear Tony," he wrote Kennedy, "I've just returned from my granddaughter's graduation and find your note. This case has sharply divided the Court from the beginning. I really think the thought expressed in the first paragraph of my amended concurrence,* I should express. I will, however, substitute for the word 'steals' in the second line the word 'takes.' Sincerely, Bill."

That same day, Kennedy wrote Rehnquist informing him that his reply, by footnote, to Brennan's first paragraph was at the printer and that Brennan had seen it. Later that Monday, Kennedy received a one-sentence reply from the chief: "I agree with your response."

"Dear Bill and Tony," Justice Stevens now wrote Brennan and Kennedy. "May we at least wait until tomorrow to decide whether to bring this case [*Patterson*] down on Thursday. I did not see Bill's revised page 1 until this morning, and was in the process of drafting an addition to my opinion [in dissent] when I received Tony's new footnote on pages 20–21. Probably we would all be better off with some deletions rather than any more writing, but I would at least like to have time to think the problem through. . . ."

Later that day, Stevens wrote Brennan a cordial two-paragraph note suggesting editorial changes that would eliminate the acrimony of Brennan's first paragraph. "Is there any possibility that you would consider revising page one of your latest draft to omit the sentence beginning with the words 'The Court's fine phrases' together with the three citations and the first three lines of the next sentence," Stevens wrote Brennan. "Then the transition would read something like this: 'The Court's formalistic method of interpretation is plainly antithetical to Congress' vision of a society. . . .' "

---

* Brennan concurred on the *Runyon* issue but dissented on the racial harassment issue.

Stevens's final sentence in his note to Brennan was designed to persuade his longtime colleague to accept his drafting advice. "I know I have no standing to make this suggestion because I have not joined this part of your opinion," Stevens wrote, "but I am sufficiently troubled by it to be thinking seriously of joining Tony's footnote response. Respectfully, John."

Stevens's polite pressure on Brennan had the desired effect. In the fourth draft of his opinion in *Patterson*, dated June 13, Justice Brennan deleted much of the language from his first paragraph that had so aroused Justice Kennedy and concerned Stevens. He substituted "takes" for "steals" in the first sentence, eliminated the fourth sentence and citations altogether (as Stevens had recommended) and modified the fifth sentence so that his references to "fine phrases" (referring to the Court's stated commitment to the eradication of racial discrimination) that "disappear" were omitted.

Kennedy responded to Brennan's accommodations by deleting the long footnote of his opinion that had lashed out at Brennan's questioning the majority's "understanding of the necessity to eradicate racial discrimination." The final draft of Kennedy's majority opinion was sent to the printer on June 14.

One day later, Justice Kennedy announced the Court's opinion in *Patterson* in open court. He reported that *Runyon v. McCrary* had been reaffirmed unanimously, but then said that a five-member Court majority (Rehnquist, White, O'Connor, Scalia and Kennedy) would not extend the application of the post–Civil War statute to the charges of racial harassment raised by Brenda Patterson.

The reaction to Kennedy's *Patterson* opinion divided along a natural political fault line. Paul Kamenar, executive legal director of the conservative Washington Legal Foundation (which had filed an amicus brief in *Patterson* arguing that the Court should have removed *all* private discrimination from the law's scope), considered *Patterson* "a field goal rather than a touchdown." But it was a victory by any measure, according to Kamenar, since it cut back on the application of the 1866 statute. A contrary opinion of *Patterson* was held by Benjamin Hooks and Ralph Neas of the Leadership Conference on Civil Rights. After *Patterson*, they pronounced the Court term "a disaster for all those committed to equal employment opportunity."

The man who represented Brenda Patterson at the reargument of her case, Julius Chambers, offered the most soberly realistic assessment of all. The fact that the Court had not overruled *Runyon v. McCrary* was "a victory in a battle that never should have been fought," he said. And the final result in *Patterson*, added Chambers, was no victory at all. The *Patterson* decision, he concluded, "has the practical effect of denying to those who suffer the emotional pain and indignity of on-the-job racial harassment any effective remedy."

After the Court's decision, Marshall Patterson continued to work for the United Parcel Service in Winston-Salem, North Carolina. His wife, Brenda, never stepped inside the McLean Credit Union office again and was unemployed for many years. Later, she organized a day-care program for preschool children in her home.

Although unsuccessful in her lawsuit, Brenda Patterson could take some satisfaction in the ultimate vindication of her legal position. For almost immediately after Justice Kennedy announced the decision for a five-member majority that Brenda Patterson's racial harassment claim was not covered by the 1866 Civil Rights Act, Congress repudiated the Court's *Patterson* decision. Reacting to *Patterson* and other controversial civil rights decisions by the conservative majority that term, Congress drafted new civil rights legislation amending both the Civil Rights Acts of 1866 and 1964.* The legislation finally passed as the Civil Rights Act of 1991 two years after it was introduced,† and it effectively reversed the Court's employment discrimination decision, *Wards Cove Packing Co. v. Atonio*, as well as the five-member majority decision in *Martin v. Wilks*.

And for those like the NAACP Legal Defense Fund's Julius Chambers who had supported Patterson's legal cause, the new civil rights statute provided that racial harassment on the job is a federal violation for which damages can be awarded. With the passage of the Civil

---

* At the request of Senator Ted Kennedy, Brenda Patterson testified at congressional hearings on the proposed new civil rights legislation.

† President Bush originally vetoed the legislation, labeling it a "quota" bill.

Rights Act of 1991, Congress guaranteed that future civil rights plaintiffs with claims of racial harassment will not suffer the same fate as Brenda Patterson.

Clearly, the conservatives on the Rehnquist Court did not create a revolution in civil rights law. The threatened reversal of *Runyon v. McCrary* provoked a furious defense of the decision by the Court's liberals as well as civil rights attorneys, scholars and congressmen, and the precedent was preserved. Most of the conservatives' narrow victories in civil rights cases, moreover, were blunted by the Civil Rights Act of 1991.

But there was a second, far less salutary, signal from the perspective of the civil rights bar. For more than three decades, the modern Supreme Court had served as the crucial national institution that had encouraged the civil rights movement by broadly interpreting the Constitution and federal laws to protect racial minorities. The 1988 Court term, in which *Patterson* was decided, marked the end of that historic judicial era. With the advent of the conservative Rehnquist Court majority, Congress, not the Court, became the channel for civil rights activism.

P A R T   I I

ABORTION

I rue this day. I rue the violence that has been done to
the liberty and equality of women. I rue the violence
that has been done to our legal fabric and to the
integrity of this Court. I rue the inevitable loss of public
esteem for this Court that is so essential. I dissent.

From the unpublished dissenting opinion of
JUSTICE HARRY A. BLACKMUN
in *Webster v. Reproductive Health Services* (1989)

CHAPTER FOUR

A BULL BY THE
TAIL

On September 17, 1971, shortly before the Court's new term was to begin, Justice Hugo Black sent word to President Richard Nixon that, after thirty-four years of distinguished service on the Court, his bad health forced him to resign. Six days later, Black's ailing colleague and close friend, Justice John M. Harlan, submitted his resignation.

The vacancies caused by Black's and Harlan's resignations presented an enormous problem for Chief Justice Warren E. Burger's leadership in only Burger's third term on the Court. The chief justice was concerned that the remaining seven members of the Court would have to decide controversial cases on the docket, such as *Roe v. Wade*, a constitutional challenge to Texas's abortion statute, without a full court. If the Court split 4 to 3 in *Roe* or other controversial cases, the position of four justices would become the law of the land.

Soon after the Court's 1971 October term had begun, President Nixon announced the nominations of Lewis F. Powell, Jr., a prominent Richmond corporate lawyer and former president of the American Bar Association, and William H. Rehnquist, an assistant attorney general in the Nixon Administration, to fill the Court vacancies. Although the Nixon nominations had been sent to the Senate in late October, there was no guarantee that Powell and Rehnquist would be confirmed in time to hear the oral argument in *Roe v. Wade* and *Doe v. Bolton*, the companion abortion case from Georgia. With memories of the president's recent failed nominations of Judges Clement F. Haynsworth, Jr., and G. Harrold Carswell still fresh,* no one could accurately predict when the Court would have its full complement of nine justices.

The prospect of a seven-member Court deciding controversial cases such as *Roe* and *Doe* prompted Chief Justice Burger to suggest to his colleagues that they screen pending cases and schedule oral arguments only for those cases that were unlikely to split the Court 4 to 3. Burger's purpose was to avoid the most difficult cases in which division among the seven justices might create a decision by a minority (four justices) of the full Court. The chief justice, therefore, appointed a small screening committee of the justices to assure that only the relatively uncontroversial cases would go forward for argument.

The committee, chaired by Potter Stewart and which included Harry Blackmun, let *Roe v. Wade* and *Doe v. Bolton* go forward. "It was a serious mistake," Blackmun later said. "We did a poor job. I think the committee should have deferred them [the abortion cases] until we had a full Court."

The Court set oral argument in the two abortion cases for Monday morning, December 13, 1971. Two weeks before the scheduled oral argument, Jay Floyd, the assistant attorney general of Texas who represented the state in *Roe*, asked the justices to postpone oral argument in the abortion cases until Powell and Rehnquist could be confirmed and take their seats on the Court. It was reasonable for Floyd to as-

---

* In 1970, President Nixon announced his intention of appointing a southerner to replace Justice Abe Fortas on the Court and nominated Clement Haynsworth of South Carolina, the chief judge on the U.S. Court of Appeals for the Fourth Circuit. After the Haynsworth nomination was defeated by Democrats charging the nominee with conflicts of interest and an unacceptable civil rights record, Nixon named Judge Carswell of the U.S. Court of Appeals for the Fifth Circuit. But the Carswell nomination sunk after his earlier racist declarations were made public—paving the way for Nixon's appointment of Judge Harry Blackmun of the U.S. Court of Appeals for the Eighth Circuit.

sume that both Powell and Rehnquist, whom the president had praised as judicial conservatives, would be sympathetic to arguments that Texas's and Georgia's laws regulating abortions should be upheld as constitutional.

On December 7, one day after Powell was confirmed by the Senate 89 to 1, the justices denied Floyd's request. Three days later, the Senate, by a much closer vote (68 to 26), confirmed Rehnquist's nomination. But the confirmation votes would do Floyd no good, at least as far as his initial argument before the Court on December 13 was concerned. Although confirmed shortly before the scheduled oral arguments in the abortion cases, Powell and Rehnquist would not officially take their seats on the Court until the first week in January.

Sarah Weddington, the attorney who would oppose Jay Floyd at the oral argument in *Roe* on December 13, 1971, had confronted the dark side of the abortion controversy four years earlier. As a frightened, pregnant law student at the University of Texas in Austin in 1967, Sarah and her future husband, Ron Weddington, had driven to the dusty border town of Piedras Negras, Mexico. There the couple followed a man in brown pants and white guayabera shirt down a succession of dirt alleys until they arrived at the small office of the doctor who performed an abortion on Sarah. "I did exactly as I was told," Weddington recalled. "When I felt the anesthesia taking effect, my last thoughts were, I hope I don't die, and I pray that no one ever finds out about this."

Two years later, Weddington placed a telephone call to her law school classmate Linda Coffee in Dallas to ask if she would be willing to join her in her legal challenge to Texas's abortion statute, which prohibited an abortion except to save the life of the mother. Coffee enthusiastically agreed, and the two women began the arduous process of building a constitutional test case. First, Weddington and Coffee knew, they needed an appropriate plaintiff—a pregnant woman who resided in Texas, wanted an abortion and would be willing to be listed as a party in their lawsuit.

After Coffee had been given Norma McCorvey's name by another Dallas attorney, Weddington and Coffee met McCorvey, the future

Jane Roe, in a Dallas pizza parlor. A petite woman in her early twenties, McCorvey wore jeans and an oversized, peasant-style blouse for her meeting with the two attorneys. McCorvey had one child already and did not want another.* Her mother had taken her daughter away from her, and Norma had rarely seen her since. Now she was pregnant again, unmarried, and certain that if she remained pregnant she would lose her job as a waitress. Without the job, Norma McCorvey felt that her already depressingly bleak life would get much worse.

Weddington and Coffee assured McCorvey that if she agreed to be a plaintiff in their lawsuit, very little would be required of her in return. It would cost her nothing, since Coffee and Weddington were absorbing the legal expenses. She would sign a one-page affidavit swearing to her condition, but would not have to testify in court. And she would be given a pseudonym for purposes of the lawsuit: Jane Roe.

On the clear, crisp morning of December 13, 1971, Sarah Weddington, twenty-five years old, joined the legendary figures of the American bar who had presented oral arguments to the Supreme Court of the United States. Weddington's task was to convince the justices that the Texas law that made abortion a crime unless it was necessary to save the life of the mother was unconstitutional, a position taken by a three-judge federal appeals panel.†

Weddington had dressed conservatively for the occasion, wearing a three-piece dark blue suit, long-sleeve blouse, and a single-strand pearl necklace. But at five feet seven inches, this attractive young woman, with strawberry-blond hair flowing below her shoulders, was hardly inconspicuous as she climbed the steps to enter the imposing Supreme Court Building.

"Go get 'em, Sarah," shouted one well-wisher as Weddington passed by.

---

* McCorvey had originally claimed that she had been gang-raped, but later admitted that that story was false, and that she had become pregnant in the more usual way.

† In *Doe v. Bolton*, the companion abortion case from Georgia, a lower federal court had invalidated portions of the state law that prohibited abortions except those performed by a physician who concluded that in his best clinical judgment a continued pregnancy would endanger the mother's life or health, the fetus would likely be born with a serious defect or the pregnancy was the result of a rape.

At 10:07 that morning, Chief Justice Warren Burger peered down from the center seat of the elevated bench in the ornate courtroom. "Mrs. Weddington," Burger intoned, "you may proceed whenever you are ready."

With those words from the chief justice, all of Weddington's pent-up nervousness evaporated, and she began the argument that she had, in effect, been preparing since that traumatic day in 1967 in Piedras Negras. Speaking with emotion, Weddington explained the effects of an unwanted pregnancy on a woman's life: "It disrupts her body, it disrupts her education, it disrupts her employment, and it often disrupts her entire family life. And . . . because of the impact on the woman, this certainly, in as far as there are any rights which are fundamental, is a matter . . . of such fundamental and basic concern to the woman involved that she should be allowed to make the choice as to whether to continue or terminate her pregnancy."

But what was the precise constitutional basis for her claim? Justice Potter Stewart wanted to know. Was she relying on the Due Process Clause of the Fourteenth Amendment? he asked.

"We originally brought suit alleging the Due Process Clause, the Equal Protection Clause, the Ninth Amendment, and a variety of others," Weddington replied.

"And anything else that might have been appropriate," Stewart added, provoking laughter in the audience.

Weddington responded spontaneously with a laugh. "The truth was," she later recalled, "that we included every argument we could think of."

Stewart had poked at the most vulnerable spot in Weddington's argument—the constitutional basis for a woman's right to control her own body.

Jay Floyd followed Weddington to the lectern and attempted to break the tension of the moment with a joke. Referring to Weddington and her cocounsel, Linda Coffee, who sat at the counsel table to his left, Floyd said, "It's an old joke, but when a man argues against two beautiful ladies like this, they're going to have the last word."

No one laughed.

As his argument progressed, Floyd found the deceptively incisive questioning of Justice Thurgood Marshall, delivered in a gruff drawl, particularly troublesome.

"When does an unborn fetus acquire constitutional rights?" Marshall asked Floyd.

"At any time, Mr. Justice," Floyd replied. "We make no distinction. There is life from the moment of impregnation."

"And do you have any scientific data to support that?" Marshall asked.

Floyd referred to the state's brief, which discussed the fetus's rights from "about seven to nine days after conception."

"Well, what about six days?"

"We don't know," answered Floyd.

"But this statute goes all the way back to one hour," said Marshall, acutely aware of the attorney's obvious discomfort with his line of questioning.

"I don't—Mr. Justice, it . . . ," stammered Floyd. "There are unanswerable questions in this field. . . ." His words trailed off as a wave of laughter rippled through the courtroom.

"I appreciate it, I appreciate it," said Marshall.

Justice Harry Blackmun was troubled on two counts. First, he didn't think the cases were very well argued. But more important, he shared the chief justice's concern that the justices would have to decide the controversial abortion cases without a full Court. The issues raised by *Roe v. Wade* and *Doe v. Bolton* would undoubtedly provoke division among the seven sitting justices. Blackmun sensed that "we had a bull by the tail."

At the justices' conference following oral arguments in *Roe* and *Doe*, Chief Justice Burger first discussed the facts and the lower court decisions in the two cases. He then devoted much of the remainder of his time to the issue of "standing": whether the lead female plaintiffs, neither of whom was still pregnant, could press their cases before the Court. On the merits of the Texas case, *Roe v. Wade*, Burger criticized the state statute but indicated that he was not prepared to declare it unconstitutional. "The balance here is between the state's interest in protecting fetal life and the woman's interest in not having children," the chief justice said. He concluded, "I can't find the Texas statute unconstitutional, although it's certainly archaic and obsolete."

Some of Burger's colleagues thought this meant the chief justice favored upholding the Texas statute, but Burger later contended that his position was not settled in conference and that he had wanted to await the "writing" by his colleagues before taking a final position in *Roe*.

The senior member of the Court, Justice William O. Douglas, spoke after the chief justice, and there could be no mistake in understanding his position in *Roe*. "The abortion statute is unconstitutional," Douglas declared. "This is basically a medical, psychiatric problem" not to be controlled exclusively, Douglas suggested, by state regulations.

Brennan was the third member of the Court to speak, and he agreed with Douglas that the Texas statute was unconstitutional.

"I agree with Bill Douglas," said Justice Potter Stewart. But Stewart, who usually anchored the center of the Burger Court on controversial constitutional issues, characteristically qualified his support. "The state can legislate," he said, to the extent of requiring a doctor to perform the abortion. And after a certain period of pregnancy, Stewart added, a pregnant woman should not be free to have an abortion.

"On the merits," Justice Byron White told his colleagues, "I am on the other side." White was not persuaded by Sarah Weddington's argument that there was a firm basis in the Constitution for the claimed woman's right to control her own body.

"I go with Bill Douglas," Justice Thurgood Marshall said, "but the time problem concerns me." Following up on Stewart's point that a woman's constitutional right to an abortion should not be unqualified, Marshall spoke of his concern for the constitutional interests of an unborn fetus as it approached term. The last justice to speak in conference on *Roe v. Wade* was the junior member of the Court, Harry Blackmun.

Exhibiting the cautious deliberation that had been his judicial hallmark on the U.S. Court of Appeals for the Eighth Circuit before his Court appointment a year earlier, Blackmun recited aloud his conflicting thoughts on *Roe*. "Can a state properly outlaw all abortions?" Blackmun asked. "If we accept fetal life, there's a strong argument that it can. But there are opposing interests: the right of the mother to life and mental and physical health, the right of parents in case of rape, the right of the state in case of incest. I don't think there's an absolute right to do what you will with your own body." But Justice Blackmun ended his discussion of *Roe* with a condemnation of the Texas statute. "This statute is a poor statute," he said, "that impinges too far on her [the pregnant woman's] Ninth Amendment rights."*

The justices' discussion of the Georgia statute broke along similar lines to *Roe*. The chief justice said that he favored upholding the statute as constitutional. Although he considered the Georgia abortion statute better than Texas's, Douglas still had serious doubts about its constitutionality. "We don't know how this statute operates," he said. "Is it weighted on the side of only those who can afford this?" Douglas asked. "What about the poor?" He suggested that *Doe v. Bolton* be returned to the lower federal court "to find out." Brennan did not share Douglas's doubts and would have affirmed the decision below, but would have gone further "to strike down the three-doctor thing† as too restrictive." White, Stewart and Marshall deviated little from the basic positions they had expressed in *Roe*.

"Medically, this statute is perfectly workable," Blackmun told his colleagues. But he was also sensitive to the competing constitutional interests. "I would like to see an opinion that recognizes the opposing interest in fetal life and the mother's interest in health and happiness," he said. But he appeared to share some of Douglas's concerns. "I would be perfectly willing to paint some standards and remand [to the lower court] for findings as to how it operates: does it operate to deny equal protection by discriminating against the poor?"

Douglas and Burger offered radically different versions of the judicial conference on the abortion cases, a disagreement that plunged the Court into internal crisis. Shortly after the justices' con-

---

* The Ninth Amendment provides: "The enumeration in the constitution of certain rights shall not be construed to deny or disparage others retained by the people."

† Brennan's reference was to a requirement that a three-member committee of doctors review the decision before an abortion could be performed. The Georgia law also required that the abortion be performed in an accredited hospital.

ference, Burger had circulated majority opinion assignments for recently discussed cases and included the assignment of the abortion cases to Justice Blackmun. When Douglas learned of the assignment, he wrote the chief justice a curt letter of protest. Douglas told Burger in his letter of December 18, 1971, that his notes showed that there had been four votes for declaring provisions of the Georgia statute unconstitutional (Douglas, Brennan, Stewart and Marshall).* There were only three "to sustain the law as written—you, Byron White and Harry Blackmun," Douglas continued. "I would think, therefore, that to save future time and trouble, one of the four, rather than one of the three, should write the opinion."

Responding to Douglas's letter two days later, Burger wrote, "At the close of the discussion of this case I remarked to the Conference that there were, literally, not enough columns to mark up an accurate reflection of the voting in either the Georgia or the Texas cases. I therefore marked down no votes and said this was a case that would have to stand or fall on the writing, when it was done. That is still my view of how to handle these two sensitive cases [*Roe v. Wade* and *Doe v. Bolton*], which, I might add, are quite probable candidates for reargument. However, I have no desire to restrain anyone's writing even though I do not have the same impression of views."

Justice Blackmun supported Burger in the controversy to the extent that he later said he understood the chief's assignment was for him to compose a memorandum discussing the issues in the abortion cases, rather than to write a majority opinion. "The confusion surrounding the *Roe* conference was, unfortunately, symptomatic of pervasive problems during the Burger Court era," Blackmun recalled. "We ended up in *Roe*, as we so often did with a situation of that kind in Chief Justice Burger's time, that one of us was assigned to do a memo, and I caught it," Blackmun said. "None of us ever liked this, because to do a memo takes as much effort and investment of time as does a full-fledged opinion."

Despite Douglas's protestations, Burger held to the course he had

---

* Blackmun himself recalled that he had voted with the majority, making the vote 5 to 2.

set in the abortion cases: Justice Blackmun was to prepare a memorandum for his colleagues that would be the basis for further writing.
The thoughts and intentions of Justice Harry Blackmun in *Roe v.
Wade*, therefore, were a matter of considerable concern to the Court's
two most senior members, Justices Douglas and Brennan, both of
whom had voted at the conference to strike down the state abortion
regulations. They had been supported by Justices Marshall and Stewart. But the outcome in the abortion cases might rest on the untested
shoulders of Blackmun. There was the possibility that Blackmun
might be open to persuasion by the chief justice; Burger had appeared to exercise considerable influence over Blackmun (who had
been a close childhood friend of Burger's) during Blackmun's first
term on the Court. And the chief's position in *Roe* was, at best, ambiguous. At the very least, Blackmun, a famously slow writer whose
own position in the abortion cases was none too clear, might be tem-
porarily paralyzed by indecision.

Any delay would give impetus to the chief's position, suggested in
his letter to Douglas after the conference, that the abortion cases
should be reargued before a full Court the next term; at that time
President Nixon's new appointees, Justices Powell and Rehnquist,
might well vote to uphold the Texas and Georgia abortion statutes.
Douglas, in particular, also suspected that the chief justice might be
engaged in dilatory tactics in the abortion cases calculated to protect
Richard Nixon—whom Douglas despised—in an election year. If the
potentially explosive abortion decisions could be delayed until after
the November 1972 election, Nixon's chance to serve a second term in
the White House might be enhanced.

The question in the final weeks of 1971 for Douglas and Brennan,
Douglas's closest ally in the abortion cases, was how best to come to
closure in the abortion cases on their constitutional terms, and before
the chief could effectively lobby for reargument among his colleagues. A second, related question for these two liberal veterans,
who between them had served forty-seven years on the Court, was
how to deal with the unpredictable Harry Blackmun.

Douglas's first notion was simply to ignore both Blackmun and the
chief. Shortly after he received the chief justice's letter refusing his

request to allow Douglas to assign the majority opinion, Douglas sent Justice Brennan a first draft of an opinion in the Georgia case that could serve as a basis for *his* four-member majority opinion, should Blackmun fail to draft an opinion satisfactory to Douglas and Brennan. In his draft, Douglas laid out a theory for a broad constitutional right to privacy that would cover a woman's right to have an abortion in the early stages of her pregnancy.

"The right to privacy described in *Griswold*,"* Douglas wrote, "is a species of 'liberty' of the person as that word is used in the Fourteenth Amendment. It is a concept that acquires substance, not from predilections of judges, but from the emanations of the various provisions of the Bill of Rights, including the Ninth Amendment." The constitutional right to privacy, Douglas continued, was broad enough to encompass the right of a woman to terminate an unwanted pregnancy in its early stages, by obtaining an abortion. Douglas conceded, however, that the woman's right was not absolute, though it was fundamental. To invade a fundamental right, Douglas wrote, a state must draw its statute narrowly and must show a "compelling" state interest in support of the limitation.

On December 30, 1971, Brennan responded to Douglas, reminding the senior justice that they had agreed not to circulate any of their own draft opinions until they received Blackmun's. It was sound strategy, since allowing Douglas's draft to be circulated to the brethren might appear to challenge the chief justice's authority and might alienate, among others, Justice Blackmun.

Having cautioned Douglas against brash action, Brennan wrote Douglas an eleven-page critique of the Douglas draft. While agreeing with Douglas's broad constitutional theory, Brennan suggested an elaboration that would identify three groups of fundamental freedoms that "liberty" would encompass: "first, freedom from bodily restraint or inspection, freedom to do with one's body as one likes, and freedom to care for one's health and person; second, freedom of choice in the

---

* Justice Douglas had written the Court's opinion in the 1965 decision *Griswold v. Connecticut*, which established a constitutional right to privacy for married couples who chose to use contraceptives as a means of birth control.

basic decisions of life, such as marriage, divorce, procreation, contraception, and the education and upbringing of children; and, third, autonomous control over the development and expression of one's intellect and personality."

Brennan concluded that "the decision whether to abort a pregnancy obviously fits within each of the categories of fundamental freedoms" he had outlined and could only be overcome by a showing of a "compelling" state interest. In the early stages of pregnancy, Brennan insisted, the decision to abort was "that of the woman and her alone."

In January, shortly after Powell and Rehnquist had taken their seats on the Court, Chief Justice Burger circulated a letter to his colleagues asking them to indicate which cases that had already been argued that term should be reconsidered. Blackmun's response to the chief's letter gave Douglas and Brennan an additional reason to be nervous about his position in the abortion cases: "I nominate for reargument the two abortion cases," Blackmun wrote his colleagues.

A formal decision on reargument was postponed until Blackmun, who was working alone on the second floor of the Supreme Court library, produced his drafts. Douglas risked showing Blackmun a copy of his revised draft (incorporating a number of Brennan's suggestions) in February 1972, but Blackmun continued to labor alone for three more months. Finally, on May 18, 1972, Blackmun circulated a first-draft memorandum* in the Texas case. It was an admittedly tentative effort by Blackmun to find a narrow common ground of agreement among a majority of his colleagues. His notes indicated, Blackmun wrote his colleagues, "that we were generally in agreement to affirm [the lower court decision finding the Texas statute unconstitutional] on the merits"—reinforcing Douglas's view that there had been a majority in conference to strike down the statute.

The good news in the Blackmun draft for Douglas and Brennan was that Blackmun was prepared to overturn the Texas abortion statute. The bad news was that the junior justice attempted to pin the decision

---

* Significantly, Blackmun labeled his draft a "memorandum" rather than a Court "opinion," corroborating his view that the chief justice had assigned him to write a memorandum, not a majority opinion for the Court.

on the narrowest possible grounds. The Texas abortion statute failed, not because it deprived a woman of her constitutional right to privacy, Blackmun wrote, but because it was "unconstitutionally vague." What does "saving the life of the mother" mean? asked Blackmun. "Does it mean that he [the physician] may procure an abortion only when, without it, the patient will surely die? . . . Or when there is a mere possibility that she will not survive?"

In his covering memorandum to his colleagues, Blackmun suggested that his vagueness argument "would be all that is necessary for disposition of the case," so that he concluded that it was unnecessary to discuss the broader constitutional issues. His hope was that a narrow ruling would produce a unanimous Court. "This may or may not appeal to you," Blackmun added. "I am still flexible as to results, and I shall do my best to arrive at something which would command a court."

Brennan and Douglas were not happy with the Blackmun draft memorandum and wasted no time in telling him so. In a "Dear Harry" letter the very day that Blackmun had circulated his draft, Brennan suggested that Blackmun had avoided "the core constitutional question" (the pregnant woman's right to privacy in her decision to have an abortion), which a majority in conference had agreed to settle. "My recollection of the voting on this and the Georgia case," Brennan wrote, "was that a majority of us felt that the Constitution required the invalidation of abortion statutes save to the extent that they required that an abortion be performed by a licensed physician within some limited time after conception."

A day later, Douglas followed up with his own letter to Blackmun making the same point: "[W]e should meet what Bill Brennan calls the 'core issue,'" Douglas wrote, as his conference notes indicated was the clear intention of the majority. Douglas could not resist a further dig at the chief justice, writing that "the Chief had the opposed view, which made it puzzling as to why he made the assignment at all except that he indicated he might affirm on vagueness."

In his circulated draft a week later on the Georgia abortion case, the embattled Justice Blackmun did confront the constitutional issue, as Brennan and Douglas had urged. But he did so on much more circumscribed terms than either Douglas or Brennan had advocated in their written analyses. While Blackmun wrote that the Court recognized that a "woman's interest in making the fundamental personal decision whether or not to bear an unwanted child is within the scope of personal rights protected by the Ninth and Fourteenth Amendments," he emphasized that the right was not absolute. "The heart of the matter," wrote Blackmun, "is that somewhere, either forthwith at conception, or at 'quickening' or at birth, or at some point in between, another being becomes involved and the privacy possessed has become dual rather than sole. The woman's right of privacy must be measured accordingly. It is not for us of the judiciary, especially at this point in the development of man's knowledge, to speculate or to specify when life begins. . . ." The woman's "personal" right, Blackmun insisted, "must be balanced against the State's interest."

Having concluded that the state had a legitimate constitutional interest during the pregnancy cycle, Blackmun conceded that Georgia could require that an abortion be performed in a state-licensed hospital by a physician who was willing to sign a written statement that the operation was necessary "based upon his best clinical judgment." A woman's privacy rights, even in the early stages of pregnancy, were subject to restrictions imposed on the physician performing the abortion.

Both Douglas and Brennan anticipated that the Blackmun drafts would inspire additional debate on the abortion cases, exactly what they wanted to avoid. Further debate at that late date in the Court term would play into the hands of the chief justice, who had made no secret of his view that the cases should be reargued the next term.

On May 25, the day Blackmun had circulated his draft memorandum in the Georgia case, Douglas suddenly recognized the intrinsic wisdom of the Blackmun drafts, praising his newest colleague's work in a letter, and announced that he would proudly support both Blackmun drafts. Brennan's support quickly followed, as did that of Marshall and Stewart. By Douglas's count, that made five—Douglas, Brennan, Marshall, Stewart and Blackmun—for holding both the Texas and Georgia statutes unconstitutional on the narrow grounds that Blackmun had outlined in his drafts. Better to have two state abortion statutes overturned on narrower grounds than Douglas would have wished than on no grounds at all.

But while Douglas was lobbying hard for a majority to produce final decisions in both abortion cases, the chief justice was just as insistent that both *Roe v. Wade* and *Doe v. Bolton* be reargued. And in the final sprint, the chief crossed the finish line ahead of Douglas.

On May 31, the members of the Court received a memorandum from Chief Justice Burger stating that "these cases . . . are not as simple for me as they appear to be for others." He then formally proposed reargument of both the Texas and Georgia abortion cases. That same day Justice Blackmun wrote: "Although it would prove costly for me personally, in light of energy and hours expended, I have concluded, somewhat reluctantly, that reargument in both cases at any early date in the next term, would perhaps be advisable."

But Douglas was not yet prepared to concede defeat. He wrote Blackmun on May 31 to applaud his "fine job" on the abortion opinions and reassure his colleague that his opinions will "stand the test of time." Given the high quality of Blackmun's opinions, Douglas felt "quite strongly" that the cases should not be reargued. He gave two reasons. First, the abortion cases "have been as thoroughly worked over and considered as any cases ever before the Court in my time." Second, Douglas noted that there was "solid agreement of the majority" and it was, therefore, time to "let the result be known so that the legislatures can go to work and draft their new laws."

Meanwhile, the two newest members of the Court, Justices Powell and Rehnquist, had also approached Blackmun, asking him if he objected to reargument since he did have a majority. Blackmun told Powell and Rehnquist that he did not object. In fact, he said that he would welcome it, since it would give him the opportunity to do additional research at the Mayo Clinic in the summer.

Powell followed up the meeting with Blackmun with a memorandum to his colleagues on June 1 stating that, though "from a purely personal viewpoint I would be happy to leave this one to others," he felt it was appropriate for him to participate. "I am persuaded to favor reargument," Powell wrote, "primarily by the fact that Harry Blackmun, the author of the opinions, thinks the cases should be carried over and reargued next term." Justice Rehnquist, in a similar memo the same day, also voted for reargument.

The chief had found his majority for reargument—Blackmun, White, Powell, Rehnquist and Burger.

That was not the end of the matter for Douglas. On the same day that both Powell and Rehnquist had announced their support for reargument, Douglas dashed off a two-sentence threat to the chief justice, warning that if the justices voted for reargument in the abortion cases at their conference, Douglas would file a dissent which would, of course, be made public, "telling what is happening to us and the tragedy it entails."

It was not the first time during his thirty-two years on the Court that Justice Douglas had stirred controversy.

One of William O. Douglas's favorite quotations was from the Persian poet Jalal-ud-Din Rumi (1207–1273), who wrote: "All your anxiety is because of your desire for harmony. Seek disharmony; then you will gain peace."

Douglas did his part to create disharmony. Throughout his illustrious career as a law professor, New Deal insider and justice of the Supreme Court, William O. Douglas had teased the establishment with such intuitive skill and timing that he always seemed to advance his professional ambitions as he flouted conventional norms. As a young Columbia University law professor, Douglas loudly quit the faculty in protest over what he considered an unprincipled power play to appoint a new law school dean by the university's imperious president, Nicholas Murray Butler—only to accept a pending offer from Dean Robert Hutchins at the Yale Law School. Hutchins later called Douglas "the outstanding professor of law in the nation."

In 1935, Douglas, an expert in business law, became the aggressive chairman of the Securities and Exchange Commission, attacking the governors of the New York Stock Exchange for running the Exchange like a private club rather than an institution responsible to individual security-holders. His public attacks infuriated the business establishment but delighted the one man who counted most, President Franklin D. Roosevelt, who invited Douglas to join both his poker parties and his inner circle of economic advisors.

After Roosevelt appointed the forty-year-old Douglas to the Supreme Court in 1939, Douglas was frequently mentioned as Roosevelt's running mate for his third and fourth presidential terms. The rumors infuriated Douglas's nemesis on the Court, Justice Felix Frankfurter, who considered it injudicious for Douglas, unlike Frankfurter himself, to clutter his mind with political thoughts. But while repeatedly denying political ambition, Justice Douglas did not seem pained by the attention.

When he wasn't writing one of his many travel books or taking hikes in his beloved Cascades, Douglas produced some of the most prophetic judicial opinions of his or any other generation. It was Douglas, for example, who declared that there was a fundamental right to procreate, in a decision preceding *Roe v. Wade* by thirty-one years. He also spoke about the constitutional right to be left alone more than two decades before Harry Blackmun wrote the Court's *Roe* opinion. And he wrote the Court opinion in *Griswold v. Connecticut,* establishing for the first time a constitutional right to privacy. His was an original mind, one of the most creative ever to grace the Court.

But for all his judicial creativity, Douglas sometimes seemed to take perverse satisfaction in diluting his influence on his colleagues, often ignoring their collective enterprise. He was a loner, happiest walking ahead of the pack on wilderness trails—and in his work on the Court. "I have only one soul to save, and that's my own," Douglas said. Douglas's colleague Potter Stewart put it differently: "Bill Douglas is positively embarrassed if anyone agrees with him."

Douglas's contrariness did not please his colleagues, and not just those, like Frankfurter, who loathed his person every bit as much as his philosophy. Others, like Brennan, voted with Douglas regularly but seethed privately over Douglas's lack of consideration for his colleagues. Douglas was indisputably the Court's resident curmudgeon, capable of producing shafts of stark constitutional insight but more often satisfied with idiosyncratic positions calculated to appeal to not a single colleague.

In his off-the-Court activities, Douglas was no less controversial. In the early spring of 1970, Douglas published *Points of Rebellion*, a miniature time bomb of protest (ninety-seven pages) directed at excesses of government and inspired by President Nixon. "We must realize that today's establishment is the new George III," Douglas wrote. "Whether it will continue to adhere to his tactics, we do not know."

Representative Gerald R. Ford, the Republican minority leader in the House, used the Douglas book as a wedge to try to remove him from the Court. Only a few weeks after President Nixon's Court nomination of Judge G. Harrold Carswell had been defeated in the Senate, Ford announced that he would initiate impeachment proceedings against Douglas. (Douglas privately was convinced that the president, not Gerald Ford, was behind the impeachment move.) Ford suggested that *Points of Rebellion*, which he described as an "inflammatory volume" that subscribed in spirit to "the militant hippie-yippie movement," was not the only indication of Douglas's unfitness to serve on the Court. Ford also condemned Douglas for his work for the "leftish" Center for the Study of Democratic Institutions, his sale of an article to *Fact* magazine for $350 while its publisher, Ralph Ginzburg, was a defendant in a libel suit pending in a lower federal court, and his service as a paid trustee of the Parvin Foundation (whose benefactor, Albert Parvin, reputedly had ties to organized crime figures).

Douglas survived Ford's impeachment attack but was privately shaken by the experience. He feared further attacks by the Nixon Administration and suspected that, with that purpose in mind, federal authorities had secretly bugged his chambers. *Roe v. Wade*, however, focused Douglas's attention on the Court as few other cases in years had done.

On June 2, 1972, the day after Douglas had sent his two-sentence note to Chief Justice Burger protesting Burger's proposal to have the abortion cases reargued, he sent Brennan a proposed draft of his threatened dissent if the majority voted for reargument in the abortion cases. The Douglas draft did not spare the chief justice's feelings or reputation:

... The Chief Justice represented the minority view in the Conference and forcefully urged his viewpoint on the issues. It was a seven-man Court that heard the cases and voted on them. Out of that seven there were four who took the opposed view. Hence traditionally the senior Justice in the majority would make the assignment of the opinion. The cases were, however, assigned by the Chief Justice, an action no Chief Justice in my time would ever have taken. For the tradition is a longstanding one that the senior Justice in the majority makes the assignment. . . .

When, however, the minority seeks to control the assignment, there is a destructive force at work in the Court. When the Chief Justice tries to bend the Court to his will by manipulating assignments, the integrity of the institution is imperiled. . . .

The plea that the cases be reargued is merely strategy by a minority somehow to suppress the majority view with the hope that exigencies of time will change the result. That might be achieved, of course, by death or conceivably retirement. But that kind of strategy dilutes the integrity of the Court and makes the decisions here depend on the manipulative skills of a Chief Justice.

The *Abortion Cases* are symptomatic. This is an election year. What both parties say or do is none of our business. We sit here not to make the path of any candidate easier or more difficult. We decide questions only on their constitutional merits. To prolong these *Abortion Cases* into the next election would in the eyes of many be a political gesture unworthy of the Court.

Each of us is sovereign in his own right. Each arrived on his own. Each is beholden to no one. Russia once gave its Chief Justice two votes; but that was too strong even for the Russians. . . .

I dissent with the deepest regret that we are allowing the consensus of the Court to be manipulated for unworthy objectives.*

Justice Brennan, the coalition-builder *extraordinaire*, knew that the Douglas dissent, if published in that incendiary form, could only do severe damage to the Court. "Dear Bill," Brennan wrote Douglas. "If anything is to be made public (& I have serious reservations on that score) I hope the pencilled out portions can be omitted." In pencil, Brennan then bracketed substantial segments of the proposed Douglas

---

* Justice Stewart shared Douglas's outrage over the "high-handed way" in which he considered Burger to be manipulating the Court's business, but there is no written record of his directly confronting the chief justice.

dissent, including all references to Chief Justice Burger's motives. Finally, he substituted as the final word in the Douglas draft "frustrated" for the original phrase "manipulated for unworthy objectives."

By the sixth draft of his dissent, Douglas had eliminated all references to the chief justice's motives, but he nonetheless exposed the Court's internal frictions in rancorous detail. As so often happens in a small group where collegiality is an important prerequisite for effective work, various members of the group, in this instance the Supreme Court of the United States, took turns trying to dissuade the spoiler— Justice Douglas—from creating public, perhaps irrevocable, havoc.

"Douglas literally exploded and inveigled against putting the cases over," Blackmun recalled. "He may have thought that the two new appointees, Powell and Rehnquist, might vote the other way and Burger, who was shaky in his vote, might switch his vote and influence me in so doing. Bill made a lot of noise and it was rather ugly."

Douglas refused to withdraw his dissent until Blackmun personally assured him that his position of declaring the abortion statutes unconstitutional was firm, and that he had no intention of reversing that position after reargument. Blackmun gave Douglas that assurance. Shortly after Blackmun spoke to Douglas, the senior justice withdrew his dissent and requested that all circulated copies be returned to his chambers.

Who won the internal tug-of-war? The chief justice could claim victory since he succeeded in having the abortion cases reargued in the early part of the October 1972 term, with Justices Powell and Rehnquist participating. Douglas's colleagues could also claim success since Douglas withdrew his dissent, saving the Court much embarrassment and possibly a long period of awkward internal relations.

But as it turned out, Justice Douglas was the biggest winner of all. His prolonged tantrum had produced a firm commitment from Justice Blackmun to hold to his original position of voting to strike down the Texas and Georgia statutes. And seven members of the Court eventually endorsed a woman's fundamental right to privacy that was broad enough to cover her decision to have an abortion in the early stages of her pregnancy—a position Douglas had taken in his original draft in December 1971.

In any event, Douglas's bitterness toward the chief justice was re-markably short-lived. After a report of Douglas's proposed dissent in the abortion cases was leaked to the *Washington Post* and published on July 4, 1972, Douglas sent Burger a personal, handwritten letter from his Cascade Mountain retreat in Goose Prairie, Washington. "I am upset and appalled," Douglas wrote Burger, over the "nasty story about the abortion cases" (in the *Post*). "I have never breathed a word concerning the cases or my memo to anyone outside the Court," Douglas assured the chief justice. "We have our differences; but so far as I am concerned they are wholly internal; and if revealed, they are mirrored in opinion files, never in 'leaks' to the press." He con-cluded the letter with an invitation to Burger and his wife, Vera, to visit him and his wife, Cathy, in Goose Prairie. He signed the letter "With affectionate regards."

Douglas received an icy reply from the chief justice on July 27, marked "Personal" and "Confidential," in which Burger devoted four typewritten pages "simply to keep the record straight" on the abortion cases. Burger wrote that "there are a number of factual errors in the printed dissent, now withdrawn, that should not be allowed to stand uncorrected. With the circulation of at least 18 copies of what was la-beled '6th Draft,' there was an obvious risk that the subject would, as it did, get outside the security of the Court, albeit in a garbled form. That being so, something akin to 'due process' suggests that the facts be clarified of record."

The chief justice then reiterated in more detail his recollection of the controversial December conference on the abortion cases. He in-sisted that it was not accurate, as Douglas had stated in his dissent, that Burger represented the minority view. The chief justice contin-ued to maintain that "there was no majority for any firm position" and that final assignment of a majority opinion would have to await the writing by members of the Court.

"Your unprecedented proposed dissenting statement, now with-drawn, seems to imply bad faith if positions are not firm, fixed and fi-nal when a Conference adjourns," Burger wrote. "If a single member of the Court would endorse your view on this, I would be astonished. The record, which I reexamined in detail after the surprising statement in your dissent, shows that I have never undertaken to assign from a minority position. Thus there is not the slightest basis for your statement."

Douglas responded with a brief letter a week later, again assuring the chief justice that he had nothing to do with the leak to the *Post*. As to the issues raised in Burger's four-page letter and Douglas's dissent, "that chapter in the *Abortion Cases* is for me gone and forgotten." Even so, Douglas did add that his conference notes "obviously differ from yours. I think, quite respectfully, that mine are more complete."

While the chief justice attempted "to keep the record straight" for constitutional historians, a mildly contrite Justice Douglas vacationed in Goose Prairie. Meanwhile, Justice Harry Blackmun had worked alone in an upstairs room of the library of the Mayo Clinic in Rochester, Minnesota. There he searched for the answer to what he considered a crucial unanswered question in the abortion cases: how should the physician's Hippocratic Oath, which had been interpreted to forbid performing an abortion, affect the Court's decision?

Blackmun had shown his concern about the issue at the December oral argument when he asked attorney Margie Hames, who represented the plaintiff in the Georgia case, to explain the significance of the Hippocratic Oath for a doctor who was asked to perform an abortion. But neither Hames nor any other attorney who argued the cases gave an answer that satisfied Blackmun. And so, six months after the oral argument, Blackmun spent two solid weeks in the Mayo Clinic library researching the question, studying the practices of physicians in both ancient and modern times, the recorded positions of medical associations on abortion and the history of state abortion statutes. By the end of his study, Blackmun was satisfied that he had found the answer: most physicians, even in Hippocrates' time, did not consider the Oath's antiabortion reference to be binding on them. The Oath, he concluded, should not critically affect the Court's decision in the abortion cases.

The reargument of the abortion cases took place on October 11, 1972, and one day later the justices met to discuss and vote in *Roe v. Wade* and *Doe v. Bolton*. Douglas and Brennan announced that their views remained essentially the same as they had expressed the previous term. Then they listened for any crack in their majority from the previous term. Justices Stewart and Marshall held fast to their views that both state abortion statutes should be declared unconstitutional, though the precise grounds were still to be worked out. But now, with two new members participating, the majority needed a fifth vote. Would Justice Harry Blackmun, the least secure member of the earlier majority, be true to his private word to Douglas? "I am where I was last spring," Blackmun told his colleagues at the October conference. He added that he would make *Doe v. Bolton* the lead case.

The majority picked up an unanticipated sixth vote*—that of Justice Lewis Powell. "Basically, I am in accord with Harry's position," Powell told his new colleagues, although he expressed concern about state regulations that would allow a physician to perform an abortion for reasons that were not directly related to health. On the Texas case (*Roe v. Wade*), Powell said that he "wouldn't go on the vagueness ground," which had been the basis for Blackmun's original draft. He also suggested that *Roe* be the lead case, a suggestion that Blackmun accepted.

The other recent Court appointee, Associate Justice William Rehnquist, supported Justice Byron White's dissenting position, expressed in conference, that the Court should not "second-guess state legislatures in striking the balance in favor of abortion laws."

On November 21, 1972, Blackmun circulated his first draft in *Roe* since his much-criticized May memorandum. He announced it as the "1972 fall edition," and admitted to his colleagues that the assignment had been "both difficult and elusive." Blackmun apologized for the "rambling character of the memorandum and for its undue length." And he ended on a prophetic note: "It has been an interesting assignment. As I stated in conference, the decision, however

---

* Chief Justice Burger, who ultimately voted with the majority in *Roe*, did not expressly declare his support for Blackmun's majority opinion until the week before the decision was announced to the public in January 1973. At the October conference, his position was not clear. He told his colleagues that the state "has a right to legislate in the field of abortion," and asked, "Is there a fetal life that's entitled to protection?"

made, will probably result in the Court's being severely criticized."

Blackmun's prediction proved to be true, but grossly understated. The Court's decision in *Roe* ignited a firestorm of public protest that spread over two decades. The reaction to *Roe* was unlike anything that Blackmun had prepared for in his life.

Harry Blackmun's father opened a hardware store on St. Paul's east side and moved his family just six blocks from the family of Warren E. Burger, the future chief justice of the United States. Harry Blackmun and Warren Burger first met at Methodist Sunday school, and the two boys soon discovered that they had much in common, not the least their modest economic circumstances.

The boys attended kindergarten and grade school together and, outside of class, they shared tennis games and camping trips in their formative years. Like all close friends (Blackmun would serve as best man at Burger's wedding), they had their disagreements. Blackmun, a committed Republican, supported Calvin Coolidge in 1924, while Burger backed the Progressive Party candidate, Robert La Follette.

The Harvard Club of St. Paul offered Blackmun a tuition scholarship to Harvard, which he accepted. When he arrived in Cambridge as an undergraduate, Blackmun arranged for a constant series of odd jobs to pay for his living expenses—he painted the university handball courts, caulked Harvard's half-dozen crew shells, drove the coach's launch and tutored in his undergraduate major, mathematics. Managing his jobs and his studies with maximum efficiency and success, Blackmun earned a Phi Beta Kappa key and graduated summa cum laude.

Although he considered becoming a doctor, Blackmun chose law instead and stayed in Cambridge another three years to study at the Harvard Law School. One of his most influential law professors was Felix Frankfurter, although Blackmun was not one of Frankfurter's favorite students. "Felix would get five or six students whom he liked, put them down in the front row, and carry on a Socratic dialogue with them," Blackmun recalled. "Those of us in the outer circle thought he was pretty arrogant."

After his law school graduation, Blackmun accepted a clerkship with Judge John B. Sanborn of the U.S. Court of Appeals for the Eighth Circuit, whom he succeeded on the bench twenty-six years later. Between his clerkship in 1933 and his appointment to the federal appellate court in 1959, Blackmun advanced in his professional career with characteristic meticulousness and determination. In 1934, he began a sixteen-year career with a prominent Minneapolis law firm, concentrating in the fields of taxation, estates and general litigation.

Blackmun's law firm had always done substantial legal work for the Mayo Clinic, the world-famous medical treatment and research center in Rochester, Minnesota, and had traditionally sent one of its members to Rochester to be the clinic's general counsel. In 1950, Blackmun was chosen for the assignment and remained in that position until his appointment to the federal appellate court nine years later.

On the U.S. Court of Appeals for the Eighth Circuit, Judge Blackmun was considered a moderate conservative, tough on convicted criminals in their procedural appeals, a centrist on civil rights, and generally reluctant to break new judicial ground. Among judges in Minnesota, Blackmun was known as a quietly effective jurist, a careful lawyer and considerable legal scholar, who produced learned treatises on both factual and legal issues raised in the cases argued before him.

Like President Nixon's first Court appointee and Blackmun's old friend Chief Justice Warren Burger, Judge Harry Blackmun had compiled a judicial record that comfortably fit Richard Nixon's job description for a Supreme Court justice. He took a hard line on criminal defendants' appeals, reassuring to Nixon, who in his successful 1968 presidential campaign had attacked the Warren Court's liberal criminal law decisions. Blackmun was also an appellate judge who approached his professional assignment with humility, eschewing broad judicial pronouncements in favor of what Nixon had termed "strict construction" of the Constitution.

Blackmun's hearings before the Senate Judiciary Committee lasted only three hours. After the tumult surrounding the Haynsworth and Carswell nominations, Judge Blackmun's introduction to the American public was a deeply welcomed anticlimax. Dressed in dark suit, white shirt and conservative tie, Blackmun seemed perfectly cast in the professional role of careful lawyer and cautious judge that he had performed for thirty-seven years. The senators on the Judiciary Committee took their turns with polite, dutiful questions of the nominee. In his flat, upper-midwestern twang, Harry Blackmun responded to each inquiry with a calm, thoughtful and detailed answer. It was as if he were fielding the questions of another nervous estate client at his old Minneapolis law firm.

The Judiciary Committee voted unanimously in favor of Judge Blackmun to serve on the Supreme Court. The full Senate, after less than an hour of debate, confirmed Blackmun's appointment by a vote of 94 to 0.

During his freshman year on the Burger Court, Justice Blackmun gave liberal senators who had supported his nomination cause to question their judgment, and his. Writing for the Court majority, Justice Blackmun rejected the claim of a welfare mother who had sued the State of New York for cutting off her payments after she had refused entry to her apartment to a state social worker. Blackmun's opinion for the five-man Court majority dismissed the mother's argument that the coercive effect of the state's depriving her of welfare money for food and shelter violated her Fourth Amendment rights to be free of unreasonable searches. Welfare recipients, Blackmun suggested, were in a position no different from those receiving private charity. "One who dispenses purely private charity naturally has an interest in and expects to know how his charitable funds are utilized and put to work," he wrote. "The public, when it is the provider, rightly expects the same."

In similarly detached fashion, Blackmun wrote a concurring opinion supporting the Court majority's decision to uphold the decision by the City of Jackson, Mississippi, to close its public swimming pools rather than to desegregate them and, according to the city, risk financial ruin. Noting that Jackson's public pools had operated at a deficit, Blackmun wrote that the city had shown its good intentions by desegregating all other municipal services and that swimming pools represented a "nice-to-have-but-not-essential variety" of public service.

In virtually all civil rights and liberties decisions that term, Blackmun and Chief Justice Burger voted together, a cohesion of views that surprised almost no one. When Blackmun had been nominated to the Court, the nominee's close friendship with the chief justice was thoroughly covered in the media. It was frequently noted that Blackmun had been best man at Burger's wedding, and widely reported that Blackmun owed his judicial appointments to the court of appeals and to the Supreme Court to Burger's influence. Who better than the chief justice would be able to persuade his old friend on issues before the Court?

In 1970, both Blackmun and Burger appeared unshakably conservative judges, just right, so it seemed, for the president who appointed them. They were dubbed "the Minnesota Twins," which did not please either man on the roster. But the statistics in that first Burger-Blackmun term bore out the pundits' characterization. Burger and Blackmun were in agreement in 89.1 percent of the cases where the Court was sharply divided (with three or four dissents), an unusually high figure for any two members of the Court.

In a *New York Times Magazine* article on the "Burger-Blackmun Court" in December 1970, Justice Blackmun was described as a "White Anglo-Saxon Protestant Republican Rotarian Harvard Man from the Suburbs."

Then came Blackmun's opinion in *Roe v. Wade.*

Justice Blackmun began his November 1972 draft memorandum in *Roe v. Wade* with a lengthy discourse on the history of abortion, traced back to the ancient Persian Empire. The history lesson was followed by a discussion of the question that he had devoted many summer hours researching. He asked the question in his admittedly "rambling" way: "What then of the famous Oath that has stood so long as the ethical guide of the medical profession and that bears the name of the great Greek who has been described as the Father of Medicine, the 'wisest and the greatest practitioner of his art,' and the 'most important and most complete medical personality of antiquity,' who dominated the medical schools of his time, and who typified the sum of the medical knowledge of the past?" His research had led Blackmun to the conclusion that the Hippocratic Oath was not uncontested, even in Hippocrates' day, and represented only a small segment of Greek opinion, including that of ancient physicians. Physicians, in ancient as well as modern times, were not required to adhere rigidly to a ban on abortion, he suggested. They could be true to the spirit of the Hippocratic Oath and still perform legally proscribed abortions.

While his discovery of the origin and meaning of the Hippocratic Oath continued to be central in Justice Blackmun's subsequent discussions of *Roe v. Wade*, it did not hold his colleagues' attention in the fall of 1972 for very long. Instead, they focused on the core holding of the Blackmun draft. And here they discovered that he had abandoned his earlier "void for vagueness" rationale in *Roe* in favor of a declaration of a fundamental constitutional right to privacy that covered the decision to have an abortion.

In expansive language that had been totally missing from his earlier *Roe* draft, Blackmun wrote that "the right of privacy, however based, is broad enough to cover the abortion decision." He adopted a "strict scrutiny" review of the "fundamental" interest in privacy which then demanded that a state show "a compelling interest" in any regulation of the abortion decision. Again, Blackmun used strong, sweeping language in defense of the abortion decision that was not contained in his earlier draft.

In his November draft, Blackmun was not yet ready to adopt the controversial trimester analysis of the final *Roe v. Wade* opinion. That analysis divided constitutional protection into the three trimesters of a woman's pregnancy. During the first trimester, a pregnant woman and her physician were protected against any interference from the state. In the second trimester, a state could only regulate to protect the health of the mother. Only in the third trimester, at the point of viability (when the fetus was capable of survival outside the womb), could the state regulate on behalf of the unborn fetus.

Blackmun's November draft opinion suggested that there be a single demarcation between the right to have an abortion and the state's authority to regulate that right. For Blackmun, the division would come at the end of the first trimester. "You will observe that I have concluded that the end of the first trimester is critical," Blackmun had written his colleagues in his covering note. "This is arbitrary, but perhaps any other selected point, such as quickening or viability, is equally arbitrary."

In discussing the constitutional right to privacy in the first trimester, Blackmun placed much greater emphasis on the physician's right than on the pregnant woman's. During that first trimester, the state, Blackmun wrote, "must do no more than leave the abortion decision to the best medical judgment of the pregnant woman's physician." After the first trimester, "the state may, if it chooses, determine a point beyond which it restricts legal abortions to stated reasonable therapeutic categories."

Blackmun's judgment on this critical—and highly controversial— point was seriously challenged by four of the members of his majority —Brennan, Douglas, Marshall and Stewart. Interestingly, Blackmun appeared to be heavily influenced on the point in his final draft by a letter written to him from the junior member of that quartet, Justice Thurgood Marshall.*

On December 12, 1972, Marshall wrote Blackmun:

> I am inclined to agree that drawing the line at viability accommodates the interests at stake better than drawing it at the end of the first trimester. Given the difficulties which many women may have in believing that they are pregnant and in deciding to seek an abortion, I fear that the earlier date may not in practice serve the interests of those women, which your opinion seeks to serve.
>
> At the same time, however, I share your concern for recognizing the state's interest in insuring that abortions be done under safe conditions. If the opinion stated explicitly that, between the end of the first trimester and viability, state regulations directed at health and safety alone were permissible, I believe that those concerns would be adequately met.
>
> It is implicit in your opinion that at some point the state's interest in preserving the potential life of the unborn child overrides any individual interests of the women. I would be disturbed if that point were set before viability, and I am afraid that the opinion's present focus on the end of the first trimester would lead states to prohibit abortions completely at any later date.

---

* Marshall's clerk Mark Tushnet drafted the letter, which Marshall sent to Blackmun without making significant changes.

In short, I believe that, as the opinion now stands, viability is a better accommodation of the interests involved, but that the end of the first trimester would be acceptable if additions along the lines I have suggested were made.

Two days after Blackmun received Marshall's letter, Justice Stewart voiced a criticism of Blackmun's *Roe v. Wade* analysis that would reverberate in public debate and subsequent dissenting opinions for two decades. "One of my concerns with your opinion as presently written is the specificity of its dictum—particularly in its fixing of the end of the first trimester as the critical point for valid state action," Stewart wrote. "I appreciate the inevitability and indeed wisdom of the dicta in the Court's opinion, but I wonder about the desirability of the dicta being quite so inflexibly 'legislative.' " Despite his reservations, Stewart ultimately accepted Blackmun's "legislative" division of constitutional interests by trimesters, as did the other members of the majority.

Rehnquist and White, in dissent, attacked the Blackmun opinion on the grounds that the Court's decision weighing the interests of the pregnant woman and the state was properly one for the legislature to make. To demand a balancing of competing interests on the abortion issue, Rehnquist wrote, "is far more appropriate to a legislative judgment than a judicial one."

"I anticipate the headlines that will be produced over the country when the abortion decisions are announced," Blackmun wrote his colleagues on January 16, 1973. He then attached an eight-page statement that he proposed to be circulated to the media before the Court announced its decision in *Roe v. Wade.* Justice Brennan, however, persuaded Blackmun to withhold the statement until the official announcement of the Court's decision. In the statement, which Blackmun later read from the bench, he conceded that the abortion issue "is a most sensitive, emotional and controversial one, perhaps one of the most emotional that has reached the Court for some time."

After reciting in detail the basis for the Court's *Roe* decision, Blackmun asked that attention be paid to what the Court did not decide:

I fear what the headlines may be, but it should be stressed that the Court does not today hold that the Constitution compels abortion on demand. It does not today pronounce that a pregnant woman has an absolute right to an abortion. It does, for the first trimester of pregnancy, cast the abortion decision and the responsibility for it upon the attending physician. Thereafter, the decisions permit the state, if it chooses, to impose reasonable regulations for the protection of maternal and fetal health. And, after viability, they give the same full right to proscribe all abortions except those that may be necessary, in appropriate medical judgment, for the preservation of life or health of the mother.

The *Roe* decision, which was announced on January 22, 1973, did not cause the instant furor that Justice Blackmun had predicted. The reason was not that *Roe* was calmly accepted, but that on the same day *Roe* was announced, former President Lyndon B. Johnson died, a news event that diverted media attention from the Court's decision. But the attacks would come soon enough, in recurring torrents of rage that would plague the Court and Justice Blackmun for more than two decades.

CHAPTER FIVE

ANYONE WHO CAN COUNT

Although the justices did not invite further controversy in the 1970s over their decision in *Roe*, they did not avoid the abortion issue either. They had little choice. Political opponents of *Roe*, in addition to pressing for an anti-*Roe* constitutional amendment, lobbied furiously in the corridors of state legislatures. With considerable success, they persuaded state representatives to pass restrictive abortion legislation calculated to challenge the basic tenets of *Roe*.

The Court issued its first post-*Roe* directive in 1976 when it rejected provisions of a Missouri statute that gave a veto to the man who shared responsibility for the woman's pregnancy or, in the case of a woman who was a minor, to her parents. Justices Rehnquist and White dissented, as they had in *Roe* three years earlier.

Despite Rehnquist's and White's continued opposition to *Roe*, they did not attract support among the other justices throughout the 1970s. But that situation would change during the 1980s, and the change would be precipitated by the New Right and Ronald Reagan.

By opposing *Roe* and supporting a constitutional amendment to reverse it, Reagan gathered a dedicated one-issue constituency, members of the right-to-life movement. Reagan also supported the Republican platform that pledged to "work for the appointment of judges at all levels of the judiciary who respect traditional family values and the sanctity of innocent human life."

As president, Reagan sent his written greetings and encouragement to the annual prolife rally held in Washington on the anniversary of *Roe v. Wade*. At the same time, the Reagan Justice Department made the dismantling of *Roe* one of its primary missions. Their first open challenge to *Roe* came in a 1982 abortion case in which the U.S. solicitor general, Rex Lee, who served as the Administration's chief advocate before the Court, boldly recommended in an amicus brief that the justices adopt a new test in abortion cases to replace Justice Blackmun's trimester analysis in *Roe*.

In his legal brief, Solicitor General Lee wrote that it was time for the Court to halt its rigidly prohibitory approach toward abortion regulations, as mandated in *Roe*, and begin to take a more benign look at restrictions such as those presented in companion cases before them from Ohio and Missouri (referred to together as *Akron*). The challenged regulations included the prohibition of abortions for unmarried minors under fifteen years old without the consent of one parent or a court order; a requirement that the physician inform the pregnant woman of the physical and emotional complications that might result from an abortion and risks associated with her pregnancy, and a twenty-four-hour waiting period after the pregnant woman signed a consent form. Specifically, Lee asked the Court to adopt an "unduly burdensome"* test that would allow states to regulate abortions throughout a woman's pregnancy so long as the regulations did not pose an undue burden on a woman's right to an abortion and were rationally related to a legitimate state objective. He urged the Court to uphold all of the regulations under an "unduly burdensome" standard.

The challenge of the abortion issue was presented by the solicitor

---

* Lee's phrase "unduly burdensome" was taken from a 1977 decision, *Maher v. Roe* ("*Roe* did not declare an unqualified constitutional right to an abortion. . . . Rather, the right protects the woman from *unduly burdensome* interference with her freedom to decide whether to terminate her pregnancy").

117

general as "the resolution of competing public policy issues" for which, in Lee's opinion, the state legislatures were much better equipped to supply the answers than courts. "The legislature has superior fact-finding capabilities," Lee wrote, "is directly responsible to the public for its resolution of the policy issues it treats, and has greater flexibility than the courts to fine-tune and redirect its efforts if a particular solution is ill-founded or unwise." The Supreme Court's role, Lee suggested, should be much more deferential to state legislative judgments than it had been in *Roe*.

At the oral argument before the justices in *Akron* on November 30, 1982, Lee reiterated the argument that he had made in his amicus brief: that the Court should uphold all of the regulations under an "unduly burdensome" test and that state legislatures, rather than the Court, should have primary responsibility for weighing the competing interests involved in the abortion controversy. The solicitor general did not mention *Roe*'s declaration of a woman's fundamental right to control her own body, but rather spoke of the need for legislatures to balance competing abortion interests.

Justice Blackmun exploded with indignation. Brandishing Lee's amicus brief, Blackmun asked angrily, "Mr. Solicitor General, are you asking that *Roe v. Wade* be overruled?"

"I am not, Mr. Justice Blackmun," Lee replied.

"Why not?" Blackmun asked.

"That is not one of the issues presented in this case, and as *amicus* appearing before the Court, that would not be a proper function for us."

"It seems to me," Blackmun persisted, "that your brief in essence asks either that or the overruling of *Marbury against Madison*." *Marbury* was the seminal Supreme Court decision written by Chief Justice John Marshall in 1803 which established the Court's authority to review federal legislation to determine if it was unconstitutional.

"Neither," replied Lee. He was only asking "that the Court at least take into account the fact that these same kinds of issues have already been faced by a legislature with superior fact-finding capabilities, and have been resolved."

A six-member Court majority rejected Lee's argument out of hand and struck down all of the challenged restrictions as unconstitutional violations of *Roe*. Speaking for the majority, Justice Lewis Powell, Jr., asserted that none of the regulations was reasonably designed to further legitimate governmental interests. The informed-consent and mandatory twenty-four-hour-waiting-period requirements, moreover, were read by the Court to be conscious efforts to place obstacles in the way of pregnant women seeking to exercise their constitutional right to have an abortion. And in a pointed reminder to those in the Reagan Administration who were eager for the Court to rip *Roe* out of established constitutional jurisprudence, Justice Powell declared that stare decisis "is a doctrine that demands respect in a society governed by the rule of law."

The major development in *Akron*, however, was not Powell's majority opinion, but the rousing dissent of the newest member of the Court, President Reagan's first appointee, Justice Sandra Day O'Connor. O'Connor, who was serving her second Court term, not only supported an "unduly burdensome" test, which had been proposed by the solicitor general as a substitute for *Roe*'s trimester analysis, but appeared disdainful of Blackmun's *Roe* analysis. In the first draft of her *Akron* dissent, O'Connor had written of Blackmun's trimester approach as "a completely unprincipled and unworkable method of accommodating the conflicting personal rights and compelling state interests that are involved in the abortion context." In her final draft in June 1983, O'Connor eliminated the reference to "a completely unprincipled" approach but retained the remainder of the sentence.

It was not the first time that Sandra Day O'Connor, the first woman to be appointed to the Court, had made her presence and views well known in a male-dominated world.

On the Lazy B Ranch in southeastern Arizona, where Sandra Day spent her early years, cowboys slept on the big screen porch of the Days' adobe ranch house and took all of their meals with Sandra and her parents. At the age of six, Sandra could shoot a .22-caliber rifle (aimed at rabbits and predators like coyotes), mend a fence and ride horseback with the cowboys on roundups from dawn to dusk on the 198,000-acre ranch. Mostly, she rode with her father. If Harry Day had to brand cattle, fix a windmill or attend to any other task on the Lazy B, he took Sandra along for companionship. Sandra did her share of chores as well, from cutting and gathering cattle during a roundup to vaccinating and earmarking a herd.

That rough, wonderful life came to an abrupt end for Sandra when she reached school age. The Lazy B was thirty-five miles from the nearest town of Duncan, Arizona, and farther still from a first-rate elementary school. Harry Day's dream of attending Stanford University and becoming a lawyer had been frustrated by the business needs of the family. His daughter's future would be different. Both Harry and his wife, Ada Mae, who read to Sandra every evening, gave their daughter's education top priority.

In what was a painful separation from her parents, Sandra was sent to El Paso to live with her maternal grandmother and attend the local public schools. Soon enough, Sandra adjusted to home life with her strong, loving Grandmother Wilkie. Sandra's grandmother was a nonstop talker who taught Sandra, out of necessity, to be a good listener.

Sandra galloped through the curriculum of the El Paso public schools, graduating from high school at age sixteen, having skipped two grades in the process. She was admitted to Stanford before she had even taken the college entrance examination, and quickly justified Stanford's faith in her. In the next six years, she earned both a bachelor's degree in economics, magna cum laude, and a law degree with honors (finishing third in her class, two slots behind the number-one graduate, Bill Rehnquist).

Upon her law school graduation in 1952, Sandra seemed ideally suited to become a pioneer in the still-nascent women's movement. She sent out her impressive résumé to scores of law firms in the West, but received no offers. Until she received the rejections, it had never occurred to her that no firm would hire her as an attorney because she was a woman. Finally, after an extensive search and much frustration, O'Connor was hired to be a deputy county attorney in San Mateo, California, and for two years represented county agencies and boards in legal disputes.

Sandra married fellow Stanford law student and law review editor John O'Connor. While John practiced with one of Phoenix's best law firms, Sandra opened her own practice with another attorney in a suburban shopping center, taking the usual run of civil cases in a small practice (e.g., landlord-tenant disputes, simple contracts), as well as her share of court-appointed criminal defense cases.

After the birth of the second of the O'Connors' three children, Sandra left practice. She continued to be engaged in law-related activities from her home, accepting bankruptcy trustee appointments and organizing a county bar association lawyer-referral service. At the same time, she compiled an impressive list of community service credits during her child-rearing years: board member of the local Salvation Army, president of the local Heard Museum, director of the Phoenix chapter of the National Conference of Christians and Jews, director of the local YMCA, national vice president of the Soroptimist Club, and board member of the Arizona State University Law School.

In 1964, Sandra Day O'Connor volunteered to be a precinct captain in the presidential campaign of Senator Barry Goldwater. It was not just neighborly friendship (both the Goldwaters and the O'Connors lived in the affluent Phoenix suburb of Paradise Valley) that attracted O'Connor to the conservative senator. She had been raised on the cautionary tales of her father, Harry Day, who deplored the social welfare policies of Franklin Roosevelt and whose own Depression-era experiences made him an economic conservative. Harry Day's daughter voted Republican and shared her father's distrust of a large federal government. She believed that a lean government was a good government. If the people couldn't solve their own problems, then better that the opportunity be given to local and state representatives, not the bureaucrats in Washington.

In 1965, O'Connor returned to full-time law practice—as an assistant state attorney general with responsibility for representing high-ranking officials in state agencies, including the state auditor and state treasurer. Four years later, O'Connor's own political career was launched when she was named to complete the unfilled term of a state senator who had been appointed by President Nixon to the National Transportation Safety Board. In the next two elections, O'Connor won the office on her own and in 1972 became the first woman majority leader of a state legislature in the nation.

Majority Leader O'Connor's legislative skills were occasionally underestimated by a new colleague, but not for long. She was an intrepid negotiator who knew the details of proposed legislation better than anyone else in the chamber. Less well prepared colleagues would soon discover her mastery of the details of legislation if they tried to slide past a drafting technicality. But she was also determinedly collegial and well liked.

On the abortion issue, O'Connor treaded a cautious moderate line in the Arizona legislature. She voted against an amendment to an omnibus piece of legislation that would have prohibited abortion operations in state hospitals. She did so, she later said, only because the amendment was extraneous to the legislation, in violation of state regulutions. More difficult to explain to members of the right-to-life movement was O'Connor's sponsorship of a state bill to provide universal family-planning services. But at the same time, O'Connor voted for legislation that allowed hospitals and doctors to refuse to perform abortions.

In 1974, O'Connor moved from the Arizona legislature to the state judiciary as a trial court judge, where she established a reputation for attention to factual detail and reluctance to think too grandly about broader philosophical issues. She also became known as a law-and-order judge, supporting the death penalty and sentencing one man to the electric chair. But she agonized, even as she handed out harsh punishments. After listening to the plea for probation from a mother who had been convicted of forging $100,000 in checks, O'Connor addressed the defendant: "You have intelligence, beauty and two small children. You come from a fine and respected family. What is depressing is that someone with all of your advantages should have known better." O'Connor then sentenced the woman to four concurrent five-to-ten-year terms. After the sentencing, the judge was observed in her chambers, still in her black robe, weeping.

In 1979, Arizona's Democratic Governor Bruce Babbitt (later President Clinton's Secretary of the Interior) appointed O'Connor to the Arizona Court of Appeals. The fact that Sandra Day O'Connor had been prominently mentioned as Babbitt's Republican opponent in the next gubernatorial election and was shown in polls to be 20 percent ahead of the governor had nothing, Babbitt has archly insisted, to do with her appellate court appointment.

For the next two years, O'Connor continued to build her reputation for thoroughness, writing exceptionally well researched decisions on the appellate court. One day in 1981, O'Connor was at home when she received a telephone call from President Reagan's attorney general, William French Smith, who asked her to come to Washington to be considered for the vacancy on the Supreme Court that resulted from the retirement of Justice Stewart.

In Washington, O'Connor was interviewed the first day of her visit by prominent members of the Reagan Administration, including James Baker and Ed Meese. The next morning, O'Connor waited outside the Peoples Drug Store at Dupont Circle in Northwest Washington until she was picked up by Attorney General Smith's secretary and driven to the White House to meet the president.

O'Connor and President Reagan met for forty-five minutes and a portion of the time was spent on pleasantries. They also talked about the Court appointment and Reagan asked her how she viewed the role of a Supreme Court justice. She told him that she had been a legislator and she had been a judge and she thought she knew the difference between the two jobs. Although she did not discuss *Roe* with the president, O'Connor said that she was personally opposed to abortion (a position that she would repeat at her confirmation hearings), and that abortion was an appropriate subject for state regulation.

Less than two weeks later, President Reagan nominated O'Connor. Public response to the nomination was overwhelmingly positive except from one Reagan constituency—the religious right. The Reverend Jerry Falwell, the Moral Majority leader, called the O'Connor nomination "a disaster" and John Wilkie, head of the National Coalition for the Right to Life, termed it "a betrayal." She was not as sure a vote as they would have liked.

But while the right-to-life leaders were complaining publicly about the O'Connor nomination, the Reagan Administration was moving quickly and effectively to make certain that the president's nominee would be confirmed. The White House issued almost daily bulletins assuring the president's New Right constituency that Judge O'Connor was personally opposed to abortion and was as tough on criminals as any man who sat on the Court. Despite a campaign by the right-to-life movement to defeat the nomination, O'Connor was confirmed in the Senate, 99 to 0.

• • •

In the first abortion opinion that she wrote after her appointment to the Court—her 1983 *Akron* dissent—O'Connor sharply attacked the *Roe* opinion: "The *Roe* framework is clearly on a collision course with itself," O'Connor wrote in her *Akron* dissent. "As the medical risks of various abortion procedures decrease, the point at which the State may regulate for reasons of maternal health is moved further forward to actual childbirth. As medical science becomes better able to provide for the separate existence of the fetus, the point of viability is moved further back toward conception. Moreover, it is clear that the trimester approach violates the fundamental aspirations of judicial decision-making through the application of neutral principles 'sufficiently absolute to give roots throughout the community and continuity over significant periods of time.' "

Applying an "unduly burdensome" analysis (later shortened to "undue burden"), O'Connor concluded that all of the regulations in *Akron* should have been upheld.

Justice O'Connor's Court debut opinion in an abortion decision did not, of course, change the Court's final result. She was joined by only two members of the Court, the original *Roe* dissenters, Justices Rehnquist and White. But the tide seemed to be moving for the first time since *Roe* was decided toward the Court's anti-*Roe* faction. A popular anti-*Roe* president was in the White House and could confidently look forward to a second term and the opportunity to nominate additional members to the Court who shared his opposition to *Roe*. Meanwhile, the *Roe* dissenters, Justices Rehnquist and White, had picked up their first recruit in ten years in Justice O'Connor—and she had staked out an aggressively critical position on *Roe*.

In 1985, two years after Justice O'Connor had written her dissent in *Akron*, she and her colleagues agreed to hear another challenge to *Roe*, and again President Reagan's solicitor general, Charles Fried, who had succeeded Rex Lee, led the attack on Justice Blackmun's *Roe* opinion.

Fried plunged into the *Roe* controversy full-tilt, writing a 1985 amicus brief for companion abortion rights cases, scornfully dismissing both lower appellate court decisions that had struck down restrictive regulations as inconsistent with *Roe*. The appellate court rulings in the two cases (referred to collectively as *Thornburgh*), Fried contended, had badly misread permissible restrictions on abortion, failing to properly balance the state's interest in maternal health and the unborn fetus against the pregnant mother's interest in an abortion. "To the extent this is so," Fried argued, "these cases and *Akron* [the 1983 decision] are not just wrong turns on a generally propitious journey but indications of an erroneous point of departure. Indeed, the textual, doctrinal and historical basis for *Roe v. Wade* is so far flawed and, as these cases illustrate, is a source of such instability in the law that this Court should reconsider that decision and on reconsideration abandon it."

It was "a very amazing brief," said Justice Harry Blackmun. Blackmun suggested that Fried, and indirectly Reagan's attorney general, Ed Meese, could save their bombast, because *Roe* was not going to be overruled. Although he conceded that there were always four votes to hear challenges to *Roe*, Blackmun said that "the other five of us heave a deep sigh and wish we didn't have to go through this traumatic experience again."

Blackmun proved to be an accurate prognosticator in *Thornburgh*; the Court voted 5 to 4 to uphold the appellate court decisions. Blackmun was given the assignment for the majority (the slenderest since *Roe* had been decided) to reiterate the guarantees set out in his 1973 opinion. The assignment was made by the senior justice in the majority, Justice Brennan, since Chief Justice Burger had officially taken the dissenters' view (joining O'Connor, Rehnquist and White) that several of his colleagues suspected he had viscerally favored all along.

The narrow margin of victory did not discourage Blackmun from laying out in unambiguous language what he perceived the Court's commitment to be and what he thought states like Pennsylvania in *Thornburgh* were doing to undercut that commitment. Blackmun wrote:

> In the years since *Roe*, states and municipalities have adopted a number of measures seemingly designed to prevent a woman, with the advice of her physician, from exercising her freedom of choice.

But the constitutional principle that led this Court to its decision in 1973 still provides the compelling reason for recognizing the constitutional dimensions of a woman's right to decide whether to end her pregnancy. The states are not free, under the guise of protecting maternal health or potential life, to intimidate women into continuing pregnancies. Appellants claim that the statutory provisions before us today further legitimate compelling interests of the Commonwealth. Close analysis of those provisions, however, shows that they wholly subordinate constitutional privacy interests and concerns with maternal health in an effort to deter a woman from making a decision that, with her physician, is hers to make.

Justice Byron White, joined by Justice Rehnquist, repeated their call for reversal of *Roe*, declaring that "this venture has been fundamentally misguided since its inception." Chief Justice Burger "regretfully" concluded that some of the concerns of the dissenting justices in *Roe*, as well as some of his own, had been realized and agreed with White and Rehnquist that *Roe* should be reexamined. In a separate dissenting opinion, Justice O'Connor again took the opportunity to promote the "undue burden" test as a substitute for *Roe*'s analysis. "I dispute not only the wisdom but the legitimacy of the Court's attempt to discredit and preempt state abortion regulation regardless of the interests it serves and the impact it has," she concluded.

Thornburgh signaled *Roe*'s raw vulnerability; the Court stood only one vote away from overruling it or seriously undermining its basic holding.

Two weeks after *Thornburgh* was decided, Chief Justice Burger announced his retirement to direct the nation's bicentennial celebration of the Constitution. President Reagan, who had been given ample notice, moved expeditiously to name Associate Justice William Rehnquist to succeed Burger. For conservatives, in general, and opponents of *Roe*, in particular, the nomination was welcome news.

For supporters of *Roe v. Wade*, the appointment of Rehnquist as chief justice was particularly ominous. Unlike Chief Justice Burger, Rehnquist had been an implacable opponent of *Roe* since it was written. Rehnquist surely would be a more effective advocate for reversing *Roe* than Burger, who never really took a forthright position on the abortion issue.

On the same day that President Reagan nominated Rehnquist to be chief justice, he named Judge Antonin Scalia of the U.S. Court of Appeals for the District of Columbia to succeed Rehnquist as associate justice. As a law professor at the University of Chicago and as a judge on the federal appeals court, Scalia had distinguished himself as a brilliant and eloquent conservative ideologue. If Rehnquist could be matched on the Court in his forceful advocacy of a conservative philosophy, including opposition to *Roe v. Wade*, friends and colleagues of Judge Scalia were certain that Reagan had made the perfect second choice. Scalia's appointment, however, did not in itself tilt any scales in abortion rulings.

But by 1989, Justice Kennedy had replaced Justice Powell, and the conservatives on the Court seemed poised to overrule *Roe*, having accepted the challenge to *Roe* posed by the case of *Webster v. Reproductive Health Services*. When *Webster* was argued before the justices in April 1989, it appeared that Chief Justice Rehnquist had finally been given the opportunity to overrule *Roe* that he had been waiting for for sixteen years.

On the eve of the oral argument before the Supreme Court in *Webster v. Reproductive Health Services*, the Missouri case in which the Court, many commentators predicted, would reverse or severely restrict *Roe v. Wade*, a *New York Times*/CBS News Poll showed that the nation was almost evenly divided between those who believed that abortion should remain legal, as provided in *Roe*, and those who did not. The *Times*/CBS Poll, conducted during the second and third weeks of April 1989, found that 49 percent of Americans favored *Roe*'s protections, while 39 percent said that abortion should be legal only in cases involving rape or incest or when the mother's life was in danger. An additional 9 percent said abortion should be illegal in all circumstances.

Outside the Supreme Court Building on April 26, 1989, the sunny spring day that *Webster* was to be argued, both prochoice and prolife demonstrators were out in force, as if to underscore the authenticity of the *Times*/CBS poll that showed a nation torn apart over the abortion issue. Passions ran high as competing protesters squared off at the courthouse steps, chanting, singing and screaming at each other.

The Court that would hear the *Webster* case included only three members of the original seven-man *Roe* majority. Gone were Justices Douglas, Stewart, Powell and Chief Justice Burger. The two original dissenters in *Roe*, Rehnquist and White, were still on the Court and were now joined by four appointees of Republican presidents. President Ford's only appointee, Justice John Paul Stevens, had indicated in several abortion opinions since his appointment in 1975 that he favored upholding *Roe*. But the three newest members of the Court, all appointees of President Reagan, had either been openly critical of *Roe* or were thought, by background and conservative judicial philosophy, to be unsympathetic to the 1973 Blackmun opinion.

Justice O'Connor, the first Reagan appointee, had written dissenting opinions in two abortion cases expressing strong criticism of *Roe*, although she had not indicated that she was prepared to overrule it. Justice Antonin Scalia had not had the opportunity to write an opinion in an abortion case. But his earlier outspoken public criticism of *Roe* left little doubt what his views were likely to be.

The third Reagan appointee, Justice Anthony Kennedy, had taken his place on the Court in 1988, one years before *Webster* was to be argued. Unlike O'Connor and Scalia, Kennedy had expressed no opinion publicly on the abortion issue. But his Irish Catholic upbringing and conservative judicial philosophy suggested that he was a good bet to contribute a fifth vote to a new majority, led by Chief Justice Rehnquist, that would either reverse *Roe* or strip it of its original protection of a pregnant woman's decision to have an abortion.

"With only four solid votes to reaffirm *Roe* [Blackmun, Brennan, Marshall and Stevens], the tenuous nature of the constitutional right to choose to terminate a pregnancy was evident to anyone who could count," Professor Laurence Tribe of the Harvard Law School observed.

The *Webster* case stimulated seventy-eight friend-of-the-court legal briefs, the most ever filed in a Supreme Court case, one indication of the importance of the case. The briefs were submitted by public officials, scientists, doctors, historians and lawyers on both sides of the issue.

The Missouri law in question proclaimed in a preamble that human life began at conception, a conclusion based on "findings" of the Missouri legislature. It prohibited abortions in public institutions, even if the pregnant woman paid her own bill and used no public funds. It also prohibited the use of public funds for counseling about abortion. Under the law, doctors who agreed to perform abortions were required to conduct tests of fetal viability, including determinations of age, weight and lung maturity, if the women seeking the operation were at least twenty weeks pregnant.

The U.S. Court of Appeals for the Eighth Circuit affirmed a federal district court decision that had held these provisions of the Missouri law unconstitutional in violation of *Roe*. The Missouri attorney general, William Webster, appealed the appellate court decision, asking the justices to uphold the challenged provisions of the state law. Webster also urged that the justices take the further step of overruling *Roe v. Wade.*

On the morning of April 26, the nine justices of the Supreme Court listened intently for an hour to three attorneys who argued the pros and cons of legalized abortion. Webster, the first attorney to stand behind the lectern, used his allotted time to argue that all of the challenged provisions of the Missouri law were constitutional. His cocounsel for the day was Professor Charles Fried of the Harvard Law School, who had been requested by the three-month-old Bush Administration to repeat the argument that he had made to the Court as Reagan's solicitor general in the *Thornburgh* case four years earlier— that *Roe v. Wade* should be overruled.

Fried immediately went to the core of his argument. He asserted that the Court should overrule *Roe* but preserve the constitutional right to privacy established in the 1965 decision of *Griswold v. Connecticut.* (*Griswold* had held that a married couple had the right to use a birth control device in the privacy of their bedroom.) "We are not asking the Court to unravel the fabric of unenumerated and privacy rights which this Court has woven in cases like . . . *Griswold*," Fried said. "Rather we are asking the Court to pull this one thread."

The reason to reject *Roe*, Fried argued, was that "abortion is different. It involves the purposeful termination, as the Court said, of potential life. And I would only add that in the minds of many legislators who pass abortion regulation, it is not merely potential life but actual human life."

Throughout Fried's argument, indeed for the entire hour that the Court heard arguments in *Webster*, Justice Harry Blackmun was silent. But his three newest colleagues, Justices O'Connor, Kennedy and Scalia, were each actively engaged in the interrogation of counsel.

"Do you say there is no fundamental right to decide whether to have a child or not?" Justice O'Connor asked Fried. "A right to procreate? Do you deny that the Constitution protects that right?"

"I would hesitate to formulate the right in such abstract terms, and I think the Court prior to *Roe versus Wade* quite prudently also avoided such sweeping generalities," Fried replied. "That was the wisdom of *Griswold*."

"How do you define the liberty interest of a woman in an abortion case?" Justice Kennedy asked Fried.

"Well, I would think that there are liberty interests involved in terms perhaps of the contraceptive interest, but there is an interest at all points, however the interests of the woman is defined, at all points it is an interest which is matched by the state's interest in potential life," Fried replied.

"I understand it is matched," said Kennedy, "but I want to know how you define it."

"I would define it in terms of the concrete impositions on the woman which so offended the Court in *Griswold* and which are not present in the *Roe* situation," Fried responded.

Frank Susman, the St. Louis attorney who was responsible for defending *Roe*, as well as the lower court decisions that struck down the restrictive provisions of the Missouri statute, was no stranger to the legal controversy over abortion. For nearly two decades, Susman, forty-seven years old, had represented abortion rights organizations; *Webster* was his fifth appearance before the Court on the issue. "Clearly the threat to abortion rights is greater now than it has ever been," Susman said to reporters shortly before his *Webster* argument, "and that gives me a tremendous responsibility."

130

Following Fried to the lectern, Susman quickly attacked Fried's sewing metaphor of unraveling fabrics, insisting that the Court could not rip out *Roe* and neatly preserve the constitutional right to privacy established in *Griswold*.

"I think the [former] Solicitor General's submission is somewhat disingenuous when he suggests to this Court that he does not seek to unravel the whole cloth of procreational rights," Susman began, "but merely to pull a thread. It has always been my personal experience that when I pull a thread, my sleeve falls off. There is no stopping. It is not a thread he is after. It is the full range of procreational rights and choices that constitute the fundamental right that has been recognized by this Court."

Susman contended that the privacy rights in *Griswold* overlapped with those in *Roe* and could not realistically be separated.

"Excuse me," interrupted Justice Antonin Scalia, "you find it hard to draw a line between those two [*Griswold* and *Roe*] but easy to draw a line between first, second and third trimester?"

"I do not find it difficult—"

Scalia interrupted again. "I don't see why a Court that can draw that line can't separate abortion from birth control quite readily."

Susman responded by saying that IUDs and low-dose birth control pills acted as abortifacients, unlike condoms and diaphragms, which were common at the time *Griswold* was decided. "The bright line, if there ever was one, has now been extinguished," Susman said. "That's why I suggested to this Court that we need to deal with one right, the right to procreate."

In his subsequent interrogation, Scalia's skepticism of Susman's argument was apparent. After Susman admitted that there was broad disagreement over the issue of when life began, Scalia bore in.

"I agree with you entirely [that there is no consensus on when life begins]," Scalia said, "but what conclusion does that lead you to? That, therefore, there must be a fundamental right on the part of the woman to destroy this thing that we don't know what it is or, rather, that whether there is or isn't is a matter that you vote upon since we don't know the answer, people have to make up their minds the best they can."

Susman was not prepared to be boxed into Scalia's corner that offered escape only through majoritarian choice in the state legislatures. "The conclusion to which it leads me," Susman replied, "is that when you have an issue that is so divisive and so emotional and so personal and so intimate, that it must be left as a fundamental right of the individual to make that choice under her then attendant circumstances, her religious beliefs, her moral beliefs and in consultation with her physician."

The justices met in conference two days later, and it was soon obvious that *Roe*'s protections were in trouble. Five members of the Court, beginning with Chief Justice Rehnquist, were ready to reverse the appellate court in *Webster* and uphold the restrictive provisions of the Missouri statute. There also was agreement among five justices— Rehnquist, White, O'Connor, Scalia and Kennedy—that the *Roe* trimester analysis was seriously flawed. Not surprisingly, the four longtime supporters of *Roe*—Blackmun, Brennan, Marshall and Stevens— defended the essential holding of the appellate court and *Roe*.

The chief justice took the position that all of the Missouri restrictions (except the "findings" of the preamble, which he said did not impose legally binding regulations on abortion) should be upheld, even under *Roe*, since they did not prevent a woman from having an abortion. The Court, he said, had never held that the government was obligated to provide funds for nontherapeutic abortions (in fact, a majority had held that there was no such obligation). Rehnquist was equally confident that the other provisions of the Missouri statute should be upheld, but did not insist, in conference, that *Roe v. Wade* be overruled, although he did not disguise his view that *Roe* was wrongly decided.

White, who with Rehnquist had been a persistent critic of *Roe*, agreed with the chief justice that the challenged Missouri provisions (except the preamble) should be upheld as constitutional and the appellate court decision reversed.

Justice O'Connor, the third member of the new conservative majority, was perceived at the time of *Webster* to be the pivotal justice, who could ultimately decide whether *Roe* survived or not. Although she had criticized *Roe* in previous opinions, at the *Webster* conference O'Connor confined her discussion to a stringent analysis of the provisions of the Missouri statute. She concluded that, under a narrow reading, they could be sustained under *Roe*. She said further that she "would adhere to her previous position," signaling that she would continue to advocate an "undue burden" standard in abortion cases, which recognized a state's interest in an unborn fetus throughout a pregnancy, as a substitute for *Roe*'s analysis.

Justice Scalia had never been fainthearted when it came to overruling precedents that he thought were wrong. *Roe* fit into his category of judicial mistakes, and he declared that he wanted "to overrule [*Roe*] when we can."

Justice Kennedy told his colleagues that *Roe*'s methodology was wrong "and that's wrong for us." A state has the authority to protect the fetus, he concluded, and he did not place the third-trimester limit on the protection that had been imposed by *Roe*. Still, Kennedy expressed reservations about overruling *Roe*. Unlike Scalia, he thought the doctrine of stare decisis (respect for precedent) "would save it." On the merits of the Missouri regulations, Kennedy supported Rehnquist's position that the legally binding provisions of the statute (but not the preamble) should be upheld.

Chief Justice Rehnquist assigned the majority opinion to himself, undertaking the task of finding common ground among the five conservatives, not just on the Missouri statute, but also on an analysis of *Roe*. Only three members of the majority—the *Roe* dissenters, Rehnquist and White, and now Scalia—were on record as favoring the outright overruling of *Roe*. Kennedy was critical of *Roe* but did not seem prepared to overrule it, having raised the stare decisis issue in the *Webster* conference. Justice O'Connor appeared to be the most tentative member of the majority, confining her position to a narrow interpretation of the Missouri statute and endorsing, once again, an "undue burden" standard in abortion cases as a substitute for *Roe*'s trimester analysis.

A longtime critic of *Roe*, Rehnquist could be confident that he would have the support of White and Scalia in any attack on *Roe* that he might make in his *Webster* opinion. If the chief justice pushed too far in his criticism of *Roe*, however, he risked losing either Kennedy or O'Connor or both. But if he treated *Roe* too gingerly, he could invite the wrath of White or Scalia.

The first draft of the chief justice's proposed majority opinion was circulated to his colleagues on May 25 and had many of the earmarks of a cautious opinion written to hold a narrow majority. For more than four-fifths of his opinion, Rehnquist presented a technical analysis of the Missouri statute, an approach calculated to appeal most particularly to O'Connor. In his draft, Rehnquist carefully parsed the language of each provision of the Missouri statute. The appellate court was wrong in declaring the preamble unconstitutional, he concluded, since that provision of the state statute did not impose legally binding restrictions on abortion. Missouri's prohibition of abortion in public facilities or with government funds was not unconstitutional, he continued, since the Court had never held that government must give financial support for abortion. For similar reasons, Rehnquist said that the appellate court had erred in striking down the statute's bar to government-financed counseling on abortion.

So far, Rehnquist had not even hinted that *Roe* was in jeopardy, and he was down to the last issue in the case—Missouri's requirement that a physician planning an abortion operation on a pregnant woman after the twentieth week of pregnancy perform various tests of viability. It was at this juncture in his opinion, presented almost as an afterthought, that the chief justice attacked *Roe*.

Missouri's viability-testing provision was a reasonable means for the state to protect the interests of the unborn fetus, Rehnquist wrote, even though the tests preceded the third-trimester requirement of *Roe*. The problem was not with the Missouri statute, but with the "rigid trimester analysis" of *Roe*, Rehnquist wrote. "In the first place, the rigid *Roe* framework is hardly consistent with the notion of a Constitution cast in general terms, as ours is, and usually speaking in general principles, as ours does," the chief justice continued. "The key elements of the *Roe* framework—trimesters and viability—are not found in the text of the Constitution or in any place else one would expect to find a constitutional principle. Since the bounds of the inquiry are essentially indeterminate, the result has been a web of legal rules that have become increasingly intricate, resembling a code of regulations rather than a body of constitutional doctrine."

Having finally unveiled his strategy of attack on *Roe*, the chief justice declared that *Roe*'s trimester analysis should be shelved. In its place, Rehnquist proposed a new standard: that the state could use all reasonable means to protect the interests of an unborn fetus *throughout* the pregnancy. The chief justice's standard, which he had advocated in his *Roe* dissent, was a less demanding test for states than O'Connor's "undue burden." The Missouri requirement of viability tests after the twentieth week of pregnancy was constitutional, Rehnquist concluded, since it was a rational means to further the state's legitimate interest in protecting potential human life. Nowhere in his discussion did the chief justice affirm *Roe*'s declaration that a pregnant woman had a fundamental constitutional right to an abortion.

The Rehnquist opinion eviscerated *Roe*, eliminating virtually every tenet of the 1973 opinion. A woman's right to control her own body was no longer "fundamental," and would now have to vie with the state's interest in protecting the unborn fetus throughout the pregnancy. Once the word "fundamental" was eliminated, the pregnant woman's right was no longer paramount, even in the first trimester, as *Roe* had stated unequivocally. A state regulation protecting the unborn fetus, on the other hand, was justified so long as it was "rational," the lowest standard of proof available in constitutional jurisprudence. Still, the chief justice said his opinion would only "modify and narrow *Roe*," not overrule it.

In a "Dear Chief" letter written shortly after the Rehnquist draft was circulated, Justice Stevens accused Rehnquist of overruling *Roe* without taking responsibility for the deed. He dismissed Rehnquist's new rationality test as a ruse. "If a simple showing that a state regulation 'reasonably furthers the state interest in protecting potential human life' is enough to justify an abortion regulation, the woman's interest in making the abortion decision apparently is given no weight at all," Stevens wrote. "A tax on abortions, a requirement that the pregnant woman must be able to stand on her head for fifteen minutes before she can have an abortion, or a criminal prohibition would each satisfy your test."

It was obvious to Stevens that the purpose of Rehnquist's test was to reject *Roe v. Wade* in its entirety. "I would think that it would be much better for the Court, as an institution, to do so [reverse *Roe*] forthrightly rather than indirectly with a bombshell first introduced at the end of its opinion," Stevens wrote. "As you know, I am not in favor of overruling *Roe v. Wade*, but if the deed is to be done I would rather see the Court give the case a decent burial instead of tossing it out the window of a fast-moving caboose."

Justice Blackmun also protested as he watched conservatives on the Rehnquist Court hover menacingly over his cherished *Roe* opinion. After he had read the first draft of Rehnquist's *Webster* opinion, he wrote a dissent that accused the chief of willfully, and tragically, abandoning *Roe*:

> Let there be no misunderstanding: the two isolated dissenters in *Roe* [Rehnquist and White], after all these years, now have prevailed, with the assent of the Court's newest members [Kennedy, O'Connor and Scalia], in rolling back that case and in returning the law of procreative freedom to the severe limitations that generally prevailed before January 22, 1973 [the day *Roe* was announced]. . . . The simple truth is that *Roe* no longer survives, and that the majority provides no substitute for its protective umbrella. . . . I rue this day. I rue the violence that has been done to the liberty and equality of women. I rue the violence that has been done to our legal fabric and to the integrity of this Court. I rue the inevitable loss of public esteem for this Court that is so essential. I dissent.

Rehnquist could afford to take Blackmun's and Stevens's tough criticism without flinching. But he could not be so stoic when criticism came from Justice O'Connor. She informed the chief that she would not support his attack on *Roe*. As she had suggested in conference, she was in favor of upholding the Missouri restrictions without reaching *Roe*. When the chief refused to omit the attack on *Roe* in his opinion, O'Connor decided to write a separate concurring opinion. Her defection reduced the chief's opinion to a plurality, not a majority opinion.

In her separate opinion, O'Connor wrote that the Missouri provisions were constitutional—and consistent with *Roe*. In her view, the Court did not have to reach *Roe* at all and, indeed, that it was sounder constitutional practice not to decide a constitutional question in advance of the necessity to do so. If Missouri's requirement for viability tests after twenty weeks was interpreted to mean that a state could employ useful tests to determine when viability was possible, then it would not impose an "undue burden" on a woman's abortion decision and would, therefore, be consistent with the basic protection of the pregnant woman provided by *Roe*.

The O'Connor opinion infuriated Scalia. Although he was not thrilled that the Court would not overrule *Roe*, he reluctantly accepted that reality. But to perpetuate the notion that *Roe* was still good law, as O'Connor's opinion did, was too much. In *his* separate opinion, Scalia sizzled with rage. "Justice O'Connor's assertion, that a 'fundamental rule of judicial restraint' requires us to avoid reconsidering *Roe*, cannot be taken seriously," he wrote.

Having warned his colleagues of the sheer doctrinal nonsense proposed by O'Connor, Scalia proceeded to lecture O'Connor on the intricacies of constitutional law as a senior professor might speak to a slightly slow-witted undergraduate. "By finessing *Roe* we do not, as she suggests, adhere to the strict and venerable rule that we should avoid 'deciding questions of a constitutional nature,' " he wrote. The question for the Court was whether the Missouri statute comported with the requirements of the Constitution. To answer that question, the Court must inevitably confront the weakness of *Roe* and, in doing so, be permitted to formulate a rule of constitutional law that goes beyond the technical interpretation of the Missouri statute. In yet another dig at O'Connor, Scalia noted that O'Connor herself had been guilty earlier in the term of what she now condemned. He reminded her that she had written for the Court in *Croson*, the decision striking down Richmond's "set aside" program for minority building subcontractors. In her *Croson* opinion, O'Connor had outlined criteria for tailoring race-based remedies, an exercise that went beyond the necessary analysis to decide the case.

"The result of our vote today is that we will not reconsider that prior opinion [*Roe*]," Scalia concluded irately, "even if most of the Justices think it is wrong, unless we have before us a statute that in fact contradicts it—and even then (under our newly discovered 'no-broader-than-necessary' requirement) only minor problematical aspects of *Roe* will be reconsidered, unless one expects state legislatures to adopt provisions whose compliance with *Roe* cannot even be argued with a straight face. It thus appears that the mansion of constitutionalized abortion-law, constructed overnight in *Roe v. Wade*, must be disassembled door-jamb by door-jamb, and never entirely brought down, no matter how wrong it may be."

Scalia's intemperate reaction to O'Connor's *Webster* concurrence did nothing to budge O'Connor, but it did put an end to speculation, circulating at the time of Scalia's Court appointment, that he would do for the conservatives on the Court what Justice Brennan had done so brilliantly for the liberals—build majorities for his firm ideological positions. A closer look at Scalia's background would have disabused conservatives of their hopeful notion that Scalia would serve as the Court's conservative counterpart to Brennan.

On every stage in his life, Antonin "Nino" Scalia had played a leading role. The only child of S. Eugene Scalia, a professor of romance languages at Brooklyn College, and his wife, Catherine, an elementary school teacher, Scalia was an ebullient academic star from his earliest school days at Xavier Military Academy, a Jesuit school in Lower Manhattan. Scalia was first in his class and valedictorian at Xavier and retained that number-one ranking through four years at the Jesuit Georgetown University. "People just competed for second," said one of Scalia's classmates, "because he was so superior academically." Scalia's classical education (six years of Latin, five years of Greek), a college friend remembered, gave him an unusually broad historical and philosophical perspective on contemporary issues. His outstanding record continued at the Harvard Law School, where he graduated in 1960 magna cum laude and served as an editor of the law review.

Besides his near-flawless academic record, Scalia's most distinguishing intellectual characteristic was his joy in debating. When

Scalia was interviewed for his first position as a lawyer with the prominent Cleveland firm now known as Jones, Day, Reavis and Pogue, the firm's managing partner remembered Scalia's performance with awe. Scalia stayed up until 3 A.M. arguing with eight members of the firm in defense of a law review note he had edited in support of blue laws (imposing store closings on Sundays). "It never bothered Nino that everybody else was on the other side," recalled one participant, Richard Pogue.

Despite his disagreement with the Jones, Day partners, Scalia was hired by the firm and worked there for six years before accepting an appointment to teach law at the University of Virginia. In 1971, Scalia, who had begun to establish a reputation as a leading young academic conservative, joined the Nixon Administration as general counsel for the Office of Telecommunications Policy. Later he was appointed assistant attorney general in charge of President Gerald Ford's Justice Department's Office of Legal Counsel (sworn in by his predecessor, Justice Rehnquist).

Scalia left the Ford Administration to join a conservative Washington think tank, the American Enterprise Institute, where he traded theories with an illustrious array of other conservative intellectuals including Robert Bork and Laurence Silberman (who would later be his colleagues on the D.C. Court of Appeals), former U.N. Ambassador Jeane Kirkpatrick and Jude Wanniski, architect of supply-side economic policy.

In one formal institute debate, Scalia rebuked liberal judges who "have found rights where society never believed they existed." Scalia gave as examples of unwarranted judicial expansion decisions by the Supreme Court on affirmative action and abortion.

After a year at the American Enterprise Institute, Scalia joined the faculty of the University of Chicago Law School, where he could enjoy the stimulating company of leading academic conservatives including Professors Richard Posner, Frank Easterbrook and Richard Epstein. He also found a fraternity house two blocks from the university campus that he and his wife, Maureen McCarthy (Radcliffe College, 1960), bought and renovated to accommodate their nine children.

During his five years at Chicago, Scalia sharpened his attacks on what he considered the excesses of liberal Supreme Court rulings. In a 1979 law review article criticizing the Court's affirmative action decisions, Scalia used his immigrant father as an example of how judicial good intentions go wrong. "Not only had he never profited from the sweat of any black man's brow," Scalia wrote, "I don't think he had ever seen a black man. To compare the racist debt [of ethnic group members] with that of those who plied the slave trade, and who maintained a formal caste system for many years thereafter, is to confuse a mountain with a molehill." Supreme Court decisions like *Bakke*, Scalia continued, established a system of restorative justice in which it is "precisely these groups that do most of the restoring."

He took satisfaction in proposing a Restorative Justice Handicapping System (RJHS) based on ancestry. Scalia awarded the highest number of points to "Aryans" like Justice Lewis Powell, Jr., author of the *Bakke* opinion, whose roots were buried deep in colonial America. Scalia conceded that his system would be difficult to implement but was confident that an adventurist liberal Supreme Court "would not shrink from the task."

With the brimming confidence of a brilliant conservative law professor who knew that his time had come (with Reagan's presidential election), Scalia turned down the Reagan Administration's first invitation to serve in the federal judiciary. Rather than accept the offer to sit on the U.S. Court of Appeals for the Seventh Circuit, Scalia waited patiently for an opening on the U.S. Court of Appeals for the District of Columbia, a more prestigious appellate court and one where his expertise in federal administrative law could be put to better use.

In 1982, Scalia received the desired appointment to the D.C. Court of Appeals and, for the next four years, produced a barrage of judicial opinions, law review articles and speeches attacking his liberal judicial adversaries. Under the Scalia judicial model, federal courts should give wide latitude to the coequal political branches of the federal government to act, particularly the executive branch, as well as to the states. In the economic sphere, Scalia advocated minimal judicial interference with the free play of market forces.

Civil rights and civil liberties petitioners learned to expect from Judge Scalia a less generous reading of civil rights statutes and the

Bill of Rights and the Fourteenth Amendment than they were accustomed to during the Warren and Burger Court eras. Scalia was not bashful in arguing for reversal of precedents established by liberal court majorities if he concluded that the decisions were wrong. When he thought a constitutional error had been made, he was unmoved by the doctrine of stare decisis. Respect for bad precedent only perpetuated the error.

Despite Scalia's rapier thrusts at the liberal dragons, practitioners of "liberal jurisprudence" on his appellate court, such as Judge Abner Mikva, insisted that Scalia "understands the doctrine of collegiality and has in fact found middle ground and I think he's good at it." After President Reagan appointed Scalia to the Supreme Court in 1986, it was suggested by the liberal Judge Mikva, among others, that Scalia possessed the potential to be a conservative consensus-builder on the Rehnquist Court. But Mikva offered one caveat: once Scalia had made up his mind, "he'll plant his flag and go down in flames with it if he needs to."

With his *Webster* blast at O'Connor, Scalia forfeited any hope of influencing the moderate-conservative O'Connor on the abortion issue. She did not take kindly to what was seen as a personal and mean-spirited attack on her professional competence.

The split among the five conservative members of the Court in *Webster* was little consolation to Justice Harry Blackmun. To be sure, it allowed him to attack the chief justice's plurality (rather than majority) opinion and to eliminate the conclusion in his first *Webster* draft dissent that "*Roe* no longer survives." Still, Blackmun's fury, which had welled up inside of him as Rehnquist and Scalia took turns pummeling his 1973 opinion, was unleashed in his final draft dissent.

It began: "Today, *Roe v. Wade*, and the fundamental constitutional right of women to decide whether to terminate a pregnancy, survive but are not secure. Although the Court extricates itself from this case without making a single, even incremental, change in the law of abortion, the plurality [Rehnquist, White and Kennedy] and Justice Scalia would overrule *Roe* (the first silently, the other explicitly) and would return to the States virtually unfettered authority to control the quintessentially intimate, personal, and life-directing decision whether to carry a fetus to term."

Blackmun then waded into the chief justice's opinion. "The plurality opinion is far more remarkable for the arguments that it does not advance than for those that it does," Blackmun wrote. Nowhere, Blackmun noted, had the chief justice conceded that many landmark decisions, including *Roe*, were based on traditionally recognized "unenumerated powers." It was true that the Constitution did not spell out a woman's right to have an abortion, Blackmun admitted. But the document also did not explicitly protect a general right to privacy, established in *Griswold* and left conspicuously untouched by Rehnquist's opinion—or a myriad of other firmly established rights, e.g., the First Amendment's protection of symbolic expression. As to what Rehnquist termed *Roe*'s "web of legal rules," Blackmun reminded the chief that in scores of Supreme Court decisions the justices laid down specific rules to be followed.

Blackmun also picked up on the point made by Justice Stevens in his private letter to Rehnquist—that the Rehnquist opinion did not contain a single justification for the chief's new standard of rationality for states attempting to protect the unborn fetus. "This 'it-is-so-because-we-say-so' jurisprudence constitutes nothing other than an attempted exercise of brute force; reason, much less persuasion, has no place," Blackmun wrote. Calling the Rehnquist standard "circular and totally meaningless," Blackmun then accused the chief justice and members of his plurality of preparing for the day when the Court would openly overrule *Roe*. "It is impossible to read the plurality opinion," he wrote, "without recognizing its implicit invitation to every state to enact more and more restrictive abortion laws, and to assert their interest in potential life as of the moment of conception. All these laws will satisfy the plurality's non-scrutiny until sometime, a new regime of old dissenters and new appointees will declare what the plurality intends: that *Roe* is no longer good law."

Harry Blackmun had requested that he be allowed to read portions of his dissenting opinion from the bench the day that the Court's decision in *Webster* was announced. On the last day of the term, Justice Blackmun read excerpts from his opinion for ten full minutes. His voice was soft but resonant and, by turns, anguished and angry. The final passage was spoken with sadness. "For today, the women of this nation still retain the liberty to control their destinies," he said. "But the signs are evident and ominous," he concluded, without looking up, "and a chill wind blows."

CHAPTER SIX

A NEUTRON BOMB

It took only a few months for Harry Blackmun's dreaded *Webster* prophesy to begin to come true. In two cases the following term, one from Minnesota and the other from Ohio, the justices decided that yet another set of restrictive state abortion regulations were constitutional (though the restrictions were not very different in intent from others that an earlier Court majority, more sympathetic to *Roe*, had rejected as unconstitutional).

As Blackmun had predicted, the old dissenters from *Roe* and new conservative appointees seemed eager to revisit *Roe* at every opportunity until, he feared, the decision would survive in formal name only. It was as if prolife forces, now with critical help from a conservative Court majority, were repeatedly driving a battering ram into the thinly protected walls of *Roe*, and that it was only a matter of time before the entire fortress would collapse.

The Minnesota statute had been drafted by one of the state's most aggressive and outspoken prolife organizations and required that both parents of a minor woman who was pregnant be notified of her intention to have an abortion forty-eight hours before the operation could be performed. It did not matter that the pregnant woman's father may have been an alcoholic or beaten her as a child or left home shortly after her birth. Indeed, it was of no consequence if her father and mother had never married or lived together. The purpose of the notification requirement, the sponsors contended, was to promote parent-child relationships at a time of "difficult and traumatic choice."

During a five-week trial, Judge Donald Alsop, a Nixon appointee, heard testimony from counselors, psychologists, juvenile court judges, and many young women who had been subjected to the statute's strictures. Even where the minor child resided in a functional family, the sudden involvement of an absentee parent who did not have custody of the child could be disruptive to the household, the district court judge concluded; in abusive or otherwise dysfunctional families, compelled notification was especially dangerous because it could provoke violent and abusive reactions.

The judge also considered the effect of the judicial bypass provision of the statute. That provision allowed a pregnant minor who was fearful of the consequences of notifying both parents of her decision to have an abortion to seek a waiver of the requirement from a judge. Judge Alsop concluded that the judicial bypass provision had no beneficial effect but served, instead, as a "traumatic distraction." He declared the statute unconstitutional, a decision that was upheld by a three-judge appellate court.

The full appeals court, with appointees of President Ronald Reagan comprising a majority, reinstated the law. They found the two-parent notification provision unconstitutional, but they upheld the statute nonetheless because of the judicial bypass provision that provided a legal means to avoid the two-parent notification requirement.

Both conclusions of the full appeals court were challenged in two separate petitions to the Supreme Court: the State of Minnesota appealed that part of the decision finding the statute's two-parent notification provision unconstitutional; Dr. Jane Hodgson, a longtime abortion rights advocate, appealed the holding of the appellate court that the judicial bypass preserved the constitutionality of the statute.

At the oral argument before the Supreme Court, on November 29, 1989, it was obvious that Justices O'Connor and Scalia had ap-

proached the issues in the Minnesota abortion case petitions differently, as they had in *Webster*.

Would the best interests of the pregnant minor necessarily be
served by the notification provision, Justice O'Connor asked John
Tunheim, Minnesota's deputy attorney general, if, say, a divorced father had been found unfit to have custody of the child?

Tunheim replied that even separated or divorced parents could be
helpful to minors at such a traumatic time. He added that about 50
percent of Minnesota's teenagers lived at home with both parents.

"Put the other way, fifty percent do not," O'Connor retorted.

Justice Scalia jumped into the fray, offering the argument that he
obviously wanted the state's attorney to make.

"Mr. Tunheim," Scalia interjected, "I had assumed the purpose of
this provision was not just to assist the child, but that . . . the biologi-
cal parents presumed to have the right to provide advice on this matter if they wanted to."

"That's correct," Tunheim replied.

"I mean there's a parental interest involved as well as a filial interest, isn't that so?" Scalia asked.

Tunheim agreed. "Both parents have those rights and responsibili-
ties," he said, and added that parents "in most cases act in the best
interest of their minor children."

Justice O'Connor waited politely for the Scalia-Tunheim dialogue
to end, then resumed her questioning.

"Well, that might be true in general," O'Connor said to Tunheim,
"but probably you would concede that there are some circumstances
in which it would not be in the best interests of the child to tell one of
the two parents of her problem and intention."

"Certainly, your Honor," Tunheim replied.

"And yet," O'Connor added, "there is no mechanism provided at
all whereby the best interests of the child can be considered."

At the judicial conference on December 1, 1989, four justices—Rehnquist, Scalia, White and Kennedy—voted to uphold the
Minnesota statute in its entirety, including the two-parent notification
provision. Blackmun, Brennan and Marshall, all staunch defenders of

Roe, voted to strike the whole statute. Stevens took a narrower position, but still voted to strike the statute, because the two-parent notification requirement was so irrational, in his view, that the judicial bypass provision could not save it.

As in *Webster*, Justice O'Connor found herself uncomfortably alone in her position. Declaring that her position was still tentative, she said that the two-parent notification provision of the Minnesota statute was irrational—the first time since her Court appointment that she had found a state regulation restricting abortion unacceptable. At the same time, however, she indicated that she favored upholding the appellate court decision (and the statute) because of the judicial bypass provision.

Three days after the justices' conference, Justice O'Connor felt it necessary to write her colleagues "to clarify" her vote. She then reiterated her position that she found the two-parent notification provision irrational but saved, constitutionally, by the judicial bypass.

The O'Connor memorandum did not change the vote in the Minnesota cases; there were still five members of the Court (Rehnquist, White, Scalia, Kennedy and O'Connor) to uphold the appeals court decision. But it prompted Stevens to write his own memorandum, elaborating on the argument that he had made at the justices' conference: a judicial bypass could not save an otherwise invalid two-parent notification provision. In Stevens's memorandum, which appeared to be aimed at O'Connor, he distinguished a single-parent-notification requirement from the two-parent notification provision in the Minnesota statute. Stevens wrote:

> In my judgment, a single-parent consent requirement for any surgical procedure performed on a minor is perfectly reasonable as a general rule, but it constitutes an undue burden if it does not contain an escape hatch for the exceptional case—e.g., a Christian Scientist who will not permit a ruptured appendix to be removed to save a child's life. The absolute veto cannot stand without some form of state authorized bypass.
>
> It seems to me, however, that a two-parent notification requirement for any surgical procedure would not survive a rational basis test because it is counterproductive in broken family cases and is

147

wholly unnecessary in the ideal family in which, as a practical matter, notice to either parent would constitute notice to both. A child who has one parent's consent to any form of surgery should not be compelled to go to court to obtain relief from a statute that is unconstitutional because it is irrational as applied in most cases.

One day later, Chief Justice Rehnquist formally assigned the majority opinion in the Minnesota cases to O'Connor. "In view of the fact that you are the only member of the Court who agrees with the result in both halves of this case," Rehnquist wrote O'Connor, "the assignment is obviously yours."

But later that same day, December 8, 1989, O'Connor wrote the chief saying that her position had changed. She had spoken to Justice Stevens about his views after receiving his memorandum and concluded that "John's views are close to my own in these two cases, and, if I understand his approach correctly, I think I can agree with it."

O'Connor's new position meant that she no longer represented the majority view on both issues (the two-parent notification and judicial bypass provisions). Instead, O'Connor's position now aligned her with the Court's four most liberal members—Brennan, Blackmun, Marshall and Stevens—to strike down the Minnesota statute in its entirety. O'Connor's switch, moreover, allowed the senior member of the Court in the majority—now Justice Brennan—to assign the majority opinion, which the chief justice conceded in the early afternoon of December 8. "As matters now stand [2:20 P.M. on Friday]," Rehnquist wrote his colleagues, "Bill [Brennan] should assign the Minnesota cases and I will assign the Ohio case [in which the chief was in the majority]."

Brennan assigned the majority opinion in the Minnesota cases to Stevens, whose views, as O'Connor had acknowledged, were closest to her own. Justices Brennan, Blackmun and Marshall understood that Stevens would be writing his majority opinion with the objective of holding O'Connor's vote. They, therefore, did not rush to join Stevens's opinion until they received word that it was satisfactory to O'Connor. But the word never came. Despite Stevens's vigorous efforts—in three drafts over a four-month period—to write an opinion that O'Connor would support, she ultimately refused to do so.

On June 11, 1990, O'Connor sent word to her colleagues of her decision that "[a]t the end of the day, I am back where I started. I agree with John that subdivision 2 [of the Minnesota statute], the 2-parent notification, is invalid. But I agree with Tony [Justice Kennedy, who had written a dissent] that subdivision 6, the 2-parent notification plus judicial bypass, passes constitutional muster."

Who, at this late date in the term, should write the opinion for the Court? Stevens no longer could speak for the majority since, without O'Connor, he was joined by only three members of the Court (Brennan, Blackmun and Marshall) who wanted to strike down the Minnesota statute in its entirety. But Justice Kennedy, who had written an opinion reflecting the position of Rehnquist, White, Scalia and Kennedy himself that the statute should be upheld in its entirety, did not command a majority either.

Stevens and Kennedy proposed a compromise solution: that the Court issue a brief, unsigned opinion upholding the appeals court decision—which had declared the two-parent notification provision unconstitutional but saved, ultimately, by the judicial bypass. Following the unsigned opinion, any member of the Court who chose to could write a separate concurring or dissenting opinion.

But Stevens, after agreeing to the unsigned opinion, remained uneasy about the compromise. He wrote his colleagues that the unsigned opinion would produce "two unfortunate consequences." First, it would mean that there would be no fully reasoned opinion for the Court. Secondly, the opinion would not be included in the syllabus in the *United States Reports*, the official repository of Court opinions and the headnote (at the beginning of the reported case) would, in Stevens's words "be meaningless."

Stevens proposed, therefore, that his signed opinion still represent the Court and promised that he would redraft it to reflect the justices' votes. His new introduction, circulated on June 15, no longer stated that "Justice Stevens delivered the opinion of the Court," but rather that "Justice Stevens announced the judgment of the Court" and that he "delivered the opinion of the Court" only for the majority that struck down the two-parent notification provision as unconstitutional.

Another majority, which included O'Connor but not Stevens, upheld the statute because of the judicial bypass. In the end, O'Connor did not support Stevens's argument that the state's requirement of notification of both parents was unconstitutional even if there was the "escape hatch" of a judicial bypass.

Justice Blackmun insisted on viewing the topsy-turvy turn of events positively, rallying the liberals around Stevens's opinion. He proposed that he, Brennan and Marshall "join as much of John's writing as possible" even though each took a more definitive position in striking down the Minnesota statute than Stevens. Brennan sent Blackmun a note approving of the strategy. "I am in wholehearted agreement with your suggestion that we all get together on as much of John's opinion as we possibly can," Brennan wrote, "especially now that Sandra has agreed to invalidate at least part of an abortion law."

Justice Scalia despaired of his colleagues' struggles in the Minnesota cases. In his own opinion, Scalia disapprovingly recounted the divergent, and irreconcilable, opinions of the justices, beginning with Justice O'Connor's. He concluded:

> The random and unpredictable results of our consequently unchanneled individual views make it increasingly evident, term after term, that the tools for this job are not to be found in the lawyer's—and hence not in the judge's—work-box. I continue to dissent from this enterprise of devising an Abortion Code, and from the illusion that we have authority to do so.

The abortion statute in the companion case from Ohio, which required notification of only one parent and also provided for a judicial bypass, proved to be an easier victory for the conservatives. The solid conservative bloc of Rehnquist, White, Scalia and Kennedy was joined by both O'Connor and Stevens in the Court's decision holding the statute constitutional. For Stevens, the only member of the majority who had dissented in the Minnesota decision, the one-parent notification requirement was reasonable, so long as there was a judicial bypass provision; a two-parent requirement, however, was not only unreasonable but counterproductive in many cases—as he had explained in his postconference memo.

The result in the Ohio case was not so noteworthy as the majority opinion written by Justice Kennedy to justify it. For the first time since *Roe*, the author of a Court majority opinion in an abortion case spoke explicitly about protecting the interests of the unborn fetus without confining the protection to the third trimester of pregnancy. In defending Ohio's restrictions, Kennedy wrote: "A free and enlightened society may decide that each of its members should attain a clearer, more tolerant understanding of the profound philosophical choices confronted by a woman who is considering whether to seek an abortion. Her decision will embrace her own destiny and personal dignity, *and the origins of the other human life that lie within the embryo.*"

In his concurring opinion, Scalia reminded his colleagues that the "Constitution contains no right to abortion." The sooner the majority ended its foolish struggle to preserve *Roe*, and sent the controversial abortion issue to the political arena, the better it would be for the Court and the country. "The Court should end its disruptive intrusion into this field as soon as possible," Scalia concluded expectantly.

A month after the decisions in the Minnesota and Ohio abortion cases were announced, Justice Brennan resigned from the Court, reducing the remaining members of the original *Roe* majority to two, Justices Blackmun and Marshall. With the right appointment, commentators predicted, President George Bush, who had supported the Republicans' anti-*Roe* platform, could produce a five-member Court majority that would overrule *Roe v. Wade*.

The president acted quickly, announcing the nomination of Judge David H. Souter of the U.S. Court of Appeals for the First Circuit three days after the Brennan resignation. At the time of Bush's announcement, little was known about the quiet, reclusive Souter outside his native New Hampshire.

During the last week of October 1990, the month that Souter was confirmed by the Senate, the newest justice listened with his colleagues to oral argument in *Rust v. Sullivan*, the latest threat to *Roe v. Wade*. The Bush Administration, represented by Solicitor General Kenneth Starr, contended that federal regulations prohibiting doctors in federally funded family planning clinics from advising pregnant women about abortion was constitutional.

Opposing the Bush Administration, Harvard Law Professor Laurence Tribe asked the justices to strike down the federal regulations on the ground that the so-called "gag rule" violated a doctor's First Amendment rights to give full medical information to his clinic patient. Tribe insisted that the reproductive rights of women, protected by *Roe v. Wade*, were not at issue; few in the courtroom took the Harvard professor's word for it. A conservative Court majority could, if it chose, take the opportunity to pronounce further negative judgment on *Roe*. For that reason, all eyes were focused on Justice David Souter.

The first opportunity to try to read Souter's intentions arose after Justice John Paul Stevens had engaged Solicitor General Starr in a brief, heated exchange. Stevens began with a hypothetical example. Suppose that one of the clinic doctors examined a pregnant woman and concluded from a purely medical point of view that abortion was the best option. Could the doctor advise his patient to get an abortion?

No, Starr replied. Under the federal regulations, Starr said, the doctor was obligated "to maintain the status quo."

"The status quo is that she's pregnant," Stevens retorted. "She doesn't need advice to stay pregnant."

Souter, who had been silent up to that point, leaned forward to address Starr. "What if the Title X [the provision at issue in the federal statute] physician in the course of his consulting or examination concludes that the woman is pregnant and in fact is in some imminent danger to her health?" Can the doctor refer her to a hospital for an abortion? he asked.

The doctor could refer the woman to the hospital for emergency care, Starr responded, but he could not refer her specifically for the purpose of an abortion.

Souter pressed the point. What if the woman faced "an imminent health risk," say high blood pressure or a heart condition, that would make a continued pregnancy extremely dangerous? Why does advising the patient of the best medical option violate the federal regulations?

Starr held his ground, insisting that a clinic doctor's advice on abortion was outside the scope of the federal regulations.

"It seems to me you are telling us that in those circumstances [when the advice is outside the objective of Title X], the physician cannot perform a normal professional responsibility," Souter said. "You are telling us that the Secretary [of Health and Human Services] in effect may preclude professional speech."

Souter's questioning suggested that he would not be led easily into the conservative camp of the chief justice. It was somewhat of a surprise, therefore, at the justices' conference on November 2, when Souter supported the chief justice's position that there was no pressing First Amendment issue and that the Court should uphold the regulations. Rehnquist, Souter, White, Scalia and Kennedy took that position at conference.

Souter did manage later to extract a concession from Rehnquist, who assigned himself the majority opinion. The chief justice added a long paragraph to his sixth draft (based on recommendations by Souter to Rehnquist in a letter) denying that the Court's *Rust* decision would make funding by government "invariably sufficient to justify government control over the content of expression." Rehnquist also included in his opinion a paragraph that conceded that a doctor might advise a clinic patient to get an abortion if it were a medical necessity, the issue that had been raised by Souter at oral argument. The chief justice wrote that such counseling did not defeat the purpose of the federal regulations; the purpose of the advice was not to encourage family planning, but to save the woman's life.

In his chambers shortly before the Court announced its decision in *Rust*, Justice Blackmun pondered the fate of *Roe*. "The votes are there to overrule *Roe* tomorrow," said Blackmun. "But they [the Rehnquist Court majority] haven't exercised that power yet. But I think this [the possible overruling of *Roe*] is part of life here," he said. "*Roe* was a 7-to-2 decision. So many people say it's a Blackmun opinion, but there were seven votes in favor of it. The sole dissenters in *Roe*, Rehnquist and White, are still here. With the two successive Presidents [Reagan and Bush] politicizing the issue, their appointees have followed along, I suppose."

Souter's vote with Rehnquist's majority in *Rust* was deeply disappointing to those who hoped that the newest justice might be a moderating influence on a Court increasingly hostile to *Roe*. But the *Rust* decision was not the worst news for prochoice advocates in 1991. Shortly after the end of Souter's first term on the Court, Justice Thurgood Marshall, eighty-two years old, announced his retirement.

Later in the summer, President Bush escorted Judge Clarence Thomas, an outspoken black conservative on the D.C. Court of Appeals, to the microphones outside Bush's vacation home in Kennebunkport, Maine, and announced that Thomas was the best person in the nation to succeed Marshall.

At his confirmation hearings the following fall, Thomas responded to an incredulous Senator Patrick Leahy that he could not recall discussing *Roe v. Wade* with his fellow Yale law students after the decision was announced. After his appointment was confirmed by the narrowest margin in Supreme Court history, Thomas sat with his new colleagues to hear oral argument in April 1992 in *Planned Parenthood of Southeastern Pennsylvania v. Casey*, Pennsylvania's challenge to *Roe v. Wade* that many believed would finally erase the 1973 court opinion from the constitutional lawbooks.

At the time of the *Casey* argument, the number of original members of the *Roe* seven-man majority had been reduced to one. Justice Harry Blackmun.

In 1986, attorney Kathryn Kolbert had persuaded a majority on the Supreme Court that restrictive provisions of a Pennsylvania statute (which included a twenty-four-hour waiting period and informed-consent requirements) violated the constitutional protections of a pregnant woman provided in *Roe v. Wade*. When she returned to the Court on April 22, 1992, to make a similar argument in *Casey*, Kolbert, a lawyer for the American Civil Liberties Union, faced a far more daunting challenge than in 1986. Three members of the 1986 five-man Court majority that had accepted her arguments had been replaced. And the pronouncements of the successors to Justices Powell, Brennan and Marshall—Kennedy, Souter and Thomas—gave Kolbert little reason to believe that she would again succeed.

The best that Kolbert could hope for, many commentators speculated, was a narrow ruling by a conservative Court majority that would not explicitly overturn *Roe*. Kolbert could claim victory against heavy odds if the Court did not throw out *Roe*, even if it upheld all of the restrictive provisions of the Pennsylvania statute (which included a twenty-four-hour waiting period and informed-consent requirement similar to those that had been struck down by the Court in 1986).

The justices and everyone else in the courtroom on April 22 were therefore stunned when Kolbert began her presentation by offering an all-or-nothing argument that the Court must strike down all of the Pennsylvania regulations. Upholding a single restriction, Kolbert told the justices, would be the equivalent of overruling *Roe*, an unthinkable result, in her view. "Never before has the Court bestowed and taken back a fundamental right that has been part of the settled rights and expectations of literally millions of Americans for nearly two decades," Kolbert said.

"Ms. Kolbert," Justice O'Connor finally said, addressing the attorney after seven uninterrupted minutes of her fervent argument, "you're arguing the case as though all we have before us is whether to apply stare decisis and preserve *Roe v. Wade* in all its aspects. Nevertheless, we granted certiorari [review] on some specific questions in this case. Do you plan to address any of those in your argument?"

Yes, Kolbert replied, she did plan to argue that the specific provisions of the Pennsylvania statute were unconstitutional. But when she did discuss the provisions of the state statute, Kolbert reminded the justices that the Court had already declared similar provisions unconstitutional under *Roe*. To uphold the Pennsylvania provisions would breach the Court's constitutional compact with millions of pregnant American women and throw them into the back alleys of yesterday.

For the sixth time in a decade, the government attorney representing the Republican Administration urged the justices to reverse *Roe*. Solicitor General Kenneth Starr adhered to the broad antiabortion argument first presented by his predecessor, Charles Fried, in the *Webster* case three years earlier. *Roe v. Wade* was a profoundly flawed opinion and should be overruled, Starr suggested. In its place, the solicitor general recommended that the Court adopt the analysis endorsed by Chief Justice Rehnquist in *Webster* that would uphold any state restriction on abortion throughout the pregnancy, including all of those in Pennsylvania's statute, so long as there was a rational basis for the restriction.

The story of *Casey*—and Rehnquist's failure to find five votes to overturn *Roe*—is one of the most extraordinary in the annals of the modern Supreme Court.

The story began in the justices' conference room in late April where the discussion on *Casey* was unusually laconic. The views of most of the justices were well known and did not need much elaboration. The chief justice, together with Justices White and Scalia, had long been on record as favoring the reversal of *Roe*. At the *Casey* conference, the chief justice reiterated the views he had expressed in his *Roe* dissent and voted to uphold the major provisions of the Pennsylvania statute. He was joined in his vote by Justices White and Scalia and the newest appointee, Justice Clarence Thomas.

On the other side, as he had been for nineteen years, was *Roe*'s author, Justice Blackmun. He was joined by Justice Stevens in his vote to strike down the Pennsylvania abortion regulations as an unconstitutional violation of *Roe*.

Justice O'Connor, a potential fifth vote for the chief, had been attacking *Roe* since her first term on the Court; she considered Blackmun's trimester analysis more medical than constitutional in its approach. For nine years, beginning with her 1983 dissent in *Akron*, O'Connor had waged a campaign to have the Court substitute an "undue burden" standard for *Roe*'s trimester analysis. As applied in abortion cases decided by the Court, O'Connor's "undue burden" test upheld most state abortion regulations. Since her Court appointment, O'Connor had found only one state restriction unconstitutional, the two-parent notification requirement in the Minnesota case (which she nonetheless upheld because of the judicial bypass provision).

But while criticizing *Roe*, O'Connor had never said that she would vote to overrule the 1973 decision—and there were good reasons for her to resist the dump-*Roe* forces on the Court. As the first woman on the Court, O'Connor took her role as a model for other women seriously, and was not eager to cast the fifth vote to overrule the Court decision. Justice Scalia's cutting *Webster* concurrence, in which he held

O'Connor's position up to scathing ridicule, had done nothing to push the proud O'Connor into the chief's camp. Finally, O'Connor, a cautious jurist, was uncomfortable with overruling precedent when an alternative—and her "undue burden" test provided it—was available. At the *Casey* conference, O'Connor voted to uphold the major provisions of the Pennsylvania statute but gave no indication that she was prepared to overrule *Roe*.

Justice Kennedy appeared to be a more promising candidate than O'Connor to provide the fifth vote. In his first full term on the Court, Kennedy had given indications, both publicly and in the privacy of the judicial conference, that he thought *Roe* was wrongly decided and that Justice Blackmun's analysis was seriously defective. In fact, Kennedy had supported Rehnquist's 1989 plurality opinion in *Webster* which, had O'Connor contributed the necessary fifth vote, would have officially decimated the constitutional analysis in *Roe*. In the *Webster* conference, moreover, Kennedy had not been gentle in his criticism of *Roe* or shy about promoting the state's interest in protecting the interest of the unborn fetus.

And two years later, in his majority opinion in the Ohio abortion regulation case, Kennedy expanded on his view that the interest of the unborn fetus throughout the pregnancy was entitled to constitutional protection comparable to that of the pregnant woman provided in *Roe*. At the *Casey* conference, Kennedy voted with the chief to uphold the major provisions of the Pennsylvania statute and appeared open to the possibility of supporting a majority opinion that would officially reject *Roe*'s analysis, including its declaration that a pregnant woman had a protected constitutional right to an abortion.

Another potential member of a majority led by the chief justice to overrule *Roe* was President Bush's first appointee, Justice Souter, although he had not yet cast a vote in a case in which *Roe* was directly challenged. At the *Casey* conference, Souter, like O'Connor and Kennedy, voted to uphold the major provisions of the state statute. But he gave no indication that he was prepared to explicitly reject *Roe*. Like O'Connor, Souter placed a high value on protecting the Court's institutional authority by preserving precedents, even those like *Roe* that were flawed. Souter would later take a leadership role in

Casey in preserving *Roe*, which surely must have shocked his supporters in the White House, President George Bush and his chief of
staff, John Sununu.

"Have I ever heard of this man?" Thurgood Marshall asked his wife
after Bush had announced the Souter nomination in July 1990. No,
she replied, and Marshall joined millions of other Americans scram-
bling to sign up for a cram course on the life and philosophy of David
Hackett Souter.

For David Souter, the small town of Weare, New Hampshire,
was an idyllic romping ground for a little boy. At first, David and his
parents, who lived in suburban Boston, visited relatives there only in
the summers. Often during those summers in the mid-1940s, Souter
and his maternal grandfather went to town, where Souter held his
grandfather's hand and watched him greet everyone by name.

Almost a half century later, Souter described Weare as "a town
large in geography, small in population. The physical space, the open
space between people, however, was not matched by the inner space
between them, because, as everybody knows who has lived in a small
town, there is a closeness of people in a small town that is unattain-
able anywhere else."

In 1950, when Souter was eleven years old, the family moved to
Weare, and the boy was never happier; he had gained permanent entrance to a secure and comfortable world that he had always loved.
While enjoying the simple pleasures of country life during his formative years, Souter also read voraciously and recorded consistently
high marks in school. The editors of Souter's high school yearbook
named him the most "literary" and "sophisticated" member of his
graduating class and prophesied that he was "most likely to succeed."

At Harvard College, Souter decided to become a lawyer after taking Professor Mark De Wolfe Howe's course, "The Role of Law in
Anglo-American History." For Souter, Howe's approach to the study
of law epitomized the highest standards of intellectual integrity. When
Howe discussed the judicial philosophy of Judge Learned Hand, for
example, Souter sensed that the professor did not agree with Judge
Hand on many issues, including Hand's criticism of the Court's deci-

sion in *Brown v. Board of Education.* Yet Howe presented Hand's views with thoroughness and utmost respect.

Souter's extraordinary mind (the small, compact Souter was once described as "about 135 pounds, 120 of which is brain") and outstanding record at Harvard enabled him to win a Rhodes Scholarship to Oxford for two years. When he came home, Souter went to Harvard Law School. In his senior year, he wrote his thesis on Justice Oliver Wendell Holmes, Jr. With two other revered exponents of judicial restraint, Judge Learned Hand and Justice John M. Harlan, Holmes headed Souter's list of judicial role models.

After graduation, Souter returned to New Hampshire, where he achieved a steady series of courtroom accomplishments (both as an attorney and a judge). His success was a result of intelligence, dedication and hard work. He was also helped mightily in his career by his professional, and later personal, relationship with Warren Rudman. In 1968, Souter was hired by Rudman, then New Hampshire's attorney general, as his assistant and, later, was made his deputy. The Rudman-Souter relationship was like "fire and ice," with Rudman, the bluff, gregarious politician, playing off Souter's more reticent, cerebral approach to law. Over the years, Rudman concluded that Souter was "the single most brilliant intellectual mind I have ever met."

Souter succeeded Rudman as New Hampshire's attorney general, and in 1978 was appointed to the state judiciary, first at the trial level and then to the New Hampshire Supreme Court (on Rudman's recommendation). When President Ronald Reagan was seeking a replacement on the U.S. Supreme Court for retiring Justice Lewis Powell in 1987, Rudman, by then a Republican senator, made certain that the White House list of highly qualified candidates included Judge Souter. Souter did not make the final cut in 1986, but a few years later Rudman's groundwork paid off handsomely.

On Friday, July 20, 1990, Judge Souter was working in his chambers in Weare, struggling to finish his last opinions as a member of the New Hampshire Supreme Court (Souter had been confirmed three months earlier for appointment to the U.S. Court of Appeals for the First Circuit). In his determination to complete his opinions, Souter had resisted all diversions, even listening to newscasts and reading newspapers. The next morning, he took a brief break to collect his mail at the Weare Post Office.

What do you think about Judge Brennan? Souter was asked by a postal clerk.

Souter first thought that the reference was to Arthur Brennan, a Weare lawyer who had been counselor to the governor. Had Arthur Brennan been appointed to the state superior court? Souter wondered to himself. But he didn't want to reveal his own ignorance of the latest state judicial appointment and replied noncommittally that the appointment was certainly something special. It certainly was, replied the clerk, who added that Brennan had been on the Court for over thirty years.

Only at that moment did Souter realize that William, not Arthur, Brennan was the subject of the conversation at the Weare Post Office—and in post offices across the country.

Later that Saturday, Souter received a call from his friend Warren Rudman to discuss the Brennan resignation. The next day, Souter's name was listed in the *New York Times* as a possible replacement for Brennan. That Sunday afternoon, President Bush's White House counsel, C. Boyden Gray, phoned Souter to ask him to come to Washington to talk about the possibility of his nomination to the Supreme Court.

After the call from Gray, Souter spoke again to Warren Rudman, who told him to be prepared for questions on a number of controversial constitutional issues, including abortion. Souter replied that he would not answer any questions about his position on abortion and, if members of the Bush Administration needed assurances on the issue, they could save the taxpayers an airfare because he would prefer to stay home. Rudman called John Sununu, the president's chief of staff and the former governor of New Hampshire, to report Souter's position. No one in the Administration was going to ask Souter about his position on abortion or any other sensitive constitutional issue, Sununu assured Rudman.

Souter flew to Washington on Sunday night, and the following Monday morning he was smuggled into the White House for a half-hour discussion with C. Boyden Gray and Attorney General Richard Thornburgh. True to Sununu's word, neither man asked Souter about his position on abortion or any other controversial issue.

At 1:30 P.M., Souter was escorted into the president's office and for the next forty-five minutes the president and Judge Souter talked about Souter's general legal interests and approach to constitutional law. By late afternoon, Bush had made his choice, selecting Souter over the other finalist, Judge Edith Jones of the U.S. Court of Appeals for the Fifth Circuit. At 5 P.M., only three and a half hours after he had met Souter, the president announced that the New Hampshire judge—a man of "keen intellect as well as wise balance between the theoretical and practical aspects of law"—would be his first nominee to the Supreme Court.

At his news conference announcing the Souter nomination, Bush, who had supported the prolife Republican platform, said nothing about Souter's views on abortion. "You might just think that the whole nomination had something to do with abortion," Bush told reporters. "It's something much broader than that. I have too much respect for the Supreme Court for that."

On the morning of September 13, 1990, the Senate Judiciary Committee and millions in the television audience were introduced to the slight New Hampshire judge who would become the 105th member of the Supreme Court of the United States. Souter was immaculately dressed for the occasion, wearing a well-tailored charcoal-gray suit, blue shirt, and crisply knotted blue-and-white-striped tie. In his opening statement, Souter spoke of his small-town roots and the closeness and caring between him and his neighbors. And he recounted with pride his representation of indigent clients and, later, as a trial judge, his admiration for juries ("the conscience of the community") that returned their sensible verdicts.

After Souter had completed his opening statement, Senator Joseph Biden, the chairman of the Senate Judiciary Committee, wasted no time in signaling that the time for tributes to the essential goodness of New Hampshire's citizenry and the duty of the state's judges to do right by them had expired. Did Judge Souter agree with Justice Harlan's opinion in *Griswold v. Connecticut*, Biden began, that there was a constitutional right to privacy for married couples using birth control?

"I believe that the Due Process Clause of the Fourteenth Amendment does recognize and does protect an unenumerated right of privacy," Souter replied.

"Now, you've just told us that the right to use birth control and decide whether or not to become pregnant is one of those fundamental rights," Biden said, interpreting Souter's response expansively. "Now, let's say that a woman and/or her mate uses such a birth control device and it fails. Does she still have a constitutional right to choose not to become pregnant?"

Less than five minutes into his confirmation hearings, Souter was confronted with the basic issue raised in *Roe v. Wade*, a decision that he had refused to discuss with members of the Bush Administration. "I think for me to start answering that question, in effect, is for me to start discussing the concept of *Roe v. Wade*," Souter replied. He would not do so, he told Biden, since the issues raised in *Roe* were likely to be reviewed by a Court on which he might sit. Later other Democratic members of the committee tried a variety of interrogative devices to pry open Souter's mind on the abortion issue. But each time Souter, with utmost courtesy, refused the entreaties.

While praising the nominee as "his own best witness," the *New York Times* was, nonetheless, perturbed that Souter did not say more about the constitutional right to privacy. "Even so," the *Times* added, "he gave decent grounds for hope that he can be fair-minded on this explosive question." Leaders of abortion activist groups, like Faye Wattleton, president of Planned Parenthood, were less impressed. "After days of evasive answers and filibusters, we know nothing more about Judge Souter's views on reproductive rights than we did before the hearings began," Wattleton told the Senate Judiciary Committee, and asked that they vote against his confirmation. At the other end of the political spectrum, one conservative activist was equally uneasy with Souter. The Bush Administration is "putting a lot of green on this shot," he said. "This is a big, big step for a guy from a New Hampshire state court. You bring guys like this on the Court, and they have a tendency to pull a Harry Blackmun on you."

Despite reservations from both liberals and conservatives, Souter won overwhelming approval by the Senate Judiciary Committee and the full Senate.

At the conference on *Casey* in late April 1992, Souter was one of seven justices (all but Blackmun and Stevens) who voted to uphold the major provisions of the Pennsylvania abortion statute. The chief justice assigned himself the majority opinion, which he expected would formally reject Blackmun's *Roe* opinion, and substitute the analysis in Rehnquist's plurality opinion in *Webster*—declaring that a state could regulate abortions throughout a pregnancy, so long as the state's regulation was rationally related to a legitimate government objective (the lowest constitutional standard of scrutiny that the Court imposed on state regulations).

But soon after the justices' conference, three members of Rehnquist's majority—Kennedy, O'Connor and Souter—met to explore the possibility of a joint opinion by the three that would preserve *Roe*. The discussions took place without the knowledge of Rehnquist or the other five justices. Kennedy, O'Connor and Souter agreed that each would draft individual sections of the proposed joint opinion. The three justices also agreed to keep their project to themselves, which assured that none of their six colleagues, including the chief, would have the opportunity to protest, or attempt to persuade them to abandon their common enterprise before it was completed.

Adding to pressure on them, Kennedy, O'Connor and Souter knew that if there was to be a joint opinion it would have to be written and ready for circulation quickly. The principal opinion by the chief justice was expected by the end of May. That meant that the three justices must be prepared to circulate their joint draft, if such a draft proved agreeable to all three, shortly after the chief's was circulated.

By late May, Kennedy, O'Connor and Souter had written their assigned sections of the draft joint opinion and circulated them to each other for editing by the other two. Justice Kennedy had been assigned the first two sections of the joint opinion. In the first section, he discussed the factual background and lower court decisions in *Casey*. His second section was considerably more difficult: to announce that the three justices—Kennedy, O'Connor and Souter—stood by the central holding of *Roe v. Wade*. In Kennedy's analysis, the substantive guarantee of "liberty" under the Fourteenth Amendment entitled a pregnant woman to have an abortion before the fetus attained viability. And though Kennedy contended that a state could regulate abortion throughout the pregnancy, he wrote that it could not do so before viability in a way that placed an "undue burden" (O'Connor's persistent point) on the pregnant woman's right to an abortion.

Justice Souter drafted the third section of the proposed joint opinion, which focused on the need for the Court to maintain its authority by adhering to precedent whenever possible. Souter discussed all of the exceptions to the general rule that the Court should adhere to its prior decisions. He found none of the exceptions to apply to *Roe* and concluded that its central holding was justified. He concluded, moreover, that the Court's legitimacy in the eyes of the public was a precious and fragile commodity, which would be jeopardized if the Court was perceived by the public to change its mind because of political pressures provoked by *Roe*.

Justice O'Connor was, in a sense, given the easiest assignment of the three since she was asked to apply her "undue burden" standard, which she had frequently done since her Court appointment in 1982. Under her "undue burden" analysis in her *Casey* draft, she found all but one provision of the Pennsylvania statute—a requirement that a spouse be notified before an abortion could take place—constitutional.

The three justices suggested editorial changes in one another's draft, but the essential ingredients of each section remained intact. Kennedy, O'Connor and Souter met their deadline and prepared to circulate their joint draft by early June.

In supporting the joint opinion, Justice Kennedy traveled considerable distance from the criticism of *Roe* that he had expressed in the justices' 1989 *Webster* conference. A devout Catholic who disapproved of abortion, Kennedy nonetheless found in *Casey* that his personal opinion on abortion was outweighed by his concern for the harm that would be done to the Supreme Court as an institution if *Roe* were overruled. In contrast to Kennedy's challenge, Souter's defense of precedent and O'Connor's application of an "undue burden" analysis had long been a part of their constitutional vocabularies.

When news of the joint opinion circulated through the Supreme Court Building during the first week of June, the reaction, as one insider put it, "was as if a neutron bomb had exploded." Chief Justice Rehnquist attempted to talk Kennedy out of his support for the joint opinion, and Justice Scalia, less diplomatically than the chief, expressed his outrage to Kennedy. But Kennedy, as well as O'Connor and Souter, held firm. And on June 29, 1992, the three read from sections of the joint opinion that they had drafted. Justice Kennedy announced:

> Liberty finds no refuge in the jurisprudence of doubt. . . . The Constitution serves human values, and while the effect of reliance on *Roe* cannot be exactly measured, neither can the certain cost of overruling *Roe* for people who have ordered their thinking and living around that case be dismissed. No evolution of legal principle has left *Roe*'s doctrinal footings weaker than they were in 1973.

Justice Souter declared:

> A decision to overrule *Roe*'s essential holding under the existing circumstances would address error, if error there was, at the cost of both profound and unnecessary damage to the Court's legitimacy and to the nation's commitment to the rule of law. It is, therefore, imperative to adhere to the essence of *Roe*'s original decision, and we do so today.

And Justice O'Connor, while adhering to the "central principle" of *Roe*—the protection of a woman's right to terminate her pregnancy before viability—nonetheless replaced *Roe*'s trimester analysis with her "undue burden" standard. Applying the "undue burden" test to the Pennsylvania statute, she concluded that all but the spousal notification provision should be upheld as constitutional.

The Kennedy-O'Connor-Souter tour de force was delivered without apology. Both Rehnquist and Scalia were left to fume in dissent. Rehnquist wrote that the Court's striving for legitimacy through adherence to *Roe* was fanciful, "a sort of judicial Potemkin village." He dismissed the joint opinion's insistence that the Court was adhering to the *Roe* precedent. "While purporting to adhere to precedent," Rehnquist wrote, "the joint opinion instead revises it. *Roe* continues to exist, but only in the way a storefront on a western movie set exists: a mere façade to give the illusion of reality." To portray *Roe* as a "statesmanlike 'settlement' of a divisive issue," Scalia added, "a jurisprudential Peace of Westphalia that is worth preserving, is nothing less than Orwellian."

With the *Casey* decision, the momentum had shifted away from the anti-*Roe* movement on the Court led by Rehnquist and Scalia. True, *Roe* was no longer the invincible shield for pregnant women that it had been in 1973. Decisive support by Kennedy, O'Connor and Souter for O'Connor's "undue burden" test guaranteed that more state regulations of abortion to protect the unborn fetus throughout the pregnancy would pass constitutional muster. But *Roe* survived, and a woman's constitutional right to control her own body during a pregnancy seemed established beyond the Rehnquist Court's recall.

Predictably, neither prolife nor prochoice advocates rushed to embrace the Court's *Casey* decision. Even before the written decision had been read to completion, leaders of both groups were urging their followers to stay the course until their cause had been fully vindicated. That vindication would not come from this Supreme Court.

Justice Harry Blackmun was not entirely displeased with the result in *Casey*. He had not been consulted by Justices Kennedy, O'Connor and Souter as they composed their opinion, and he was surprised when he learned of their joint effort. But he quickly recovered and went out of his way in his own opinion in *Casey* to praise the three for "an act of personal courage and constitutional principle."

Still, Blackmun repeated his ominous warning that *Roe* remained in jeopardy, even after *Casey*, since the chief justice needed only one more vote to reverse it. If George Bush were reelected for a second term, he might well have the opportunity to replace, among others, the eighty-three-year-old Blackmun. The choice of whether *Roe* would survive, in the final analysis, could depend on the 1992 presidential election. George Bush's opponent in the 1992 presidential campaign,

Arkansas Governor Bill Clinton, had promised that if he were elected, he would appoint to the Court justices who would not overrule *Roe*.

Around midnight on November 3, 1992, after the polls had closed in California and it was clear that Bill Clinton had won enough electoral votes to become the next president of the United States, the phone rang in Justice Harry Blackmun's apartment. The call was from the justice's youngest daughter.

"Daddy, are you going to turn in your suit [i.e., robe] tomorrow?" she asked.

"No," Blackmun replied good-naturedly.

"I guess," she added, "it would be a little unseemly if you did."

Justice Blackmun did not mind the gentle tease.

PART III

CRIME AND PUNISHMENT

For the third time, this Court disregards Warren McCleskey's constitutional claims. In 1986, McCleskey, an Afro-American defendant, presented uncontroverted evidence that Georgia murder defendants with white victims were more than four times as likely to receive the death sentence as were defendants with Afro-American victims. . . . Last term, the Court not only discounted Warren McCleskey's constitutional claim but sharply limited the opportunity of criminal defendants, even those on death row, to obtain federal habeas review. . . . Now, in the final hours of his life, Warren McCleskey alleges that he was denied an impartial clemency hearing. . . . In refusing to grant a stay to review fully McCleskey's claims, the Court values expediency over human life. Repeatedly denying Warren McCleskey his constitutional rights is unacceptable. Executing him is inexcusable.

JUSTICE THURGOOD MARSHALL,
memorandum to the Conference,
September 24, 1991, in *McCleskey v. Bowers*

CHAPTER SEVEN

A FATAL MISTAKE

The late Justice Potter Stewart, who served on the Court from 1958 to 1981, once said, only half in jest, that a telling distinction in judicial conference between the liberal Chief Justice Earl Warren and his conservative successor, Warren Burger, was the chiefs' dramatically different narratives in explaining the facts of a brutal crime to the brethren. Chief Justice Warren placed the crime in a broad social context, Stewart said, perhaps pointing out that the defendant, often an uneducated black or Hispanic youth, came from an impoverished and broken family. At his every step in the criminal justice system, Warren might note, the defendant had faced hostile and often unfair law enforcement authorities who were intent on locking him up, no matter what the price in invading his constitutional rights. Chief Justice Burger, on the other hand, might begin his narrative with the victim—say, a seventy-two-year-old widow living alone in a tiny walk-up apartment—and recount the violent and frequently tragic consequences of the crime on the innocent citizen in bloody detail.

Perspective is crucial in evaluating the Court's work in the criminal justice field and that perspective, at least from the vantage point of the Supreme Court majority, changed radically in thirty years, from the sixties when Chief Justice Warren led a liberal Court majority in expanding the constitutional rights of the criminally accused, through the more cautious Burger Court days and, finally, to the assertively conservative rulings of the Rehnquist Court majority.

A solid conservative majority of the Rehnquist Court, boldly led by the chief justice, has given constitutional endorsement to more aggressive police work against criminal suspects, allowing previously outlawed warrantless searches. In limited cases, the Court has also sanctioned the admission into evidence of coerced confessions, which was an issue in the case of Oreste Fulminante, a man convicted of the brutal murder of his stepdaughter in the Arizona desert (discussed in Chapter Eight). The Court, moreover, has systematically blocked off the federal courts from most constitutional claims of convicted criminals in state prisons, many of whom face the death penalty. The Rehnquist Court's significantly tougher stance on habeas corpus claims* was taken in the case of Warren McCleskey, a death-row inmate in Georgia's state penitentiary, whose legal arguments to save his life came before the justices three times between 1986 and 1991 (discussed in Chapters Seven, Eight and Nine).

The *New York Times*'s Linda Greenhouse observed that courtroom announcements of decisions by the conservative Rehnquist Court in criminal cases have a different tone and text than in the past. When the Court's liberals claimed a majority in criminal cases, Justice Brennan, who often spoke for the liberal majority, rarely gave a complete report on the nature of the crime and the evidence accumulated against the accused. But no one in the courtroom could mistake his basic message: the conviction was thrown out because of a flagrant violation of the defendant's constitutional rights.

By the early 1990s, the courtroom liturgy had changed. Chief Jus-

---

* Habeas corpus—literally translated from the Latin, "you should have the body"—is the court order that requires the government to produce prisoners and answer challenges to the legality of their detention. State prisoners commonly ask federal courts for the writ to pursue claims of the unconstitutionality of their convictions in a forum in which federal constitutional claims are more likely to receive serious consideration.

tice Rehnquist, frequently speaking for a conservative majority, dwelled on the crime. "On he goes," Greenhouse has written, "in a conversational tone: the date, scene, weapon, everyone's names, fact after damning fact. His presentation makes it clear that what matters most to the Chief Justice is that a crime has been committed. Someone should have to pay."

Attorney John C. Boger had not expected to be standing before the justices of the Supreme Court on October 15, 1986, only one week after William H. Rehnquist had taken his center seat as chief justice. Boger was surprised that the Court had agreed to hear oral argument in his case, *McCleskey v. Kemp*. But once on the Court's docket, *McCleskey* became the most closely watched case of the term and was considered a possible harbinger of the new Rehnquist Court's direction.

Boger's client, a black man named Warren McCleskey, had been convicted of armed robbery and the murder of a white policeman in Marietta, Georgia, and had been sentenced to death. The NAACP Legal Defense Fund, Boger's organization, had commissioned a statistical study directed by Professor David Baldus of the University of Iowa Law School to determine if blacks were more likely to receive the death penalty in Georgia than whites convicted of the same crime. The Baldus study, which analyzed every homicide in Georgia between 1974 and 1979 that resulted in an arrest, concluded that both the race of the convicted murderer and that of the victim affected the sentence. Black men convicted of killing whites were sentenced to death in Georgia in 22 percent of the cases, the Baldus study reported, while white men convicted of killing blacks were sentenced to death in only 3 percent of the cases. And regardless of the race of the murderer, the death penalty was four times more likely to be imposed if the victim was white than if he was black.

When the Legal Defense Fund petitioned the Supreme Court for review of the McCleskey case, Boger had been aware that the justices could not easily hear argument in the case without considering the ultimate issue of whether the death penalty should be abolished as unconstitutional. At the least, the Court's review would require a close look at the Georgia sentencing structure and, necessarily, of those of the three other states (Florida, Louisiana and Texas) that together carried out nearly three-quarters of the executions in the United States.

Since the review of a lower court decision required affirmative votes by four members of the Court, Boger had not rated his chances as particularly good. Certainly, Justice Thurgood Marshall would vote in favor of review and would, on the merits, vote once again to abolish the death penalty as unconstitutional. Marshall had argued that position forcefully in *Furman v. Georgia*, a 1972 Court decision in which a five-member majority struck down death penalty procedures in every state in the union as too arbitrary to comply with the strictures of the Constitution. Marshall's closest friend and ally on the Court, Justice Brennan, had also declared in *Furman* that the death penalty per se, regardless of procedures, should be struck down as cruel and unusual punishment in violation of the Eighth Amendment. But Marshall and Brennan's abolitionist position was not supported by a single other member of the Court in *Furman* or in any decision in the fourteen years between *Furman* and *McCleskey*. Indeed, the Court's *Furman* decision was significantly curtailed in 1976 in *Gregg v. Georgia* and two companion cases in which the Court upheld the constitutionality of three states' capital sentencing procedures, which had been modified since *Furman*.

In Boger's favor, the McCleskey case raised the potent issue of racial discrimination in the criminal justice system. Only a year earlier, the Court had reversed a criminal conviction because the prosecutor had systematically excluded blacks from the jury. In that decision, *Batson v. Kentucky*, Justice Powell had written for a seven-person majority that included not only Marshall and Brennan, but also Blackmun, O'Connor, Stevens and White (only Chief Justice Burger and Associate Justice Rehnquist dissented).

Any justice in the *Batson* majority might have voted to review the McCleskey case and could, Boger believed, be persuaded to support his argument that McCleskey's death sentence was a violation of both the Equal Protection Clause of the Fourteenth Amendment and the Eighth Amendment's prohibition against cruel and unusual punishment. Even the newest justice, Antonin Scalia, might appreciate the solid basis of the Baldus statistical study, Boger speculated, and spring an early surprise on his conservative supporters.

Boger was conceding only Chief Justice Rehnquist's vote against Warren McCleskey's constitutional claim. Since joining the Court as an associate justice in 1972, Rehnquist had consistently voted against capital criminal defendants, compiling a pro-prosecution record unequaled by any other member of the Court.

At 10:01 on the morning of October 15, 1986, Boger was instructed by Chief Justice Rehnquist "to proceed when you are ready." The attorney wasted no time in cutting to the heart of his argument. If the State of Georgia in 1986 enacted criminal statutes that required harsher penalties for blacks than whites, Boger began, those statutes would plainly violate the Constitution. Such discrepancies were common before the ratification of the Fourteenth Amendment, Boger noted, when blacks could be given the death penalty for the crime of assault on a white citizen of Georgia. Although such antebellum statutes had long since been eliminated, Boger argued that the Baldus study showed that Georgia prosecutors and juries in the 1980s were acting "as if some of those old statutes were still on the books." The color of a defendant's skin, and that of the victim's, still could be decisive in determining if a convicted murderer would be put to death in Georgia.

In presenting the findings of the Baldus statistical study, Boger emphasized the comprehensiveness of the study and the willingness of Professor Baldus to test rival hypotheses. (In fact, Baldus had even tested one hypothesis that had been suggested by the federal district court judge in the *McCleskey* case.) Analyzing every proposed hypothesis, the Baldus study always came to the same conclusion: a death sentence for a black convicted of murdering a white was significantly more likely than for any other racial combination (white murdering black; white murdering white; black murdering black).

As he worked his way through his argument, Boger realized that the justices had allowed him to speak, uninterrupted, for an unusually long period of time. Ordinarily, an attorney is peppered with questions within one or two minutes. Boger had spoken for more than six minutes.

175

Finally, Justice White inquired, "Who took the information for the study?"

At first, Boger was puzzled by the thrust of the question and groped for an answer. But in a series of questions to Boger, White made the point that the data had been collected by law students, not by professional lawyers. Boger did not respond, and later wished that he had, that each of the students had been professionally trained for such research.

Once the exchange with White was concluded, other members of the Court engaged Boger in dialogue along more predictable lines. Justice O'Connor wanted to know what remedy Boger was seeking. One solution, after all, was to sentence more convicted murderers to death (whites as well as blacks) so that the discrepancy that McCleskey complained of would be eliminated. Alternatively, was Boger suggesting that the death penalty be abolished altogether? she asked.

Boger answered that neither remedy suggested by O'Connor was required. The Georgia sentencing statute was not being administered evenhandedly, Boger said. Without necessarily advocating more or fewer executions, he suggested that the Court should require the state to reform its system to prevent the unmistakable pattern of racial discrimination revealed by the Baldus study.

Chief Justice Rehnquist pointed out that "this particular jury was only convened once." The Baldus statistical study did not prove that McCleskey, in fact, was sentenced to death because of his race. "I think you have to show under our cases that this particular jury would have dealt differently with a black defendant who killed a black person," Rehnquist said.

Boger responded by asserting that the Baldus study had, inferentially, made that showing.

"Well, it's hard to claim discrimination against McCleskey at the plea-bargaining stage in this case," said Justice White. "He was offered a plea bargain and turned it down."

Boger told White that the trial court record had incorrectly represented that McCleskey was offered a plea bargain and had turned it down. It was true, he conceded, that McCleskey's trial counsel had urged McCleskey to consider a guilty plea in return for a life sentence, but McCleskey had refused, insisting that he had not killed the police officer.

"So there was no offer," said White, "but there was a reluctance on Mr. McCleskey's part to consider a plea bargain?"

Yes, said Boger.

While Boger was addressing White's question, he did not hear a whispered "Mr. Boger, Mr. Boger" from the other side of the bench.

"Yes, Mr. Justice Powell," Boger responded belatedly, and apologized for failing to address the justice more promptly.

Powell's poor health had combined with his soft southern drawl to make his voice almost inaudible. The seventy-eight-year-old Powell nonetheless forced Boger into the most disconcerting exchange of the entire oral argument. Until that exchange, Boger had thought that Powell, author of the *Batson* opinion, was his best hope for a fifth vote (with Marshall, Brennan, Blackmun and Stevens).

Powell reminded Boger that Warren McCleskey was convicted of murdering a police officer in the official course of his duty while committing armed robbery. Both facts—the murder of the officer while on duty and during an armed robbery—were "aggravating" factors under Georgia law to be considered in weighing the death penalty. "You have to accept the jury verdict that the defendant shot the police officer, don't you?" Powell asked. When Boger conceded Powell's point, the justice repeated it in a slightly different way. "So this defendant was found guilty of shooting a police officer while he was in the process of committing a robbery," Powell said.

The exchange with Powell troubled Boger, and the direction of the questioning immediately became more pointed. Justice Scalia elaborated on the heinousness of the crime. "Wasn't the shot, which the police officer suffered, in the head, and at very close range," asked Scalia, "indicating that there was a conscious attempt to kill the man?"

Boger admitted that the trial record showed that there was a flurry of shots, but not necessarily at close range. No doubt the crime was serious, he conceded, but "it's not the kind of crime that gets death in Fulton County or, indeed, statewide, on any regular basis. That's what's so remarkable." Trying to regain the momentum for his statistical argument, Boger said, "Indeed, it's the torture murderers and the multiple killers in Fulton County who receive death. Out of 17 people who've killed police officers in Fulton County, this is the only death sentence during this period of time."

Georgia's assistant attorney general, Mary Beth Westmoreland, who followed Boger to the lectern, opened her thirty-minute argument by describing the horrible details of the armed robbery and murder of the police officer. She told the justices that Warren McCleskey had been convicted of armed robbery three times before and said that he had bragged to a prison inmate about the murder. She questioned the validity of the Baldus study and emphasized that, in any event, there had been no showing of intentional discrimination in McCleskey's case.

At 11:00, Chief Justice Rehnquist announced that the case of *McCleskey v. Kemp* was formally submitted for the Court's deliberations.

"They were all tough questions," Boger recalled, "but I felt I had responded." An informal poll taken immediately after the oral argument among Boger and his colleagues who had worked on the case concluded that "we had a chance." Boger was reasonably confident of the votes of the Court's most liberal members on issues of racial discrimination in capital cases—Marshall, Brennan, Blackmun and Stevens. He had no reason to think that he had lost their votes at the oral argument.

Where would he find the fifth vote? Boger, who had originally considered Powell the most likely swing vote in his favor, was less optimistic after the oral argument. Powell had dwelled on the seriousness of the crime for which McCleskey was sentenced to death.

Justice O'Connor, another possible vote for Boger, had asked about remedies, but Boger felt that he had left the door open for the Court to remand the case to the lower appellate court to review Georgia's system and focus on the sentencing disparities. Scalia understood the statistics, which Boger considered "a plus." White was always unpredictable, and even after his rough questioning, Boger still thought he might win his vote. Only Chief Justice Rehnquist remained "a lost cause," Boger concluded.

• • •

Had Boger known about the internal memorandum Justice White prepared the day after the oral argument and one day before the justices were to discuss the case in conference, his guarded optimism would have diminished even more. In his October 16 memorandum, Justice White returned to the issue that he had raised at oral argument: had McCleskey been offered a way out of a death sentence at the plea-bargaining stage? Boger had denied such an offer, quoting McCleskey's trial counsel in the transcript of the postconviction hearing in which he testified that McCleskey had refused even to consider a plea.

White quoted from another part of the transcript where McCleskey's attorney testified that the case against his client was almost "airtight" and that he had "used every amount of persuasion in my power to try to get him to enter a plea but he insisted he wasn't there and he wasn't guilty."

The quoted testimony did not really contradict Boger's reply to White at oral argument. White had asked him if a plea bargain had been offered and Boger's answer was no; the defendant insisted that he had not shot the policeman and would not, therefore, consider a plea. But for White, the testimony by McCleskey's attorney raised doubts about the overall merits of Boger's argument. "In light of this testimony," White wrote, "it would be difficult to conclude that McCleskey suffered racial discrimination at the plea-bargaining stage, and there is a reduced chance that racial considerations influenced the prosecutor to proceed to a sentencing hearing."

Rehnquist opened the justices' October 17 conference by declaring that a reversal of McCleskey's death sentence "would dismantle Georgia's whole system." Reiterating the point he had made at oral argument, Rehnquist said there was no showing that McCleskey's jury was racially prejudiced, despite the statistical study. There was "no inference of any sort that other [death penalty] cases would come out the same way." Even assuming the validity of Baldus's statistics, Rehnquist concluded that the Legal Defense Fund did not make the case for Warren McCleskey.

Brennan argued that Warren McCleskey's death sentence should be overturned as a violation of both the Eighth and Fourteenth

179

amendments. There was, he noted, a long-established pattern of racial discrimination in Georgia's criminal justice system predating the Baldus study. Baldus's study confirmed that pattern and had shown that the death penalty was imposed in Georgia in a racially discriminatory manner, a violation of the Fourteenth Amendment. Moreover, the Court had recognized since *Furman* that the death penalty was different, requiring the justices to scrutinize the sentencing procedures more carefully than with lesser punishments. Georgia's sentencing structure was demonstrably arbitrary, Brennan concluded, violating the Eighth Amendment's prohibition against cruel and unusual punishment.

Justice White followed Brennan and, like the chief justice, rejected Boger's arguments. "Baldus doesn't measure up to intentional discrimination," White said. McCleskey's claim had to fail unless intentional discrimination or "something very close to that" was shown. White concluded that there was no such showing. Two votes against McCleskey.

But Brennan picked up three additional votes—Marshall, Blackmun and Stevens—to reverse McCleskey's death sentence. Of the three, Stevens offered the most detailed rationale for his position at conference. There was a history of racial discrimination in Georgia's statutes, he said, "and it takes generations to dissipate that." Undoubtedly, there had been subconscious prejudice in the Georgia system, said Stevens, and the Baldus study proved it. He did not think proof of intent was critical, as White had suggested. Agreeing with Brennan that "death cases are different," Stevens argued that the Court should accept the Baldus conclusion that "race makes a difference and presents an unacceptable risk." He suggested further that the Court could avoid a sweeping ruling by remanding the case to the lower appellate court for review.

Justice Powell, Boger's hoped-for "swing" vote, supported the chief justice. He told his colleagues that the Court "couldn't decide criminal cases on statistics alone."

Justice O'Connor did not doubt that there was "still much societal discrimination in the country" and, further, stated that she would assume the accuracy of Baldus's statistical study. "But the petitioner

[McCleskey] wants a reduction of discretion [i.e., less flexibility in sentencing]," said O'Connor, "and that bothers me." In the end, O'Connor did not think McCleskey had made his case under either the Equal Protection Clause or the Eighth Amendment.

Scalia was the last to speak, and he admitted that we "all bring our sympathies into the courtroom." But the Court just could not abolish the death penalty on the basis of "statistics of this kind." Scalia said the Court had done as much as it could to curb the prejudices of juries and the statistics, as good as they were, did not change his mind.

Rehnquist, showing skill early in his tenure as chief justice in assigning opinions that would preserve his close majorities, asked Lewis Powell to write for the five-member majority. In his fifteen years on the Court, Powell had proved adept at articulating a position on a wide range of civil rights and liberties issues that commanded a Court majority. Powell's pivotal role on the Court mirrored the centrist role he had played as a leader in the legal profession as well as in community affairs in his native Richmond, Virginia.

Born into the southern aristocracy (the Powells were members of the Society of Cincinnati, an organization open to descendants of officers of the Revolutionary War), Lewis F. Powell, Jr., attended Washington and Lee University, where he received his bachelor's and law degrees, finishing first in his law school class. He also earned a master's degree from the Harvard Law School and counted among his most influential professors Roscoe Pound and Felix Frankfurter, whose philosophy of judicial restraint strongly influenced Powell's own concept of the proper role of the courts in the federal system.

Powell joined Richmond's most prestigious law firm after graduation from Harvard and soon established his reputation as a superb corporate lawyer and counselor (he served as director of more than a dozen corporations). As chairman of the Richmond School Board and, later, as president of the American Bar Association, Powell threaded his way through a host of protracted philosophical and practical problems.

As head of the Richmond School Board from 1953 to 1961, Powell mediated a southern city's struggle with its racist past and uncertain future. While the Faubuses and Ross Barnetts fine-tuned their demagoguery of racism, moderate Lewis Powell claimed the center and was denounced by activists on both sides. Reading the Supreme Court's instruction in *Brown v. Board of Education* that desegregation should proceed with "all deliberate speed" in the cautionary spirit in which it had been given, Powell moved Richmond slowly toward a desegregated school system. The city's militant blacks were impatient. But Powell's refusal to close the city's schools also provoked rage among the city's segregationists. Powell persevered, despite the pressures, and ultimately the Richmond schools were successfully desegregated.

In similarly pragmatic fashion, American Bar Association President Powell worked his, and his organization's, way through the issue of the proper role of government attorneys in representing the poor. Originally, Powell had been opposed to a federal government role (as part of President Lyndon Johnson's War on Poverty) in providing attorneys to bring suits on behalf of the poor. But once it was clear to Powell that local bar associations could not handle the legal problems of the poor adequately and clearer still that the legal services program was going forward with or without ABA support, Powell put the prestige of his office behind the federal policy.

Like many other moderate conservatives in the legal profession in the 1960s, Powell was publicly critical of the Warren Court's most controversial decisions in the criminal law field, such as *Miranda v. Arizona* (which required police to advise criminal suspects of their constitutional rights to remain silent and to be represented by counsel before they could be interrogated). Powell believed that fairness to criminal defendants could be preserved without broad-based rules that could frustrate the police and prosecution, as he thought the Court had done with its *Miranda* decision. He also took a dim view of civil disobedience, whether by civil rights protesters of the early 1960s or those demonstrating against the Vietnam War in the later years of that decade.

President Richard Nixon found the Powell résumé irresistible and kept him high on his list of potential Court appointees, even after the Richmond attorney politely rejected the first overtures by Attorney General John Mitchell, who had raised the possibility of a Court appointment with Powell in a telephone conversation shortly after Nixon's election. In 1971, Mitchell again spoke to Powell about a Court appointment, but this time the president himself followed up with a call to Powell (with Chief Justice Burger in the room) and asked him to accept the nomination. He did.

On the Court, Powell resided at the center, flanked to the left by Brennan and Marshall and just as far to the right by Rehnquist. Regarding law-and-order issues, Powell retained his conservative instincts but with some frequency supported a criminal defendant's argument based on the specific facts of the case. On issues of racial discrimination, Powell gravitated slowly but unmistakably toward the liberal side of the center. It was Powell who wrote the decisive opinion in *Regents of University of California v. Bakke*. Powell attached as an appendix to his *Bakke* opinion the Harvard admission plan that had expressly recognized the value of a racially diverse student body. Such a policy, Powell later said in an interview, "was not only appropriate but also highly desirable in an educational institution."

In his *McCleskey* opinion, which was announced by the Court in the spring of 1987, Powell proceeded cautiously, concentrating on the facts in the case. He emphasized that there was no evidence that racial discrimination had been involved in McCleskey's death sentence. While Powell admitted that similar statistical arguments had been accepted by the Court in other areas of the law (employment discrimination, for example), it was not, he wrote, applicable to criminal trials and sentencing where jury discretion was essential. He concluded that "the Baldus study does not demonstrate a constitutionally significant risk of racial bias affecting the Georgia capital sentencing process."

"I was unhappy with that case," Powell recalled in a 1990 interview, "and I'm still unhappy. I think it is rarely mentioned that McCleskey had committed murder when he and a colleague were robbing a store. So I don't think the case could be very sympathetic, as to him. I was troubled by the statistical argument that, on its face, was very persuasive. But I finally concluded that if we started down the road of relying on statistics to a major extent in criminal law, rather than the Constitution itself, that it would be undesirable."

In his interview three years after *McCleskey*, Powell said that he regretted his vote. Since that time, Powell had decided that capital punishment should be abolished, a position he did not hold at the time he wrote his opinion. "We are the only western country that still has capital punishment. If you keep in mind that the law is not being enforced on capital punishment [although thirty-seven states still have the death penalty, less than a quarter of that number enforce it, Powell noted], I think it discredits the whole system. And I think also it's perfectly clear that capital punishment does not deter murders." By the time Powell had changed his position on capital punishment, he had retired from the Court.

After the Court's 1987 decision in *McCleskey v. Kemp*, Warren McCleskey's attorneys continued to exhaust every available legal avenue in an effort to prevent his electrocution. Jack Boger realized that his condemned client was "at his last gasp." Boger said that he and his cocounsel, Robert Stroup, asked themselves if there was anything left for them to do to help McCleskey. Fortuitously, an Atlanta television station had in 1987 successfully been granted a federal court order to inspect the government's files in another high-profile murder case. The court decision gave Boger and Stroup an idea.

"We had always felt that the government's key witness [a prison inmate named Offie Evans] was lying in denying a relationship with the prosecution," Boger recalled. McCleskey's attorneys, citing the decision in favor of the Atlanta television station, requested the government's files in the McCleskey case.

They received, among other documents, a twenty-one-page statement by Offie Evans that laid out in detail Evans's conversations with McCleskey when Evans and McCleskey were in adjoining cells. Boger asserted that the prosecutor and state attorney general's lawyers had denied that any written statement existed throughout McCleskey's trial and appeal. After reading Evans's written statement, Boger concluded that Evans had been a government informer placed in the cell next to McCleskey for the specific purpose of actively eliciting a confession from McCleskey that he had been the trigger man in the armed robbery.

Boger's conclusion was based, first of all, on the illiterate Evans's almost total recall of his conversations with McCleskey—suggesting to him that Evans had taped the conversations. Even more suspicious was the fact that Evans's statement indicated that he was familiar with information about the robbery and murder that only police officers investigating the crimes could have known. "The only way to explain that information," Boger said, "was on the basis of a relationship between Evans and the police."

Boger and Stroup realized that Evans's statement might provide the constitutional argument that could save McCleskey's life. Once a suspect was in custody, a 1964 Supreme Court decision had held, the state could not surreptitiously question him without counsel present. In that decision, *Massiah v. U.S.*, the Court had declared that the government could not use a confession taken from a criminal suspect in custody if it was the result of an active interrogation by a government informer. The confession had to be voluntary.

In his twenty-one-page statement, Offie Evans had said that he told McCleskey that he was the uncle of a codefendant and asked McCleskey where the guns were and who did the shooting. He had also told McCleskey that he had heard that McCleskey had accused one of his codefendants of shooting the police officer, information that only the police had known from their undisclosed conversations with McCleskey.

After studying Evans's statement, Boger and Stroup asked for a second habeas hearing in federal court, where they established that Evans was a regular police informer who had been promised a lighter sentence in exchange for his cooperation with police. On the basis of new testimony at the hearing by a police officer involved in the case, they also identified a prison official named Ulysses Worthy who testified that he had been asked by the police to move Evans to the cell next to McCleskey and that Evans made his twenty-one-page statement in Worthy's office.

During the second habeas hearing, McCleskey's attorneys argued before U.S. District Judge Owen Forrester that the State of Georgia had violated McCleskey's Sixth Amendment right to counsel (citing the Court's *Massiah* decision) by placing Offie Evans in an adjoining cell to McCleskey and directing him to interrogate the defendant after McCleskey, in custody, had invoked his right to be represented by counsel at all interrogations.

Judge Forrester granted McCleskey's second habeas petition, ruling that the fact that his attorneys did not have the Evans written statement at the time of his first habeas petition excused their not making the Sixth Amendment argument in the earlier petition. On the factual record, the judge found that "police officers had not only violated *Massiah*, but had actively concealed the violation." They had, as the judge put it, "lied and lied well in a complicated conspiracy." The judge also held that the evidence that would have proven the *Massiah* violation was not reasonably discoverable by counsel. And finally, he ruled that McCleskey's attorneys were not guilty of "inexcusable neglect" or "deliberate abandonment" (legal standards that barred a second successful habeas application) of the *Massiah* claim after state proceedings because their failure to use the Evans statement was prompted not by any independent tactical considerations, but solely because of defense counsel's inability to discover the Evans statement, evidence "that state officials were in fact actively concealing" from the defense.

But McCleskey's legal success was short-lived. The U.S. Court of Appeals for the Eleventh Circuit in Atlanta overturned the district court's decision, declaring that the failure of the defendant's attorneys to raise the *Massiah* claim at the first habeas hearing constituted "deliberate abandonment" under the law (i.e., a conscious decision not to pursue the constitutional claim), thus barring McCleskey's right to a second habeas hearing. The appeals court ruled, further, that even if Evans's statement had been made available to McCleskey's attorneys at the outset, it would not have affected the outcome since the Court concluded that McCleskey would have been found guilty of murder on other evidence. McCleskey's attorneys appealed to the Supreme Court, which agreed to hear their argument.

In October 1990, Jack Boger again represented Warren McCleskey before the Rehnquist Court as he had done in 1986, and was optimistic about his second chance for success—despite the fact that Justice Brennan had been replaced by Justice David Souter. Boger was not even discouraged by Chief Justice Rehnquist's public campaign to place stricter limits on habeas corpus petitions by death penalty prisoners; the chief had in 1990 appointed a commission headed by retired Justice Lewis Powell to make recommendations to Congress for new legislation imposing new restrictions on habeas petitions to the federal courts by inmates facing the death penalty.

Boger thought the fact that the chief had recommended federal legislation to narrow the habeas remedy might, ironically, work in his favor. Court conservatives like Rehnquist and Scalia had often urged the Court to defer to legislative judgments, rather than to write broad policy decisions of its own. The McCleskey case offered the justices an opportunity to show their deference to Congress and wait for a legislative directive. Boger also hoped that the Court's conservatives would want to conserve a habeas remedy that dated back several centuries in the English common law.

Finally, Boger was confident that he had a "backup" argument, perhaps the most potent of all: the state had deliberately concealed evidence from the defense, and basic fairness demanded that the Court not allow the government to benefit from its own wrongdoing, particularly when it could cost a man his life.

"This is a case about state misconduct in a criminal trial, the *Massiah* violation," Boger began his 1990 McCleskey oral argument before the justices, "about how that conduct was hidden by certain state police officers and other officials for nine years, and about how both the underlying misconduct and the conspiracy that hid it subsequently came to light."

Boger characterized Offie Evans as "a man on a mission," a police informer who was determined to get McCleskey to confess to the shooting of the police officer. And although Evans testified at McCleskey's trial, Boger conceded, it was not clear that his testimony was based, in part, on information that he could only have gotten from the police. "At the time of the trial," Boger said, "it really sounded like McCleskey himself had volunteered most of this information. What we see in the 21-page statement is an active, aggressive questioner."

Pressed on the issue of whether the defense should have discovered Evans's written statement earlier, Boger responded, "The prosecutor turned over every other document in this case. Is there the slightest doubt why he held back this one piece of information? Is there the slightest doubt whether the state's attorney general, when we asked for all the documents, should have turned it over? I don't think so. And I think the reason it was held back is clear. It was a smoking gun."

Boger also argued that the federal appeals court had been wrong to overrule the district court judge because the appellate court began its analysis "as if the state's active concealment and its misconduct were simply irrelevant, and as if the fact findings of the district judge had never been made." The state actions "plainly impeded and impaired [defense] counsel's investigation," Boger asserted, a finding of the district court that should only have been overruled if it was "clearly erroneous," which he contended was not the case. Aside from Evans's statement, Boger said, the other evidence was so weak that "we think the court of appeals is profoundly in error to suggest that it [the Evans written statement] would have made no difference at guilt or at penalty."

In his concluding remarks, Boger argued "that here was enough state concealment, enough misrepresentations and half-truths and partial answers, that on an equitable matter of abuse of the writ,* we should not have our client go to the electric chair because he couldn't ferret through this game of 20 questions that was being played by the state. They had the statement, they knew it, they knew it bore on the *Massiah* violation, and they didn't turn it over."

After Boger sat down, his place at the lectern was taken by Georgia's now senior assistant attorney general, Mary Beth Westmoreland, who had defended the state's conviction of Warren McCleskey before the justices four years earlier. Westmoreland began by reframing the issue before the Court: it was not a case of state concealment, as the defense had claimed, but rather of bad judgment and possibly inept

---

* Abuse of the writ is the legal doctrine that under Warren and Burger Court interpretations had barred successive habeas appeals only if the defendant's attorney deliberately refrained from raising the arguments earlier or did not raise them previously through "inexcusable neglect."

legal tactics by McCleskey's attorneys. The Evans written statement had been in the state's file for years before Boger and Stroup asked for it and subsequently filed their second habeas petition on behalf of McCleskey.

"Why do you suppose counsel didn't say, 'May I see that statement?'" Stevens asked, suggesting that the defense may not have asked for the statement because they didn't know it existed.

"Your Honor, I think that is a very good question that we do not know the answer to."

How does it happen, Stevens continued, that the only document that defense counsel did not receive was Evans's statement?

Westmoreland responded by noting that the state had not been obligated to turn over the statement prior to trial and that, after the trial, it made no formal effort to prevent the defense from obtaining the document. The defense attorneys' problem, she suggested, was that they did not ask for the statement (which Boger claimed had been purposely concealed from them by the government). Defense counsel had not exercised "reasonable diligence," resulting in their failure to discover Evans's written statement, Westmoreland argued.

"May I interrupt for a minute?" Thurgood Marshall asked. "Are you trying to convince us that defense counsel was aware of the existence of this statement?"

"That he should have been," Westmoreland replied.

Was it the state's position, Marshall asked, "that counsel made a mistake?"

"Yes, Your Honor, that is absolutely correct."

"And this man shall die because of his mistake," Marshall continued. "Is that your position?"

"Your Honor, my position is that counsel made a mistake, that that constitutes an abuse of the writ, and that there is no miscarriage of justice in this case because there is no question of Mr. McCleskey's guilt in this matter. Yes, Your Honor, that is our position in this matter."

CHAPTER EIGHT

" G U I L T Y   A S   S I N "

During the month of October 1990, in which Jack Boger and Mary Beth Westmoreland made their second oral arguments before the Court in the McCleskey case, the justices listened to arguments in another case of a convicted murderer, Oreste Fulminante, whose confession also raised serious constitutional issues.

On September 14, 1982, Fulminante had telephoned the Mesa, Arizona, police department to report that his stepdaughter was missing. Two days later, the body of Fulminante's eleven-year-old stepdaughter was found in the Arizona desert, shot twice in the head, with strangulation marks around her neck. Fulminante, who had served time in prison for five felony convictions, became a prime suspect after he admitted to the police that he had argued with his stepdaughter before her murder. But Mesa police did not have enough evidence to charge him with the crime, and he left the state.

Later, Fulminante was arrested and convicted for firearms possession in New Jersey and sentenced to time in a federal penitentiary. In prison, Fulminante became friends with Anthony Sarivola, a reputed organized-crime operative who, unknown to Fulminante, was also a paid FBI informant. After rumors circulated in prison that he was a child murderer, the diminutive Fulminante (five feet three, 118 pounds) began to receive "rough" treatment by other inmates. Meanwhile, Sarivola was instructed by the FBI to pump Fulminante for information on his stepdaughter's murder. At first, Fulminante denied any role in the murder. Sarivola suggested to Fulminante that, in exchange for information on the murder, he would provide protection in prison for Fulminante. Fulminante accepted Sarivola's offer and confessed to his cell mate that he had murdered his stepdaughter.

Was Fulminante's life in danger when he accepted Sarivola's offer of protection? The answer to that question would prove critical in Fulminante's later murder trial.

"He [Fulminante] would have got out, but it wouldn't have been the way I got out—he would have went out of the prison horizontally," Sarivola explained. Why the special transportation? Sarivola was asked. "Because most organized crime figures and most criminals have some sort of scruples, regardless of what most people believe," Sarivola testified, "and children is a very soft point except for animals and, ah, the more the story began to be talked about and get around the joint a lot of people were thinking of hurting the little gentleman."

In his confession to Sarivola, Fulminante furnished his cell mate with the details of his crime. Later, he also confessed to Sarivola's wife, in a conversation during a car trip after serving his prison term, that he had killed his stepdaughter. Fulminante was arrested and brought back to Arizona to stand trial for his stepdaughter's murder. He was convicted and sentenced to death.

Fulminante's attorney appealed his murder conviction, arguing that his confession to Sarivola was coerced, since it was given in exchange for protection when he considered that his life was in danger in prison. The Arizona Supreme Court agreed with Fulminante, ruling that the confession was coerced and, further, that the admission of a coerced confession into evidence in a trial was always grounds for a reversal of a conviction, even if the admission was "harmless error," i.e., the defendant would have been convicted on other evidence. Following "an unbroken line" of U.S. Supreme Court precedents, the state supreme court reversed the conviction and ordered that Fulminante be retried without the use of the confession to Sarivola.

Before the retrial, the Rehnquist Court accepted the petition for review of the Arizona Supreme Court's *Fulminante* decision, requesting oral argument in October 1990 on two issues: (1) was the defendant's confession to Sarivola coerced, and (2) if so, could that confession be considered "harmless error" and not, therefore, be cause for overturning the conviction?

At the oral argument before the justices, Arizona's senior assistant attorney general, Barbara Jarrett, spoke first and described Oreste Fulminante as a middle-aged sociopath with low-to-average intelligence who "had absolutely no mental or physical problems that would have made him especially susceptible to coercion." Although he was small, Jarrett said, Fulminante, who was serving his third prison term, knew how to take care of himself in prison and did not need the likes of Anthony Sarivola to protect him.

A very different picture of Fulminante and Sarivola was depicted by Fulminante's defense attorney, Stephen Collins, who said that his client would not have walked out of the prison yard alive if he had not agreed to accept protection from Anthony Sarivola. The FBI informant was a former employee of the Colombo organized-crime family in New York, Collins said, and used violence to collect payments on extortionate loans made by the Colombo family. "Because of his connections with organized crime," Collins said, "the other inmates were afraid to do other than what he said." The FBI was aware, according to Collins, that their paid informer, Sarivola, "would resort to any means necessary to obtain confessions from targeted suspects." Collins did not claim that the FBI should refrain from using paid informers, "but, there is everything wrong when the Government sends a known violent criminal after a citizen."

On the "harmless error" doctrine, the government's attorney, Paul Larkin of the U.S. solicitor general's office, said that the Arizona Supreme Court's refusal to apply the doctrine to a coerced confession was "an anachronism," at odds with the general rule recognized by the Court that technical violations should not be grounds for reversal if other evidence at a trial would convict a defendant.

But Stephen Collins reminded the Court that it had declared in more than twenty-five opinions that a conviction could never stand when a coerced confession has been admitted at trial. "And the Court has stated many times that the reason for this is that no civilized system of justice can condone the use of a coerced confession," even if the confession was not essential to a defendant's conviction. The Court had recognized, Collins said, that the framers had feared an American version of the inquisitions that had occurred in Europe; they intended that the Constitution bar coerced confessions under any circumstances to underscore their commitment to a criminal justice system that was not inquisitorial. Collins argued further that the admission of coerced confessions "undermines public confidence in the entire judicial system, because it has the appearance that the courts will look the other way when the police have coerced a confession from a suspect."

At the judicial conference following the *Fulminante* oral argument, it was immediately apparent that the justices were deeply divided on both issues that had been argued in the case earlier in the week. Leading the attack on the Arizona Supreme Court decision was Chief Justice Rehnquist. He argued that the confession was not coerced. Rehnquist viewed Oreste Fulminante as a hardened criminal who was able, despite his small stature, to fend for himself in prison. He concluded that his confession to Sarivola was not involuntary, since he was not in fear of his life.

Rehnquist also argued that even if the confession were coerced, it should not be grounds for reversal under the harmless-error doctrine. The Fulminante case, he contended, gave the Court the overdue opportunity to apply the harmless-error doctrine in coerced confession cases, a position he had first advocated, unsuccessfully, as law clerk to Justice Jackson in 1953. As Jackson's law clerk, Rehnquist had written an extensive memorandum to the justice in support of his position in a New York robbery-murder case in which the three defendants claimed that their confessions were coerced and that their convictions should be reversed. The defendants were "guilty as sin," Rehnquist wrote Jackson, and there was ample evidence, apart from the confessions, to convict them. The Court should not overturn their

193

convictions, he argued, even if the confessions were coerced. By refusing to adopt the harmless-error doctrine for coerced confessions,
he contended, the Court encouraged a defense strategy devoted "not
to showing their [the defendants'] innocence but for laying the foundation of a technical reversal which this Court is often so willing to
give."

At the *Fulminante* conference in October 1990, Rehnquist again
argued that the Court should adopt the harmless-error doctrine in
coerced-confession cases. He maintained that the defendant could
have been convicted on evidence other than his confession to Anthony
Sarivola, and that the Arizona Supreme Court's decision refusing to
apply the harmless-error doctrine in Fulminante's case was wrong and
should be reversed.

Rehnquist was immediately challenged by his frequent ally in
criminal cases, Justice Byron White, who could never be accused of
being soft on criminals. Since his appointment by President John F.
Kennedy in 1962, White had viewed most of the liberal Warren Court
decisions in the criminal justice field with open hostility. White's
usual approach to the Court's criminal law cases was like the justice
himself: tough, detached and pragmatic.

Byron Raymond White grew up during the Depression in the
small town of Wellington, Colorado, where his father ran a lumber
supply business. At the age of seven, Byron, like the other boys in
town, was dismissed from school early so that he could work in the
nearby sugar beet fields, thinning and harvesting the beets by hand
for a dollar or two a day. Despite the hard financial times, White's parents, who did not complete high school, insisted that their son's studies came first. White graduated at the top of his high school class and
was awarded an academic scholarship to attend the state university in
Boulder.

At the University of Colorado, White was a junior Phi Beta Kappa
and valedictorian of his graduating class. But he was best known for
his superior talents on the football field. As a six-foot-two-inch, 190-
pound halfback, "Whizzer" White was not just fast and agile, but
tough, often preferring to run straight at defenders rather than around

them. In his senior year, he led his team to an undefeated season at the same time that he rushed for more yards than any other college player in the nation.

White won a Rhodes Scholarship to study English law and legal history at Oxford, but postponed his trip to England for a year to play halfback for the Pittsburgh Steelers. In his rookie season, White, who was paid $15,800 (the highest salary of any player in the history of the National Football League at that time), led the professional league in rushing. Afterward, he went to Oxford, but his studies were cut short in September 1939 when England went to war. He returned to the United States and enrolled in the Yale Law School, where he posted the highest grades in his first-year class. He was invited to join the school's prestigious law journal but declined so that he could devote his spare time to playing halfback for the Detroit Lions.

The bombing of Pearl Harbor interrupted White's studies and football career. He joined the Navy and became an intelligence officer based in the Solomon Islands. One of White's assignments was to write up the official report of the sinking of *PT 109*, which brought him into contact with the boat's young skipper, John F. Kennedy.

After the war, White completed his law studies at Yale and was selected to clerk for Chief Justice Fred Vinson (he was the first law clerk to later serve on the Court). Showing characteristic self-confidence and cool resolve, White turned down lucrative offers from two Washington law firms when they would not meet his demand for a partnership in two years. For the next twelve years, White developed a thriving commercial law practice in Denver. In 1960, he volunteered to work for his wartime acquaintance, Jack Kennedy, first heading the Colorado Committee for Kennedy and later the nationwide Citizens for Kennedy. Robert Kennedy was so impressed with White's administrative abilities that he persuaded the president to appoint him deputy attorney general, the second-ranking job in the Justice Department.

White's first task was to reorganize the Justice Department, which he did with quiet efficiency. Although he preferred to work behind the scenes, White could take command of a situation if he felt the circumstances demanded it. That happened in 1961 after the first "free-

195

dom riders" boarded buses traveling through the Deep South to protest continued segregation on interstate carriers. After the buses were met by rioting crowds in Montgomery, Alabama, White drafted the legal papers necessary to restore order. He then flew to Montgomery, took personal charge of the Justice Department's operation and held a terse conversation with Alabama's recalcitrant governor, George Wallace. Assured that peace had been restored, White returned to Washington.

A year later, after Justice Charles Whittaker announced his retirement, President Kennedy named White to be his first appointee to the Court. White disappointed liberals who hoped that he, like Kennedy's second appointee, Arthur Goldberg, would join the liberal-activist wing of the Warren Court. Instead, White wrote cautious, generally conservative, opinions that focused narrowly on the facts of a case and avoided broad declarations of judicial philosophy. While he was firm in his support of the Warren Court's desegregation decisions, he opposed later affirmative action rulings. He dissented in *Roe v. Wade* and repeatedly called for its reversal. And he regularly opposed the constitutional claims of criminal defendants, writing some of his most outspoken dissents to liberal rulings of the Warren Court, including *Miranda v. Arizona*.

At the *Fulminante* conference in the fall of 1990, White departed from his customary conservative position in criminal cases to support the defendant's constitutional claims, bringing him into direct conflict with the chief justice. He voted to affirm the decision of the Arizona Supreme Court, which had supported the defendant's position on the two basic constitutional issues. The Fulminante confession in prison was coerced, White argued. On the other issue, he insisted that the harmless-error doctrine should not be applied in coerced-confession cases. Permitting a coerced confession to be part of the evidence on which a jury is free to base its verdict, White asserted, was inconsistent with a basic premise of American criminal justice: that ours is not an inquisitorial system.

Blackmun, Marshall and Stevens, the remaining three most liberal members of the Court, supported White on both issues. He also received, initially, crucial support on one or both issues from O'Connor, Scalia, Kennedy and Souter. White, as the senior justice in the majority on both issues, assigned the Court opinion to himself.

An unusual transformation of the Court on the two issues after the justices' conference on *Fulminante* began in late November 1990. Almost immediately after Justice White circulated his first draft for the majority on November 28, 1990, he heard rumblings from several of his colleagues he hoped would sign on to his opinion.

On November 29, Justice O'Connor wrote White that, while she continued to think coerced confessions were not subject to harmless-error analysis, she wanted him to clarify that the Court's holding was limited "to genuinely coerced confessions—that is, confessions motivated by fear or force." She drew a distinction between "involuntary" and "coerced." "A confession can be involuntary without being coerced," she wrote, "such as a confession obtained without adequate Miranda warnings. I hope the opinion can make such a distinction."

The same day that O'Connor wrote her memorandum to White, Rehnquist sent his colleagues the first draft of what he presumed to be his dissenting opinion. Rehnquist wrote in the first sentence of his draft opinion, "I think that the Court is mistaken as to both questions it decides in this case." He asserted that the confession was not "involuntary"; the chief used the term "involuntary" rather than "coerced" in all of his draft opinions, a term most likely to appeal to his wavering colleagues. Rehnquist declared, "I am at a loss to see how the Arizona Supreme Court reached the conclusion that it did."

The chief went on to point out that the Supreme Court "has applied harmless-error analysis to a wide range of errors and has recognized that most constitutional errors can be harmless." The fact that the Court had never applied the harmless-error doctrine in coerced or "involuntary" confession cases did not deter the chief justice. He advocated the use of the harmless-error doctrine in *Fulminante*, since the defendant could have been convicted, in his view, on the later confession to Sarivola's wife.

To support his argument, Rehnquist organized constitutional errors into two categories, structural and trial. He argued that structural errors—those that pervaded the entire legal process, such as lack of counsel and judicial bias—were not subject to harmless-error analysis. But he insisted that all trial errors, including admission of involuntary confessions, fit within the harmless-error doctrine.

Eight days after Rehnquist's draft was circulated, White received another note, which was addressed to both White and Rehnquist from Kennedy. "As Byron's opinion indicates, and as we all recognized at conference," Kennedy wrote, "the coercion issue in this case is close." He then expressed his concern "that a holding that the confession is coerced on these facts will cause much difficulty in other cases." He concluded, "I now think that, based on this record, we should hold the confession to be not coerced." Kennedy joined Rehnquist's dissenting opinion on the coerced-confession issue.

Justice David Souter, in his first Court term, also had second thoughts on the coercion issue. On December 21, he wrote White and Rehnquist that he was prepared to join Rehnquist's dissent on the issue, even though at judicial conference he had voted with White. "I realize now that I did not fully appreciate the closeness of the coercion question," Souter wrote, "and after examining the record I believe the better view is that the confession probably was not a coerced one." On the basis of the trial record, Souter admitted that the question of whether the confession was "probably voluntary" or "probably involuntary" was close, but his examination of the record pushed Souter toward Rehnquist's view. "It is one thing to say that Fulminante confessed for the sake of getting whatever protection he might get in return," wrote Souter. "[I]t is quite another thing to say that his will was overborne."

Scalia was the next justice to recant on his original conference position, but he did so on the second issue—the application of the harmless-error doctrine. Scalia, who had originally voted to affirm the Arizona Supreme Court's decision on the issue, wrote the chief that he had become convinced that it would be difficult to define "a limited category of 'really' coerced confessions that alone would be excluded from harmless error." He therefore had decided to join Rehnquist's opinion on the harmless-error issue, "with apologies to Byron."

Two days after Scalia's memo, Justice O'Connor wrote the chief justice that she had changed her mind and had decided to join Rehnquist's opinion on both the confession and the harmless-error issues. On the latter issue, she wrote, "At Conference I voted to affirm in the belief that our precedents require that holding, but, like Nino, I am persuaded that admission of an involuntary confession can be, and should be, analyzed under the harmless error doctrine."

The vote now stood at four justices in favor of declaring Fulminante's confession coerced (White, Blackmun, Marshall and Stevens), four opposed (Rehnquist, Kennedy, O'Connor and Souter) and Scalia taking no position on the issue. On the harmless-error question, four justices opposed application of the doctrine (White, Blackmun, Marshall and Stevens), three supported it (Rehnquist, O'Connor and Scalia) and two justices, Kennedy and Souter, had yet to declare their positions on the issue.

On January 11, 1991, Rehnquist circulated a revised draft opinion, aware that he still lacked the votes for a majority on either issue. "I think the Court is mistaken as to both of the questions it decides in this case," he wrote. But there was one important and, for Justice White and the Court's three most liberal members, unsettling addition to Rehnquist's latest draft: the opinion was preceded by the announcement that its author was now joined by Justice O'Connor on both issues, by Justices Kennedy and Souter on the coerced-confession issue, and by Justice Scalia on the harmless-error issue.

Less than three months after their conference, the justices' lineup in the Fulminante case was thoroughly jumbled. The chief sent his colleagues a status report:

I have spoken with Byron regarding the status of votes in this case. With respect to the first issue, we are in agreement that, at present, there are four votes to find the confession involuntary and four votes to find it voluntary, with Nino not reaching the issue. On the second issue, four justices have voted to hold that harmless-error analysis cannot apply and three say that it can, with David and Tony not reaching the issue. Unless either Nino, Tony or David decide to cast a vote on these issues, the opinion will be delivered in its present state as to the second issue, with no opinion on the first issue.

The Rehnquist memo had the effect of moving Scalia toward a decision on the coerced-confession issue, though not in the direction that the chief justice had hoped. "In the interest of shaking loose the log-jam in this case," Scalia wrote White, "I am willing to take a position on the coercion issue, though it is not necessary to my judgment. I agree with you that a proper deference to the state court leads to the conclusion that this confession was coerced. Though we decide for ourselves the ultimate issue of coercion, I think we must accept the factual finding of a credible threat of physical harm, since such a finding is permissible on this record. And in my view a credible threat of physical harm always produces coercion."

But while White now could claim Scalia's crucial fifth vote to give him a majority on the coercion issue, he was in the process of losing the more important harmless-error argument. The two members of the Court who had earlier not taken a formal position on the harmless-error issue, Justices Kennedy and Souter, eventually supported the chief justice. That gave Rehnquist five votes: the chief, O'Connor, Scalia, Kennedy and Souter.

In his fifth and last draft, Chief Justice Rehnquist could finally declare that "the Court properly concludes today that the admission of an 'involuntary' confession at trial is subject to harmless-error analysis." With that statement, the Rehnquist Court majority obliterated several decades of Court precedents that had expressly prohibited the application of harmless-error analysis to forced-confession cases. Rehnquist, the chief justice, had succeeded where Rehnquist, the law clerk to Justice Jackson in 1953, had failed.

Still, the chief justice was denied the satisfaction of a clear victory. Kennedy, who supported Rehnquist's position that an involuntary confession can be deemed "harmless error" in an appropriate case, nonetheless voted with Justices White, Blackmun, Marshall and Stevens in ruling that Fulminante's confession was *not* harmless error, therefore affirming the Arizona Supreme Court's decision that Fulminante was entitled to a new trial. In a concurring opinion, Kennedy indicated that it would be the rare case in which he found an involuntary confession to be "harmless," for "apart, perhaps, from a videotape of the crime, one would have difficulty finding evidence more damaging to a criminal defendant's plea of innocence" than a full confession.

• • •

While the justices struggled with the coercion and harmless-error issues in *Fulminante*, they also had to contend with Warren Mc-Cleskey's argument urging the Court to overturn his conviction and death sentence. In 1987, Rehnquist had been a member of a five-member majority that rejected McCleskey's argument that the death penalty, as imposed in Georgia, was unconstitutionally weighted against blacks. In 1990, the chief justice again voted against Mc-Cleskey, who had asked the Court to rule that the government's use of McCleskey's incriminating statement in prison to Offie Evans was a violation of his constitutional rights. In the McCleskey case, Rehnquist had an easier time persuading a majority of his colleagues to reject the defendant's argument than he had had in the Fulminante case.

Just as Rehnquist's views as a young law clerk to Justice Jackson almost forty years earlier had foreshadowed his position in *Fulminante*, his earlier conservative views had also anticipated his position in the McCleskey case. As Jackson's law clerk, Rehnquist had written a memorandum advocating that the Court narrow habeas corpus remedies, expressing impatience with the many habeas petitions from death row inmates received by the Court. In the almost four decades that had passed since he wrote the memorandum entitled "HABEAS CORPUS, THEN AND NOW—Or, 'If I Can Just Find the Right Judge, Over These Prison Walls I Shall Fly. . . ,'" Rehnquist's views on habeas petitions had not changed.

As chief justice, Rehnquist had enthusiastically endorsed a proposal by a committee of federal judges (which he had appointed) recommending a strict limitation on habeas appeals. When the proposal failed to win widespread support of the federal judiciary, he publicly called on Congress to pass legislation that would accomplish the same result. In a speech given seven months before the second *Mc-Cleskey* oral argument, Rehnquist said that the system for handling death penalty appeals in the federal courts "verges on the chaotic," and urged the legislators to put tighter limits on death row prisoners' appeals. "At no point until a death sentence is actually carried out," Rehnquist declared disapprovingly, "can it be said that litigation concerning the sentence has run its course."

Congress had failed to act upon the chief justice's recommendation at the time the justices considered the second McCleskey case. But a strong Court opinion rejecting Warren McCleskey's second habeas petition could accomplish by judicial decision what the chief had so far been unable to achieve by legislation.

Rehnquist assigned the majority opinion to Justice Kennedy, who wrote for himself, Rehnquist, O'Connor, Scalia, Souter and White. The Kennedy opinion dismissing McCleskey's argument went far beyond the proprosecution position that Georgia's Senior Assistant Attorney General Westmoreland had put forward at oral argument. Kennedy rejected McCleskey attorney Boger's argument that the state had systematically refused for nine years to allow defense attorneys to see Offie Evans's twenty-one-page statement. And once he had rejected Boger's argument (and the district judge's findings), Kennedy expanded the abuse-of-the-writ doctrine far beyond the "reasonable diligence" standard that Westmoreland had advocated at oral argument. In the process, Kennedy opened a dramatically wider avenue for courts to reject second habeas petitions, making it easier for states to carry out death sentences quicker. Justice Kennedy's majority opinion redefined the abuse-of-the-writ doctrine so that multiple habeas petitions by prisoners could be dismissed as "abusive" unless the inmate could show "cause" why his legal point had not been raised earlier and that he had suffered "actual prejudice" from the alleged constitutional error.

McCleskey's lawyers had failed, and so would later legal challenges, unless it could be proved that a defendant's lawyer was so inept in his representation that it amounted to "constitutionally ineffective assistance of counsel." Under the Court's new standard, neither an attorney's legal error nor his bad judgment would qualify.

How significant the shift in the Court's standards might be was suggested by the fact that at the time of the second *McCleskey* decision, 40 percent of all death sentences that were overturned resulted from a federal judge's finding of constitutional error in the conviction or sentence. The new conservative Court majority, through Justice Kennedy's opinion, had fastened a stronger latch to the doors of the federal courts, at least where death row inmates were concerned. Observing that "perpetual disregard for the finality of convictions disparages the entire criminal justice system," Justice Kennedy predicted that the Court's new standard "should curtail the abusive petitions that in recent years have threatened to undermine the integrity of the habeas corpus process." The decision was not just an important victory for state prosecutors, but also for Rehnquist personally.

Jack Boger was surprised by the Court's new habeas standard and "shocked at the majority's mistreatment of the facts in McCleskey's case." There was, he said, "a cynical refusal to give weight to the state's deliberate concealment of evidence." He concluded that the Rehnquist Court majority wanted to send a message to lower federal courts not to tolerate second habeas petitions. "Warren McCleskey became a sacrificial victim on the altar of the Court's new standard."

Justice Thurgood Marshall did not describe the majority's position in *McCleskey v. Zant* in the scathing terms of Boger. But he did not spare the majority either. In the first draft of his dissenting opinion, Marshall labeled Kennedy's majority opinion "lawless." He excised "lawless" only after he received a memorandum from his fellow dissenter, Justice Stevens, gently reminding Marshall that whatever the shortcomings of the majority opinion, it was the law.

The 1990 Court term was Marshall's last year on the Court, and it was a bitterly disappointing valedictory. The *McCleskey* decision had been a particularly anguished defeat for Marshall, who had been urging the Court to outlaw capital punishment for more than twenty years. After the Court majority had ruled in *Furman v. Georgia* in 1972 that the death penalty was so arbitrarily administered that it violated the Constitution's Due Process Clause, Marshall wrote: "In striking down capital punishment, this Court does not malign our system of government. On the contrary, it pays homage to it. In recognizing the humanity of our fellow beings, we pay ourselves the highest tribute."

Marshall's mark on twentieth-century American history was made with his persistent struggle to desegregate the nation's public schools, culminating in his successful argument to the Supreme Court in *Brown v. Board of Education.* But to his mind, *Brown* was not necessarily his most important courtroom triumph. In terms of personal satisfaction, Marshall put his criminal cases, particularly those in which he defended young black men accused of capital offenses, above all of the others, including *Brown.* "They did the most good because they saved people's lives," he said. Over Marshall's illustrious career as a trial lawyer, just the word-of-mouth bulletin "Thurgood's coming" was enough to lift the spirits of an entire black community.

Thurgood Marshall was taught pride in his African-American heritage from his early days growing up in Baltimore before World War I. It was not an easy lesson for a young black man to learn in a city that was more rigidly segregated than any other in the United States, including Jackson, Mississippi. Blacks could not shop in the downtown department stores or even relieve themselves in the public toilets. Marshall remembered the embarrassment and discomfort of enduring a long trolley ride from downtown Baltimore to his house where, finally unable to control himself any longer, he "ruined" his front steps.

The Marshalls were relatively well-to-do mulattoes by the prevailing standards of Baltimore at the turn of the century. Thurgood's mother, Norma, was an elementary school teacher and his father, William, worked as a Pullman car waiter and later steward at the exclusive Gibson Island Club on Chesapeake Bay. Thurgood, who was born in 1908, showed an early independence of mind, shortening his cumbersome first name of Thoroughgood (which had been invented by his freedman grandfather to satisfy Union Army regulations that every volunteer have both a first and a last name).

In the segregated public schools of Baltimore, Marshall showed no particular academic spark. As a teenager, he spent his most animated intellectual moments arguing with his father, an exercise that led Marshall to the study of law. "He never told me to become a lawyer," Marshall recalled, "but he turned me into one. He did it by teaching me to argue, by challenging my logic on every point, by making me prove every statement I made."

After graduation from all-black Lincoln University in Chester, Pennsylvania, Marshall wanted to study at the law school at the University of Maryland, but it did not accept blacks. So Marshall enrolled at the Howard University Law School in Washington, D.C., in 1930. It was that rare instance when racial segregation produced salutary results. For at predominantly black Howard, Marshall came under the tutelage of a remarkable black attorney and administrator, Vice Dean Charles Houston.

Marshall and his classmates nicknamed Houston "Ironpants" and "Cement Shoes" in homage to the vice dean's unbending toughness. Houston not only demanded high academic standards, but also was determined to mold the law school's graduates into social engineers who would use the law to reform society in ways that would directly benefit black Americans. Marshall, who finished first in his class, recalled that Houston would "drive home to us that we would be competing not only with white lawyers but really well-trained white lawyers, so there just wasn't any point in crying in our beer about being Negroes."

Shortly after his law school graduation, Marshall teamed up with Houston, who had been appointed special counsel to the NAACP, to bring a lawsuit challenging the segregation policy of the law school at the University of Maryland. They won the suit, and Marshall soon officially joined Houston at the NAACP, as the organization's full-time assistant special counsel. In 1938, the two attorneys collaborated to win their first victory in the U.S. Supreme Court, successfully arguing that Missouri's refusal to admit a black applicant to its state law school—offering him instead an out-of-state "scholarship"—violated the Equal Protection Clause of the Fourteenth Amendment.

Shortly after that Court decision, Houston resigned his NAACP position for reasons of poor health and was replaced by his protégé, Marshall. Houston had taught Marshall the intricacies of the law as well as its broad purposes. Marshall brought to the NAACP his own tactical shrewdness and a salty sense of humor that, besides providing thousands of hours of laughter for his colleagues, enabled him to preserve his sanity and perspective through his many difficult years of pathbreaking legal work. "I intend to wear life like a loose garment and not worry about nothin'," Marshall once said. That casual bravado disguised the nerves of a lion tamer and the steely determination of a man who would change constitutional history.

During one of his many suits challenging the discriminatory salaries paid to black public school teachers throughout the South, Marshall learned that "the powers that be cannot afford to let a 'northern nigger' win a case against them, so they want to settle." Marshall noted archly in a report to his home office, "Will you please respect the fact that I am a *northern* nigger." Over a fifteen-year period, beginning in the thirties, Marshall and other NAACP attorneys won fifty cases dealing with the equalization of teachers' salaries, worth over $3 million to black teachers.

Marshall's hectic schedule in the late thirties and early forties always included a substantial number of criminal trials. In 1941, he defended a young black farmer named W. D. Lyons in a trial that would profoundly influence Marshall's views on the need for strong constitutional safeguards for criminal defendants. The twenty-year-old Lyons had been arrested outside of Hugo, Oklahoma, for the brutal murders of a white couple and their four-year-old son, who had been shot, their bodies chopped up with an ax and then their house set on fire. After stories spread through the black community of Hugo that Lyons had been savagely beaten into confessing to the murders, Marshall was brought to Oklahoma to defend him.

When Marshall took his seat at the defense table on Monday morning, January 27, 1941, he became the first black attorney to practice in Judge J. R. Childers's Hugo courtroom. For the rest of the week, hundreds of spectators jammed into the courtroom to watch the "nigger lawyer from New York"—the first time, Marshall wrote, "that they had seen such an animal." Students from the local white elementary and high schools were given a day off to attend the trial. It was, Judge Childers announced, a "gala day."

"Imagine it," Marshall wrote Walter White, the NAACP's national secretary, "a Negro on trial for his life being considered a 'gala' day." He reported that the law enforcement officers that he cross-examined "became angry at the idea of a Negro pushing them into tight corners and making their lies so obvious."

Under Marshall's cross-examination, the officers admitted that Lyons had been beaten for more than six hours and that a special investigator assigned to the case had ordered the bones of the deceased woman to be placed in a pan on Lyons's lap and then rubbed on his hands and arms. At 2:30 A.M., shortly after the deceased woman's bones had been placed in his lap, Lyons signed his first confession. He was then taken to the state penitentiary at McAlester, where, twelve hours later, he again signed a confession, this time to the warden, who, Lyons testified, told him that if he didn't admit to committing the murders, "you'll be the fortieth man I've sent to the chair."

Marshall made motions to suppress both confessions, arguing that they were inadmissible because they were coerced. The judge ruled in Marshall's favor on the first confession, because "the defendant may have been frightened during the long hours of investigation and seeing the bones." But he allowed the second confession to be admitted into evidence. After testimony in the trial was completed, the state prosecutor asked the jury to return a guilty verdict and sentence Lyons to the electric chair. The jury returned the expected guilty verdict, but sentenced Lyons to life imprisonment.

Marshall considered the life sentence a victory. "You know," he wrote Walter White, "that life for such a crime as that—three people killed, shot with a shotgun and cut up with an axe and then burned— shows clearly that they believed him innocent." He added, "I think we are in a perfect position to appeal." (Marshall was overly optimistic; he lost Lyons's appeal in both the state appellate court and in his appeal to the U.S. Supreme Court.)

The Lyons case represented a critical turning point in the future Justice Marshall's thinking about the criminal justice system. As a defense attorney, Marshall always listened with a healthy dose of skepticism to a prosecutor's claim that a confession was voluntary. Based on his investigation of the 1943 race riot in Detroit, which left 34 killed and 600 injured (three-quarters of them black), he also had reason to question more broadly the conduct of white law enforcement authorities. "Many Negroes guilty of no crime were shot and others beaten, cursed and threatened indiscriminately," Marshall wrote in his Detroit report, and "the reckless disregard for innocent people by white policemen caused at least two deaths."

In 1946, Marshall again was drawn into the caldron of race-inspired violence, defending twenty-five black men accused of assault and murder during a race riot in rural Tennessee. After he won acquittals for twenty-four of his clients and a conviction of a lesser offense for the twenty-fifth, he very nearly ended up being lynched for his efforts. Local white police officers, enraged by the verdicts, followed Marshall and his two cocounsel out of town. Three patrol cars, their sirens blaring, motioned Marshall to pull over. They searched Marshall's trunk for liquor but found none. Marshall was allowed to continue his trip but was stopped two more times. Finally, he was arrested for drunk driving.

"[T]he mob got me one night," Marshall said, recalling the frightening events that night, "and they were taking me down to the river, where all of the white people were waiting to do a little bit of lynching."

The police caravan with Marshall in tow pulled off the main highway and sped toward the nearby river. But the two other defense attorneys, who had been ordered to continue their drive to Nashville on the main highway, refused to obey the police and, in what Marshall would later call an extraordinary act of courage, followed the patrol cars. Their pursuit, Marshall believed, saved his life. Not wanting any witnesses, the police ultimately abandoned their plan and headed back to Columbia with their "drunken" prisoner. A local magistrate, further frustrating the police, said Marshall was not drunk and ordered his release.

While Marshall's criminal defense work continued throughout the forties, he was also pursuing an aggressive strategy of challenging racial discrimination—with spectacular results. He successfully argued before the Supreme Court that Texas's all-white Democratic primary was designed to deprive blacks of their constitutional right to vote. The Court also endorsed Marshall's argument in *Morgan v. Virginia*, declaring in 1946 that a state statute requiring segregation on interstate buses was unconstitutional. And in *Shelley v. Kraemer* in 1948, the justices again ruled in Marshall's favor, holding that state courts could not enforce racially restrictive covenants in real estate contracts. At the same time, he was patiently laying the legal groundwork for a direct challenge to public school segregation. And in 1954, Marshall won *Brown v. Board of Education*, his most celebrated victory in the Supreme Court. "Separate educational facilities are inherently unequal," Chief Justice Warren declared for a unanimous Court in *Brown*.

But even at the height of his civil rights successes, Marshall did not forget his criminal cases, or the look on the face of one defendant's mother who told him sternly, "Lawyer, don't let my boy die." After Marshall was appointed to the Supreme Court in 1967, he remained vigilant in his insistence on sturdy constitutional safeguards for the accused. For Marshall, the criminal justice system worked best when a poor defendant's presumption of innocence was backed by competent representation and a legal process that, girded by constitutional guarantees, eliminated the chance of covert or subtle intimidation by state and federal law enforcement authorities. Even with constitutional protections, Marshall believed that the system could never be foolproof, one reason that he consistently called for abolition of the death penalty.

During the 1990 Rehnquist Court term, Marshall found himself increasingly isolated on a Court hostile to his liberal views of the broad constitutional protections guaranteed to criminal defendants. During the term, the conservative Court majority had brushed Marshall's positions aside as it rewrote critical doctrines in *Fulminante* and *McCleskey*. But these were not the only aggressively proprosecution decisions handed down that term.

In *Coleman v. Thompson*, the conservative majority threw out a habeas petition because the defense lawyer had filed formal papers one day late. That majority also found, in Johnny Paul Penry's case, that there was no constitutional barrier to the execution of mentally retarded people. Similarly, the conservative majority sanctioned the execution of Heath Wilkins, who was sixteen years old when he stabbed a convenience-store employee to death during a robbery.

The Court also dismissed the argument that a life sentence should be related to the magnitude of the crime. It ruled against Ronald Harmelin, a first-time offender who had been sentenced to life imprisonment for possession of 672 grams of cocaine that were found in the trunk of his car. Michigan's mandatory sentence of life imprisonment for drug offenders did not, Justice Scalia declared for the majority, violate Harmelin's rights to be protected against cruel and unusual punishment under the Eighth Amendment.

Aggressive police investigations were encouraged in a spate of decisions in the spring of 1991, including the reversal of a twelve-year-old Court precedent that gave police much greater discretion to conduct warrantless searches. In the opinion of the new Court majority, police could search a closed container in an automobile without a warrant so long as they had probable cause to believe it contained contraband. In another decision, the Court held that suspects could be detained by police for up to forty-eight hours without a probable cause hearing. And in yet another, the Court decided that bus passengers could be searched by police officers even if they lacked reasonable suspicion, so long as the passengers consented to the search. The Court majority ruled that a bus passenger who had allowed a police search—without being informed that she had the right to refuse—had given her consent.

Justice Marshall was joined in his resentment of the conservative majority's juggernaut by the normally unflappable Justice John Paul Stevens. Stevens accused the majority of becoming "a loyal foot soldier in the Executive's fight against crime," responding politically, rather than on the basis of objective constitutional standards.

On the last day of the term, June 27, 1991, Justice Marshall announced his retirement from the Court. That same day, he signed off on his last Court opinion, a scorching dissent in another criminal law decision. The Marshall dissent followed a Rehnquist-led conservative majority opinion that made constitutional history by sanctioning, for the first time, the admission of statements by relatives of the victim at a convicted defendant's sentencing hearing before a jury, when he could face the death penalty.

In the decision, *Payne v. Tennessee*, the Court overturned two recent decisions (*Booth v. Maryland* in 1987 and *South Carolina v. Gathers* in 1989), permitting for the first time the introduction of "victim impact" statements at sentencing hearings where the death penalty could be imposed. Justice Powell had stressed in his majority opinion in *Booth* that the purpose of the sentencing hearing was to focus on the crime and criminal; the introduction of statements by the victim's family and friends would not only inject a highly emotional element into the proceeding, Powell wrote, but could favor socially connected defendants over the poor and ignorant.

In *Payne*, however, the chief justice's majority opinion reversing *Booth* and *Gathers* dismissed the precedents as poorly reasoned and wrongly decided. The chief declared that stare decisis was not "an inexorable command" and that precedent was more important in property and contract right cases than in those involving individual rights. In his *Payne* opinion, Rehnquist demonstrated once again (as he had in his initiative to reconsider the civil rights precedent *Runyon v. McCrary*) that he was not a judicial conservative who necessarily respected precedent; he was, rather, a conservative-activist, who seemed prepared to reverse liberal precedents he disapproved of whenever he had the votes to do so.

"Power, not reason," Marshall wrote in his last bitter dissent in *Payne*, "is the new currency of this Court's decision-making. In dispatching *Booth* and *Gathers* to their graves, today's majority suggests that an even more extensive upheaval of this Court's precedents may be in store. The majority today sends a clear signal that scores of established constitutional liberties are now ripe for reconsideration."

This was the grim judicial farewell of a man who had spent more than fifty years in courtrooms as attorney and judge defending the rights of criminal defendants.

CHAPTER NINE

DEPRECIATING LIBERTY

The call to Judge Clarence Thomas came from White House Counsel C. Boyden Gray on June 28, 1991, one day after Marshall had announced his retirement. Gray informed Thomas that he was being considered for the Court vacancy. Gray himself had already made up his mind that Judge Thomas, who had served on the U.S. Court of Appeals for the District of Columbia for only fifteen months, should be President George Bush's next appointee to the Court. Attorney General Richard Thornburgh wanted the president to consider conservative Hispanic candidates as well. Judge Emilio M. Garza, a little-known member of the U.S. Court of Appeals for the Fifth Circuit, was flown to Washington from Texas to meet the president. But Bush, who already knew and was impressed with Thomas, was convinced that Thomas should have the nomination and become the second African-American to serve on the Court.

On July 1, after a crabmeat salad luncheon, the president and his Court appointee Thomas stepped outside the Bush summer home at Kennebunkport, Maine, and Bush introduced Thomas as his nominee to be the 106th justice of the Supreme Court.

Fighting back tears, Thomas said, "Only in America could this have been possible." He recalled, "As a child, I could not dare dream that I would ever see the Supreme Court—not to mention be nominated for it."

Clarence Thomas was born in 1948 in the sultry river town of Pin Point, Georgia, near Savannah. He and his older sister, Emma Mae, lived with their mother in their aunt's rotting wooden shanty, where the floor was dirt and newspapers served as wall insulation. Clarence's mother, Leola, worked nearby, plucking the meat from crab shells at 5 cents a pound, and as a $10-a-week maid for wealthy white Savannah families.

When Clarence was two, his father left his mother, who was pregnant with her third child. Leola moved her family to a one-room tenement in east Savannah in 1954, where they shared a kitchen and an unworkable outdoor latrine with other poor tenants. "It was hard," Thomas remembered, "but it was all we had and all there was." A year later, Thomas's mother dispatched him and his younger brother, their belongings stuffed into two grocery bags, to live in another part of Savannah with their grandfather, Myers Anderson, and his wife.

Grandfather Anderson believed that hard work and the Bible were man's best hope in overcoming life's adversities and temptations. Both stern and kind, Anderson was the dominant influence in young Clarence's life. Thomas learned discipline by his grandfather's example, and from his gruff aphorisms. "Old man Can't is dead," Anderson told his grandson. "I helped bury him." But just in case Clarence was slow to take up the challenge, Anderson's thick leather belt was at the ready. If Clarence faltered in his schoolwork or so much as dropped a candy wrapper on the floor at home, he was whipped or sent to his room. But beneath the harsh discipline lay an inspired purpose. "Boy, you are going to school today," he told Clarence. "You're goin' to do better than I'm doing."

A devout Catholic, Anderson wanted his religion to be central in Clarence's life as it was in his own. Clarence was sent to the all-black St. Benedict the Moor (Catholic) Elementary School where he was taught by Franciscan nuns. Like Grandfather Anderson, the nuns instilled purpose in Clarence and his uniformed classmates, assisted, when necessary, by a straight ruler deftly rapped over a transgressor's knuckles.

After St. Benedict's, Anderson sent his grandson to all-white St. John Vianney Minor Seminary, a Catholic boarding school, where Clarence played quarterback on the football team and continued to earn excellent academic marks. His achievements, however, did not insulate him from ugly incidents of racism. "Smile, Clarence, so we can see you," one of his bunkmates yelled after lights were out. The worst of it, Thomas later recalled, was that no one told the racist to shut up. Later, at the Immaculate Conception Seminary in far-off northwestern Missouri, where Thomas planned to study for the priesthood, he still could not escape the stains of racism. In April 1968, the night that the Reverend Martin Luther King, Jr., was shot, a fellow seminarian, unaware of Thomas's presence, yelled, "Good. I hope the son of a bitch dies."

The remark turned Thomas away from the priesthood. He transferred to the Jesuit Holy Cross College in Worcester, Massachusetts, where he was only one of twelve blacks in his class. Confused about his life and future, Thomas scribbled his anxieties in a notebook: "Turn 20 summer of 1968 . . . MLK shot previous spring . . . Bobby Kennedy assassinated . . . depressing, scared, serious, angry, confused . . . years of rage."

At war with his former model-seminarian image, a rebellious Clarence Thomas tramped across the Holy Cross campus in combat boots and battle fatigues, his once-short hair sprouting into an Afro. Thomas helped found the college's black student union, nailed a poster of Malcolm X on his dormitory room wall and stomped off campus in protest when some students were suspended for obstructing a recruiter from General Electric (which held military contracts).

By his senior year in college, Thomas had decided to study law in hopes, he later said, of righting some of the wrongs he had seen and endured over the years. As a black graduate with an outstanding academic record (he stood ninth in his class), Thomas was admitted to several law schools. He chose Yale, which, like Holy Cross, had instituted an affirmative action admissions policy to attract promising blacks. At an Episcopal church in Worcester the day after his graduation from Holy Cross, Thomas married Kathy Ambush, who attended a black Catholic school for women in Worcester, and the newlyweds headed for New Haven.

As a first-year law student at Yale, Thomas always felt that he was being judged by the color of his skin. "You had to prove yourself every day because the presumption was that you were dumb and didn't deserve to be there on merit," he later remembered. "Every time you walked into a law class at Yale, it was like having a monkey jump down on your back from the Gothic arches."

Throughout his three years at Yale, Thomas seemed to wrestle with contradictions. He wore overalls, a signal of his solidarity with the masses, and he worked at a New Haven legal aid office that provided assistance to welfare recipients. But he appeared to make a conscious effort to be inconspicuous in class, sitting in the back of the classroom and never volunteering an opinion. He avoided civil rights courses, preferring the drier subjects of tax and commercial law. At the same time, he became close friends with Harry Singleton, a black student with strong conservative views, and his politics began to swing from the radical left of his Holy Cross days to the militant, but no less angry, right.

Failing to receive the offer that he sought from one of the major Atlanta firms after graduation, Thomas accepted a job with Missouri's attorney general, and fellow Yale alumnus, John C. Danforth, after Thomas had been recommended to Danforth by Yale Law Professor Guido Calabresi. Thomas requested that he not be given legal assignments in traditional civil rights areas, but rather in the fields of environmental and commercial law. He dressed in conservative dark suits and prominently displayed a Georgia flag (which incorporated the stars and stripes of the Confederacy) on his desk.

After Danforth was elected to the U.S. Senate, he arranged for Thomas to join the legal staff at the St. Louis–based Monsanto Company. There he drafted environmental impact statements and performed other technical legal tasks for the chemical company for two and a half years. In 1979, he left Monsanto to work for Danforth in Washington. By that time, Thomas was beginning to develop his own ideas and ambitions. In the late seventies, Thomas had become an advocate of the economic theories of black conservative Thomas Sowell and the Republican politics of Ronald Reagan. A new Clarence Thomas emerged, confident, outspoken and dedicated to a national conservative agenda.

Like Reagan, Clarence Thomas wanted to take the government off the backs of the people, to return to the basic virtues that had made the country great in the first place: self-reliance, discipline and a free-market economy. By 1980, when Reagan was elected president, Thomas already had confided to a reporter for the *St. Louis Post-Dispatch* that he aspired to sit on the Supreme Court.

In 1981, the Reagan Administration offered Thomas his first political appointment, as assistant secretary in the Department of Education. Eight months later, he left that position for the more prestigious and powerful chairmanship of the Equal Employment Opportunity Commission, where he spent the next eight and a half years. Established by the Civil Rights Act of 1964, the EEOC had wielded a legal club against reluctant employers who were slow to obey the nondiscrimination tenets of the 1964 statute.

Under Thomas's direction, the EEOC changed its focus to fit the conservative political ambitions of the Reagan Administration. The president had denounced federal affirmative action programs; Thomas's EEOC, in turn, abandoned large class action suits against employers who had suspiciously low numbers of minorities in their workforce. Instead of bringing sweeping class action suits, Thomas concentrated on individual legal challenges to discriminatory practices. At the same time, the EEOC largely ignored the demands by women's organizations and the elderly for more aggressive prosecutions of sex- and age-based discriminatory practices. Any suggestions of quotas or group solutions to employment discrimination were exorcised from the EEOC vocabulary.

In interviews and lectures, EEOC Chairman Thomas drew on his personal experiences and observations to expand on his burgeoning conservative philosophy. He told the *New York Times* in 1982 that "I am unalterably opposed to programs that force or even cajole people to hire a certain percentage of minorities. I watched the operation of such affirmative action policies when I was in college, and I watched the destruction of many kids as a result." A year later, he told another reporter: "I'll put the bottom line on you. I don't think we [black Americans] caused our problem, but we're damn sure going to have to solve it." In a lecture at the conservative Heritage Foundation in 1987, Thomas recalled his upbringing: "The most compassionate thing [my grandparents] did for us was to teach us to fend for ourselves and to do that in an openly hostile environment. . . . Self-sufficiency and spiritual and emotional security were our tools to carve out secure freedom. Those who attempt to capture the daily counseling, over-sight, common sense, and vision of my grandparents in a governmental program are engaging in sheer folly."

By the late eighties, Thomas—bright, articulate, resolutely conservative—was destined for higher office. The grooming began in 1990 when Thomas was appointed by President Bush to a seat on the U.S. Court of Appeals for the District of Columbia. There was, by then, already talk that if the Republicans remained in the White House much longer, Judge Thomas would soon become Justice Thomas.

On September 10, 1991, the first day of Thomas's Supreme Court confirmation hearings before the Senate Judiciary Committee, the nominee was greeted with shouts of encouragement from supporters lining the corridors outside the Senate Caucus Room. Judge Thomas smiled broadly and enthusiastically shook hands as he made his way to the front of the room. Dressed in dark gray suit, white shirt, and red-patterned tie, Thomas sat nervously erect at the witness table. His expertly crafted opening statement emphasized the genuinely heartrending story of his rise from a disheveled Georgia shanty to the chandeliered elegance of the historic Senate Caucus Room. With obvious emotion, Thomas spoke of his family's one-room tenement in east Savannah, carting his grocery bag of belongings to his Grandfather Anderson's, and the humiliation of hearing his wonderful grandfather called "boy."

He gave credit to the Franciscan nuns who had reinforced the importance of religion in his life and "were unyielding in their expectations that we use all of our talents no matter what the rest of the world said or did." He also made a point of expressing gratitude to the civil rights movement and leaders like Thurgood Marshall, an expression that had been noticeably absent from his many speeches and articles while he was President Reagan's EEOC chairman.

Finally, Thomas addressed the committee members directly, imploring them to judge him and, hopefully, to conclude "that I am an honest, decent, fair person."

Clarence Thomas's credibility, for which the nominee had explicitly asked to be judged, immediately became the central issue of his confirmation hearings. During the five days in which he was interrogated by the committee, Thomas's responses to questions were riddled with awkward circumlocutions. Despite his many public proclamations of adherence to conservative dogma, Thomas told the committee that he held no strong views or overarching ideology that would influence him on the Court. For years, Thomas had expressed his belief in natural law (i.e., governing principles that transcend man-made law) in articles and speeches, and had applied the concept specifically to constitutional issues. Yet he told the committee that his prior statements were the musings of an amateur, not those of a wholly serious political theorist. Asked about his endorsement of an antiabortion attack by conservative businessman Lewis Lehrman, Thomas replied that he had not actually read Lehrman's article, which he had publicly praised. Nor, he said, had he read the 1986 report of the White House Working Group, which he signed as a member and which concluded that unwed teenage mothers should be denied welfare benefits.

When asked about basic constitutional concepts, Thomas gave stiff responses, exhibiting none of the facility for discussion that had served the two previous Court nominees, Anthony Kennedy and David Souter, so well. In response to the question of whether he recognized a constitutional right to privacy, Thomas repeated the position taken by Kennedy and Souter before him. Yes, said Thomas, he supported *Griswold v. Connecticut*, the Court decision that had established the right to privacy of married couples in the intimacy of their bedroom. But he provided no evidence that he had thought about the doctrine or considered its theoretical underpinnings.

Thomas was heavily fortified to repel the inevitable inquiry about his opinion of *Roe v. Wade*. In response to a question from Committee Chairman Joseph Biden, Thomas respectfully declined to discuss the decision, as had Kennedy and Souter, since the issue might come before the Court in the future. Later, Senator Patrick Leahy pressed him. Since Thomas was a law student when the Court decided *Roe v. Wade*, Leahy assumed that Thomas had discussed the decision with other law students.

Actually, Thomas replied, he was so busy as a working married student that he really had no time for such discussions.

Well, Leahy said, he, too, had been married and working when he was in law school; nonetheless, he had found time to discuss important Supreme Court cases. Are you suggesting, asked Leahy, that you *never* discussed *Roe v. Wade*?

"Senator," Thomas replied, "I cannot remember personally engaging in those discussions."

Leahy stared in disbelief at the nominee, stretching out the most awkward moment of the interrogation. It was obvious that Thomas was determined to stonewall the committee on any questions that might force him to reveal an opinion on *Roe*. But in his brittle response, Thomas did not present himself as a nominee committed to judicious discretion so much as one who would defend his statements rather than risk a damaging concession. Throughout the questioning, Thomas maintained his minimalist strategy. "My motto is, 'Don't get mad, don't get even, get confirmed,'" Thomas would tell CIA Director-designate Robert Gates, when he, too, was undergoing a rough interrogation at his confirmation hearings.

In the end, Thomas's unimpressive performance produced a 7-to-7 tie on the committee. Six of the seven negative votes came from Democratic senators who had a year earlier voted in favor of the confirmation of David Souter. With the tie vote, the Senate Judiciary Committee could not recommend Thomas's confirmation to the full Senate.

While Clarence Thomas's nomination languished, the justices heard one last plea from Warren McCleskey. It came after the Georgia Board of Pardons and Paroles had listened to two jurors who had originally sentenced McCleskey to death and had changed their minds. Both said that they would not have voted to send the defendant to the electric chair had they known at the time that Offie Evans was a police informer who had been promised a lighter sentence for his incriminating statements about McCleskey. One of the jurors, Robert Burnette, a forty-nine-year-old postal worker, said the fact that Evans stood to gain by his incriminating statement would have changed his vote, had he been privy to that information at the time of McCleskey's sentencing. "I believe if you take a life, death is the right punishment," Burnette said after the parole board hearing. "But when you take that person's life you have to be sure beyond a shadow of a doubt that person committed the crime, and I don't feel that way about this case. If we knew more about Offie Evans, his credibility would have been shot to hell." A second juror, Jill Darmer, called the proceedings "an outrage."

Based primarily on the statements of Darmer and Burnette, McCleskey's attorneys argued before the parole board that the information withheld from the jurors had compromised the entire process; Warren McCleskey's execution should be stayed, they said, and his sentence commuted to life imprisonment. In further support of their plea, McCleskey's attorneys furnished the board with statements from prison clergymen and the condemned man's relatives that spoke of McCleskey as a model inmate who was deeply involved in the prison's religious programs.

Georgia's attorney general, Michael Bowers, was not impressed. "We had a young policeman in the flower of his life gunned down with no compunction whatsoever," said Bowers, "and now we hail this guy as the poster child for Amnesty International. It's ridiculous." Bowers told the parole board that jurors could not impeach their own verdicts. He urged the board to ignore the jurors' belated doubts and last-minute testimonials to McCleskey's good character and allow the state to proceed with the execution. The board ruled in Bowers's favor, and the scheduled execution continued on track.

McCleskey's attorneys immediately went to the federal district court to ask for a stay of McCleskey's scheduled execution, and the court granted the stay until 7:30 P.M., the evening of September 24,

1991. An emergency motion was subsequently filed with the justices of the Supreme Court to prevent Georgia from carrying out the death sentence on the grounds that the parole board had acted under the improper influence of Michael Bowers, the state attorney general.

After receiving McCleskey's emergency motion, Justice Anthony Kennedy wrote in a memorandum to his colleagues that "there is no substantial factual showing and no substantial legal basis for this claim." Kennedy voted to deny the motion for an emergency stay and "absent any different showing or new circumstances, I will vote to deny relief based on any further filings." A six-member Court majority supported Justice Kennedy's position (Justices Blackmun, Marshall and Stevens dissented).

Thurgood Marshall was still sitting on the Court when McCleskey's final plea came before the justices, since Judge Clarence Thomas's appointment had not yet been confirmed. In one of his last judicial pronouncements, Marshall offered a passionate plea for Warren McCleskey's life. His memorandum to his colleagues noted that he had long held the view that the death penalty was in all circumstances cruel and unusual punishment prohibited by the Eighth and Fourteenth amendments. Then Marshall assessed the McCleskey claim and concluded, as he had for many years, that the death penalty was imposed in a racially discriminatory fashion. Marshall wrote:

> For the third time, this Court disregards Warren McCleskey's constitutional claims. In 1986, McCleskey, an Afro-American defendant, presented uncontroverted evidence that Georgia murder defendants with white victims were more than four times as likely to receive the death sentence as were defendants with Afro-American victims. Despite such clear and convincing evidence of irrationality in sentencing—irrationality we have consistently condemned in our Eighth Amendment jurisprudence—the Court somehow rejected McCleskey's claim and upheld the constitutionality of Georgia's death penalty. See *McCleskey v. Kemp* (1987). Since then, the factual record has continued to show that the death penalty is not and cannot be administered fairly: white lives are routinely valued more than Afro-American lives.

Last term, the Court not only discounted Warren McCleskey's

constitutional claim but sharply limited the opportunity of criminal defendants, even those on death row, to obtain federal habeas review. See *McCleskey v. Zant* (1991). In radically redefining the content of the "abuse of the writ" doctrine, the Court repudiated a long line of judicial decisions and unconscionably denied defendants such as McCleskey the judicial protections the Constitution requires. The Court, in essence, valued finality over justice.

Now, in the final hours of his life, Warren McCleskey alleges that he was denied an impartial clemency hearing because the Attorney General threatened to "wage a full scale campaign to overhaul the pardons and paroles board" if the Board granted relief. McCleskey also alleges that to counteract this assault, the Board's chairman announced, even before the hearing, that there would be "no change" in McCleskey's sentence. In refusing to grant a stay to review fully McCleskey's claims, the Court values expediency over human life.

Repeatedly denying Warren McCleskey his constitutional rights is unacceptable. Executing him is inexcusable.

Warren McCleskey died in the electric chair in the early morning of September 25.

On Monday, October 7, one day before the Senate's scheduled vote on Judge Clarence Thomas's confirmation, Professor Anita Hill of the University of Oklahoma Law School called a press conference in Norman, Oklahoma, to declare that "the ugly issue" of sexual harassment by a nominee to the Supreme Court must be made public. Hill promised that she would cooperate with the Senate Judiciary Committee so that the American people would be given the full story.

With only two hours' sleep on Friday morning, October 11, Thomas prepared for a return appearance before the Judiciary Committee to deny Anita Hill's allegations that he had sexually harassed her while she worked for him at the Department of Education and EEOC in the early eighties.

Before the committee, with millions watching on television, Thomas issued an angry denial of the charges and a personal plea for an end to his ordeal: "I have never, in all my life, felt such hurt, such pain, such agony. My family and I have been done a grave and irreparable injustice." He denounced members of the media, who were tracking down every possible damaging rumor in his private and public life. "This is not America," he said. "This is Kafkaesque. It has to stop. It must stop for the benefit of future nominees and our country. Enough is enough."

After Thomas finished his testimony and responded to committee members' questions, Professor Anita Hill replaced the Court nominee at the witness table. Speaking in a flat, deliberate voice, Hill recounted the lurid details of her charges. Clarence Thomas had tried to date her, Hill said, after she joined his staff in 1981 at the Department of Education. She refused to go out with him and repeatedly turned down his requests for dates, even though she continued to work for him at the EEOC. Although Thomas never physically abused her, Hill testified, he subjected her to verbally debasing sexual conversations in his office. According to Hill, Thomas spoke to her suggestively about the size of his penis and about the exploits of a pornographic movie star, Long Dong Silver. He also described to her in vivid detail the sexual acts of women with wild beasts in pornographic films he had seen. Once when Hill was in his office, she said he suddenly looked up and exclaimed, "Who has put pubic hair on my Coke?"

For eight hours, Hill provided the committee with details of her charges of repeated acts of sexual harassment by the nominee. During the entire session, Hill maintained her composure, responding politely to all questions, including those from Republicans on the committee who attempted, with both subtle and bullying tactics, to destroy her character and her story. Hill was such an effective witness on her own behalf that Thomas returned to the Senate Caucus Room that evening to refute her charges.

This time, Thomas made no attempt to hide his rage, or his contempt for the Democrats on the committee: "This is a circus. It's a national disgrace and from my standpoint as a black American . . . it's a high-tech lynching for uppity blacks. It is a message that you will be lynched, destroyed, caricatured by a committee of the U.S. Senate rather than hung from a tree."

With his bald charges of racism, Thomas thoroughly intimidated the committee's Democrats. After his explosive statement, they poked gingerly around the circumference of his testimony denying Hill's charges, but they never forced him to defend the details of his statements. For his part, Senator Ted Kennedy, usually the most aggressive interrogator among liberals on the committee, was conspicuously quiet (Kennedy had his own problems with his role in accompanying his nephew, William Kennedy Smith, to a bar on the night that Smith was later accused of raping a woman he had met at the bar and who returned with him to the Kennedys' Palm Beach compound).

By the end of the extraordinary session, the Thomas-Hill hearings had secured a place in modern American political-legal folklore no less historic than two other events that had taken place in the same Senate Caucus Room: the 1954 Army-McCarthy hearings and the 1987 Bork confirmation hearings. There were, however, important differences. In both prior hearings, clear winners emerged—in 1954, a charming and very clever Boston lawyer named Joseph Welsh, and, in 1987, the liberal opponents of Judge Bork's confirmation. And there were also losers: after the 1954 hearings, Senator Joseph McCarthy never again was able to effectively stir the pot of anti-Communist hysteria; in 1987, Judge Bork never realized his ambition to sit on the Supreme Court.

After the Thomas-Hill hearings, both sides claimed victory, of course. But if the purpose of the hearings was to test the truth of Hill's charges, the committee and the nation were no closer to a conclusive judgment afterward than they had been before the session began. The debate has continued, however, with the publication of new analyses and investigations of Hill's charges. In the most objective recent work, Jane Mayer and Jill Abramson's *Strange Justice: The Selling of Clarence Thomas,* the authors report that the Senate Judiciary Committee refused to hear witnesses who could have corroborated Hill's story. Despite the failure of the committee to resolve the issue, Anita Hill did succeed in awakening Americans to the long-repressed secret of sexual harassment in the workplace, and her testimony made her a heroine of the women's movement. As for Clarence Thomas, after the second series of hearings were completed, the Senate confirmed him by a vote of 52 to 48, the narrowest margin for confirmation in Court history.

The October 1991 Court term had officially opened on the first Monday in October, but one member of the Court, Justice John Paul Stevens, still had some unfinished business from the October 1990 term to take care of. During the previous term, Stevens's dissents in the criminal law area had been uncharacteristically strident. Stevens had accused the Rehnquist Court majority, in one instance, of "unabashed judicial activism." His dissents that term were not the end of the argument, for Stevens had devoted part of the summer of 1991 to gathering his thoughts for a renewed attack on the conservative majority. Throughout the summer months, he faxed ideas to his law clerk, a few pages at a time, for an October 25 centennial keynote address at the University of Chicago's law school.

Wearing a dark suit and his trademark bow tie, Stevens opened his Chicago lecture innocently enough with a quotation from an obscure tax opinion written by Justice Oliver Wendell Holmes, Jr. "A word," wrote Holmes, "is the skin of a living thought." Stevens used the Holmes quote as his theme for a wide-ranging discussion of civil liberties—and a warning of the dangers presented by the conservative Rehnquist Court majority.

"As years pass, an idea may mature, changing its shape, its power, and its complexion, even while the symbols that identify it remain constant," Stevens observed. To make his point more vivid, Stevens invited his audience to travel in time and space—from the huge pillars of Stonehenge in prehistoric southern England to Gettysburg, Pennsylvania, where President Lincoln in 1863 called for a "new birth of freedom" and, finally, to the Supreme Court of the United States in 1991. Neither the primitive astronomers at Stonehenge nor the embattled Civil War president, Stevens said, could have known the full implications of their expression for later generations. So, too, the framers of the Bill of Rights and the Fourteenth Amendment could not have foreseen the essential dynamic quality of their words for twentieth-century America.

The term "liberty," as used in the Fourteenth Amendment's Due

Process Clause, possessed such a dynamic quality, said Stevens. It permitted the modern Court to expand on the constitutional concept far beyond anything conceived by the framers in 1868. Among other important contributions of the "liberty" clause, as Stevens referred to it, was the modern Court's recognition of a constitutional duty that required states as well as the federal government to treat criminal defendants fairly.

The aggressively conservative Rehnquist Court majority of the October 1990 term, Stevens asserted, had reneged on the promise of liberty guaranteed by the Bill of Rights and the Fourteenth Amendment. He then proceeded to list his grievances against the Court majority:

> The prosecutor's use of a coerced confession—no matter how vicious the police conduct may have been—may now constitute harmless error (*Arizona v. Fulminante*). In a totally unnecessary and unprecedented decision, the Court placed its stamp of approval on the use of victim impact evidence to facilitate the imposition of the death penalty (*Payne v. Tennessee*). The Court condoned the use of mandatory sentences that are manifestly and grossly disproportionate to the moral guilt of the offender (*Harmelin v. Michigan*). It broadened the powers of the police to invade the privacy of individual citizens and even to detain them without any finding of probable cause or reasonable suspicion. And, in perhaps its most blatant exercise of lawmaking power marching under the banner of federalism, it completely rewrote the procedural rules governing post-conviction proceedings to foreclose judicial review of even meritorious constitutional claims in capital cases (citing both *Coleman v. Thompson* and *McCleskey v. Zant*). . . .

"In this country, while dozens of universities throughout the land are celebrating the bicentennial of the Bill of Rights," Stevens observed, "an extraordinarily aggressive Supreme Court has reached out to announce a host of rules narrowing the Constitution's protection of civil liberties." Stevens deplored the Court's criminal law decisions in which, he asserted, the majority had "depreciated the value of liberty."

For Stevens to publicly vent his professional fury, as he did at the

University of Chicago, was highly unusual. Unfailingly polite to colleagues and clerks alike, Stevens had long been considered a maverick on the Court who did not garner the headlines, or votes, of a Rehnquist or a Brennan. But behind his mild demeanor lay a powerful and resourceful intellect which, when aroused, could command instant attention.

After President Gerald Ford's announcement in 1975 of the nomination of Judge John Paul Stevens of the U.S. Court of Appeals for the Seventh Circuit to replace the retiring Justice William O. Douglas, the immediate judicial line on the nominee was that he was smart, hardworking and noncontroversial, neither a partisan nor an ideologue. The profile seemed to meet President Ford's political needs. After his pardon of Richard Nixon, Ford could not risk being buffeted by criticism of his first Court nominee if he hoped to be successful in the 1976 presidential campaign. Stevens appeared made-to-presidential-order, as the media groped vainly for a firm ideological handle to attach to the nominee.

Stevens was born in 1920 into a prominent Chicago family that prospered in the insurance business and once owned a downtown hotel, which later became the Chicago Hilton. A brilliant student, Stevens graduated Phi Beta Kappa from the University of Chicago and first in his class from the Northwestern University Law School, where his grades were the highest then on record at the school. During World War II, Stevens served in the Pacific as an intelligence officer analyzing intercepted Japanese communications and was awarded the Bronze Star for his outstanding work.

After the war, Stevens clerked for Supreme Court Justice Wiley Rutledge, whose "ivory-tower jurisprudence" was dismissed as hopelessly naive by a later Court clerk, Bill Rehnquist. But Stevens came to respect and admire Justice Rutledge, who impressed his law clerk with his dedication, broad knowledge of the law and, most of all, determination to reach a fair result based on the facts of each case.

Justice Rutledge wrote unusually long opinions in the criminal procedure area, in part, Stevens observed, to assure himself that he had considered every argument advanced by the parties to the litigation. He was vigilant in spotting any procedural unfairness toward a criminal defendant. In one case, Justice Rutledge wrote an opinion declaring that the Illinois attorney general's technical objections had made the appeals process so complicated that he had undermined the defendant's constitutional rights. The approach was typical of Justice Rutledge, who became frustrated with overly technical legal obstacles that prevented what he considered a sensible and just result.

When he returned to Chicago after his judicial clerkship for Justice Rutledge, Stevens soon earned a reputation as a first-rate lawyer in his specialty of antitrust law. He also found the time for public service—as associate counsel for a congressional subcommittee studying monopolies and a member of the attorney general's National Committee to Study the Antitrust Laws. In 1969, he accepted the sensitive assignment of general counsel to a special Illinois Supreme Court commission that was investigating allegations of misconduct against two state supreme court justices. The investigation resulted in the resignation of the two justices, and public recognition of Stevens's scrupulously fair professional performance.

Appointed to the U.S. Court of Appeals for the Seventh Circuit in 1970, Stevens proved impossible to typecast ideologically. Judge Stevens demonstrated, nonetheless, a steady concern for fairness to defendants in criminal proceedings, reflecting Justice Rutledge's influence as well as his own conviction. In one opinion, Stevens reversed an Illinois corruption conviction—even though the evidence of guilt was strong and the crime reprehensible—because the procedure for conviction was not fair to the defendant. "This case brings to mind the trial of Titus Oates,* a guilty man who was convicted by improper means," Stevens wrote. "Macaulay's observation about that trial is worth repeating: 'That Oates was a bad man is not a sufficient excuse, for the guilty are almost always the first to suffer those hardships which are afterward used as precedents against the innocent.' "

---

* Oates was a seventeenth-century Church of England clergyman whose accusation that there was a papist plot to assassinate King Charles II led to the execution of a number of prominent English Catholics. Oates was later tried and convicted of perjury. He was fined, whipped, stripped of his clerical robes and sentenced to life imprisonment.

On the Supreme Court, Justice Stevens continued to confound the categorizers: early in his tenure, he rejected rigid quotas in civil rights cases. But Stevens always built his position from the ground up, concentrating on the facts and on constitutional doctrine relevant to the particular case. And these factors sometimes led him to a "liberal" conclusion, as happened in a 1987 Court decision in which he joined a Court majority that found that the goal of a more diverse workforce justified adoption of voluntary affirmative action plans even by employers with no history of discrimination. He approached each case with a fresh perspective and frequently produced the Court's most original opinions. In the 1989 *Webster* abortion decision, for example, Stevens alone wrote that the preamble of the Missouri law declaring that human life began at conception violated the First Amendment's prohibition against the establishment of religion.

For Stevens, the Rehnquist Court's determined proprosecution decisions had provoked alarm—first in his dissents in the spring of 1991 and six months later in his address at the University of Chicago. Unfortunately for Stevens, if there was to be movement on the Court during the October 1991 term, as he had urged in his Chicago address, it was not likely to be in Stevens's libertarian direction. In the same month that Stevens delivered his Chicago speech, Judge Clarence Thomas was confirmed by the Senate.

Like his predecessor Thurgood Marshall, Thomas brought to the Court the scars of racism. But that was where the similarities ended. Based upon his professional experiences, Marshall had urged a broad interpretation of the Bill of Rights and the Fourteenth Amendment that provided unprecedented protections for the poor and ignorant, the powerless in society. Thomas possessed a very different constitutional vision, one tightly controlled by his conservative values which, even in rudimentary judicial form, promised less "liberty" in Justice Stevens's terms and more "order" along the lines dictated by the criminal law decisions of the conservative Rehnquist Court majority.

Liberals looked anxiously for hopeful signs in Clarence Thomas's background or public statements. Dean Guido Calabresi of the Yale Law School, who had supported Thomas's confirmation, said that he

229

had found in his conversations with Thomas a sensitivity to the less fortunate. Calabresi, who described himself as a liberal, acknowledged that he did not agree with much that Thomas had written or said. "What matters most, though," Calabresi wrote, "is that, unlike many on the Court, he does know the deep need of the poor and especially poor blacks, and wants to help."

Others had been encouraged by Thomas's response at his confirmation hearings to a question from Senator Herbert Kohl. "I would like to ask you why you want this job," Kohl said. Thomas replied:

> It is an opportunity to serve, to give back. That has been something that has been important to me. And I believe, Senator, that I can make a contribution, that I can bring something different to the Court, that I can walk in the shoes of the people who are affected by what the Court does. You know, on my current court (the D.C. Court of Appeals), I have occasion to look out the window that faces C Street, and there are converted buses that bring in the criminal defendants to our criminal justice system, busload after busload. And I look out, and I say to myself almost every day, "But for the grace of God there go I."

On November 29, 1991, Chief Judge Emeritus A. Leon Higginbotham, Jr., of the U.S. Court of Appeals for the Third Circuit, a prominent black jurist, wrote Justice Thomas a letter that he made public, questioning how Thomas could be so ignorant of past civil rights leaders, such as Thurgood Marshall, and their struggles that had made both Higginbotham's and Thomas's professional successes possible. Higginbotham told Thomas that he had read virtually every article Thomas had published and every speech he had given. To his dismay, Higginbotham continued, "I could not find one shred of evidence suggesting an insightful understanding on your part of how the evolutionary movement of the Constitution and the work of civil rights organizations have benefitted you."

At the end of Higginbotham's letter in which he challenged the basic premises of Thomas's conservative ideology, Higginbotham looked to Thomas's future role on the Court: "I wonder whether (and how far) the majority of the Supreme Court will continue to retreat from protecting the rights of the poor, women, the disadvantaged minorities, and the powerless. And if, tragically, a majority of the Court continues to retreat, I wonder whether you, Justice Thomas, an African-American, will be part of that majority."

Four months after taking the oath of office, Justice Thomas began to furnish answers in the criminal law field to the questions that Higginbotham and others had asked. The Court had agreed to review the constitutional claim of Keith Hudson, a Louisiana prisoner who was shackled and beaten by two guards while their supervisor, who watched, warned them only against having "too much fun." A seven-member Court majority opinion written by Justice O'Connor ruled that the beating, which resulted in bruises, swelling and loosened teeth, violated the Eighth Amendment's prohibition against cruel and unusual punishment. "When prison officials maliciously and sadistically use force to cause harm, contemporary standards of decency always are violated," wrote O'Connor, and that was so even if there was no permanent injury (Hudson did not require medical attention).

In dissent, Justice Thomas, joined only by Antonin Scalia, waded into the O'Connor opinion, chiding the majority for converting the Bill of Rights into "a national code of prison regulation." Thomas wrote that neither the text nor history of the Eighth Amendment permitted the Court to indulge its contemporary humanitarian instincts. "Today's expansion of the cruel and unusual punishment clause beyond all bounds of history and precedent is, I suspect, yet another manifestation of the pervasive view that the Federal Constitution must address all ills in our society," Thomas wrote. The strong words, with more than a hint of a hard-drive conservative ideology behind them, were delivered by the justice who had told the Senate Judiciary Committee only six months earlier that, if confirmed, he would not bring to the justices' deliberations any preconceived views or ideology.

A second glaring discrepancy between the words of Justice-designate Thomas at his hearings in September 1991 and the opinions of Justice Thomas six months later concerned the doctrine of stare decisis. Respect for judicial precedent was important, Thomas had said. He had read someplace, Thomas had told the judiciary committee, that respect for precedent should be greater when property rights

231

were at issue than when personal rights were at stake. He said that he disagreed with that view of precedential values although he could not recall the source (it was Chief Justice Rehnquist's majority opinion in *Payne v. Tennessee*, the victim-impact statement decision announced the previous June). In the Louisiana prison-beating case, Justice Thomas urged the Court to discard precedents protecting personal rights that did not conform with an original understanding of constitutional intent.

Later during the term, Thomas again showed independence, rejecting the constitutional approach of his more moderate conservative colleagues like Justice O'Connor. O'Connor had written another opinion for a seven-member majority ruling that a state could not force a mentally ill defendant to accept antipsychotic medication during trial without an "overriding justification." Thomas, in dissent, saw nothing "fundamentally unfair" about forcing medication on a mental patient at trial. Any legal grievance that the inmate might have, Thomas suggested, could be pursued in a damage suit against prison officials.

In another decision announced the same day, the Court invalidated a Louisiana law that required inmates at a mental institution who had been found guilty of a crime by reason of insanity to remain in the institution until they could prove that they were no longer dangerous to themselves or others. Once an inmate was no longer mentally ill, the majority held, dangerousness alone was not a constitutionally adequate rationale for continued confinement. Thomas again dissented, declaring that removing formerly insane inmates from mental institutions "may make eminent sense as a policy matter," but it was not a permissible interpretation of the Due Process Clause, which "does not require the states to conform to the policy preferences of federal judges."

A 1993 Thomas opinion demonstrated that his outspoken conservative pronouncements in criminal justice cases were not a one-term phenomenon. In a Texas death penalty case, the Court turned down the appeal of a man convicted of committing a murder at the age of seventeen who claimed that the Texas death penalty law had not given the jury sufficient opportunity to consider youth as a factor mitigating against the death sentence. The five-member majority opinion was written by Justice White (and supported by the chief justice and Justices Kennedy, Scalia and Thomas), but Thomas filed a separate concurring opinion issuing a broad challenge to the modern Supreme Court's approach to the death penalty. In Thomas's view, the Court should abandon its current judicial position allowing defendants to present evidence of mitigating circumstances in death penalty cases. He preferred mandatory death penalty laws to eliminate possible irrational factors in the jury's judgment.

Those few people in whom Justice Thomas confides say that he still suffers from the humiliation of his Senate hearings. He is pleasant to his colleagues (and close, ideologically, to Justice Scalia), but is the least engaged of the nine members of the Court. He says little from the bench or in the justices' conferences. One member of the Court said that he did not know Thomas any better after serving with him for several terms than he did when Thomas first joined the Court. He is the least influential justice, increasingly isolated on the far right wing of the Court, with only Justice Scalia matching his conservative ardor.

Outside the Court, Thomas has given highly visible support to activist conservative political groups. In April 1993, for example, he made a brief but spirited appearance on satellite television to praise Paul Weyrich, founder of the conservative Heritage Foundation, whose Free Congress Foundation brings together groups to fight abortion and work for other conservative causes. He also presided at the wedding in his home of conservative talk-show host Rush Limbaugh.

For his hard-edged conservative judicial opinions, Thomas relies heavily on the work of his law clerks, who are reputed to be the most ardently conservative in the Supreme Court Building. Thomas has told friends that he intends to serve on the Court for precisely forty-three years, his age when he barely survived what he considered the unfair attacks on him by the liberal establishment.

PART IV

THE FIRST AMENDMENT

Because I believe the majority's view of the
Establishment Clause reflects an unjustified hostility
toward religion, a hostility inconsistent with both
history and precedent, I must dissent from this holding.

From the first draft of
JUSTICE ANTHONY KENNEDY'S opinion
(dissenting, in part) in *Allegheny County (Pa.) v.
Greater Pittsburgh Chapter of the American Civil
Liberties Union*, circulated on June 16, 1989

Although Justice Kennedy repeatedly accuses the
Court of harboring a "latent hostility" or "callous
indifference" toward religion, nothing could be further
from the truth, and the accusations could be said to be
as offensive as they are absurd.

From the second draft of
JUSTICE HARRY BLACKMUN'S
Court opinion in *Allegheny County (Pa.) v. Greater
Pittsburgh Chapter of the American Civil Liberties
Union*, circulated on June 26, 1989

CHAPTER 10

JEFFERSON'S WALL

During the twelve years that Ronald Reagan and George Bush occupied the White House, conservative politics were transformed into constitutional argument in an extraordinary number of civil liberties cases. Two of the most important and fiercely fought issues involved the religion and speech clauses of the First Amendment.* With First Amendment issues, as those in other civil liberties areas, the political agendas of Reagan and Bush were often linked with their Justice Department's constitutional challenges.

Although devotion to God and country had rarely become the political preserve of the presidential candidates of a single party, in the 1980s Republicans Reagan and Bush appeared to appropriate those attachments for themselves alone. They wooed conservative religious constituencies with vows to increase the presence of religion in public life. And they exuded patriotic fervor during the last days of the Cold War. Bush made patriotism a central theme of his 1988 negative

---

* The First Amendment provides: "Congress shall make no law respecting an establishment of religion, or prohibiting the free exercise thereof; or abridging the freedom of speech. . . ."

campaign, repeatedly impugning the loyalty of his opponent, Massachusetts Governor Michael Dukakis.

In the early months of 1989, both religion and patriotism were the focus of First Amendment arguments before the Rehnquist Court. In the first case, the outgoing Reagan Administration supported the contention of Allegheny County (Pennsylvania) that a government-sponsored holiday display, which included the Christian nativity scene, did not violate the First Amendment's prohibition against the government's establishment of religion. In supporting Allegheny County's argument, the Reagan Administration openly urged the Rehnquist Court to abandon a central premise of established modern Supreme Court precedents—that there must be a clear separation between church and state.

A month after oral argument in the Allegheny County case, the justices were asked to decide if the ceremonious burning of an American flag by Gregory "Joey" Johnson, a self-described revolutionary, was political expression protected by the Free Speech Clause of the First Amendment. Johnson had set fire to the flag in Dallas in 1984 as a protest against the "Rambo-mania" mentality of the Reagan Administration, while President Reagan, at another location in the city, was accepting his party's nomination for a second presidential term.

Both of those First Amendment cases, and others that the Rehnquist Court considered in later terms, deeply divided the justices. The turmoil generated by the challenges produced unpredictable results, with the final alignments sometimes far different from the justices' coalitions in abortion, capital punishment and civil rights decisions.

Chief Justice Rehnquist still anchored the right wing of the Court in the First Amendment area, as he had done in the other civil rights and civil liberties fields. Since joining the Court in 1972, Rehnquist had urged a more permissive view of government-sponsored religious displays and programs in public life, calling Thomas Jefferson's famous metaphor of a wall of separation between church and state under the First Amendment "misleading." He had rejected Jefferson's interpretation of the Establishment Clause and offered his own narrow reading of the First Amendment prohibition in a 1985 dissenting opinion, *Wallace v. Jaffree*, in which he declared that the framers' intentions were confined to prohibiting the establishment of a national church and the preference of one religious sect over another. As chief justice, he supported arguments in favor of government-sponsored crèche (the Christian nativity scene) displays, public school commencement prayers and a special school district drawn to accommodate an ultra-Orthodox Jewish community.

In First Amendment challenges to statutes that prohibited the burning of the American flag, Rehnquist contended that the government had the right to prevent the desecration of the flag, even if it was burned as an expression of political protest.

Just as consistent was Justice Brennan, who had served as the Court's liberal counterweight to the chief justice in the First Amendment cases, as he had in every other civil rights and civil liberties area. He was the Court's most outspoken separationist, insisting that Jefferson's wall between church and state remain impregnable. Brennan found that the crèche, as well as a Christmas tree and a Chanukah menorah, were religious symbols. These displays in downtown Pittsburgh violated the First Amendment's clause prohibiting the establishment of religion.

In two flag-burning cases, Brennan was no less vigilant in protecting symbolic expression under the First Amendment. In 1989, he wrote the Court's majority opinion in *Texas v. Johnson* declaring that political expression—even symbolic expression as detestable as the burning of the American flag—was protected by the First Amendment. With a carefully crafted opinion, Brennan was able to hold a tenuous majority. Among Brennan's supporters from conference to the final majority opinion was not only Justice Kennedy, but Justice Scalia.

The balance of power in both the church-state and political-expression cases did not reside with Rehnquist or Brennan, but with their colleagues who arranged themselves at various points along the Rehnquist-Brennan constitutional axis. In the 1989 challenge to Pittsburgh's holiday displays, *Allegheny County (Pa.) v. Greater Pittsburgh Chapter of the American Civil Liberties Union*, for example, the Court's crucial votes were cast by Blackmun and O'Connor, who were attacked from both the right and the left.

239

• • •

Every year for forty-five days during the holiday season, a crèche depicting the Christian nativity scene was placed on the Grand Staircase of the Allegheny County Courthouse, which was considered the main display and most public part of the courthouse. The manger in the display had at its crest an angel bearing a banner proclaiming GLORIA IN EXCELSIS DEO (GLORY TO GOD IN THE HIGHEST). The crèche was donated by the Holy Name Society, a Roman Catholic group.

A block away, a forty-five-foot decorated Christmas tree and an eighteen-foot Chanukah menorah stood outside a government building jointly owned by the City of Pittsburgh and Allegheny County. At the foot of the Christmas tree was a sign bearing the name of Pittsburgh's mayor and declaring the city's "salute to liberty." The city owned the Christmas tree; a Jewish group owned the menorah, but it was stored, erected and removed each year by the city.

The Greater Pittsburgh Chapter of the American Civil Liberties Union and seven Pittsburgh residents filed suit asking a federal court to stop the county from displaying the crèche and the city from exhibiting the Christmas tree and menorah on the grounds that the displays violated the Establishment Clause of the First Amendment (which the Supreme Court had applied to state governments under the Fourteenth Amendment).

A federal court judge denied the ACLU's motion, but later the Court of Appeals for the Third Circuit reversed the district court's judgment, holding that the displays were an impermissible governmental endorsement of Christianity and Judaism. The City of Pittsburgh and Allegheny County appealed to the Supreme Court. Charles Fried, President Reagan's solicitor general, joined in their appeal in an amicus brief.

Fried's brief offered legal support for the strong political views of the president, who had complained that for too long government-sponsored forms of religious expression had been prohibited. Just as he had made his opposition to the Court's abortion decision in *Roe v. Wade* a winning political issue, Reagan had found that his call for more government sponsorship of religion—endorsing public school prayer, for example—struck a resonant political chord. The president's theme was picked up by his attorney general, Ed Meese, who said that any government assistance to religion was constitutional so long as it did not establish a national church and did not favor one sect over another.

Solicitor General Fried, who had enthusiastically argued in favor of the Reagan Administration's position that *Roe v. Wade* should be overruled, took a more cautious approach to the Establishment Clause issue raised in *Allegheny*. Nonetheless, he left no doubt in his legal brief that the federal appeals court was wrong in forbidding the holiday displays. From the earliest days of the Republic to the present, Fried wrote, the federal government had recognized the central role that religion played in American life. Although he conceded that "Jefferson's celebrated reference to a 'wall of separation between church and state' may suggest that all governmental acknowledgments of religion must be condemned," Fried noted that the Supreme Court had never taken such a rigid separationist view.

What was forbidden under the Establishment Clause, Fried contended, were government practices that coerced religious orthodoxy or involved the government directly in religious exercises (daily Bible reading in public schools, for example). But allowing Allegheny County and the City of Pittsburgh to participate in holiday celebrations with religious as well as secular meaning, Fried argued, was well within the permissible boundaries of the First Amendment.

On February 22, 1989, attorney Peter Buscemi addressed the justices of the Supreme Court on behalf of Allegheny County and the City of Pittsburgh. He immediately called the Court's attention to its five-year-old decision in *Lynch v. Donnelly*. In *Lynch*, the Court had found the Pawtucket, Rhode Island, Christmas display (including a crèche) constitutional. The Rhode Island display, Buscemi reminded the justices, contained "a rather large nativity scene with figures as big as five-feet-tall." Later in his argument, Buscemi stressed that the Court in *Lynch* had viewed the crèche in the larger context of a holiday display.

If a Catholic mass were held in Pittsburgh's City-County Building as an additional way to celebrate the holiday season, would that violate the Establishment Clause? asked O'Connor.

"I think that probably tests the limits of the Court's decision in *Lynch*," Buscemi responded, "but I would say that would be appropriate as long as it were a noncoercive ceremony. That is, it did not involve any compulsion and it did not involve anything more than a de minimis expenditure of public funds."

Buscemi argued that the nativity scene in the Allegheny County Courthouse as well as the Christmas tree and menorah displays were "passive symbols," and could not be considered coercive.

"Are all symbols passive?" Kennedy asked Buscemi. "Would a cross be passive? Or a swastika, which brings forth powerful emotions?"

"Yes, I think the symbol itself is a passive device," Buscemi replied, although he later conceded that a symbol that dominated a community (a large cross permanently erected on a city's tallest building, for example) might be different. But in the case before the Court, Buscemi insisted, the displays were passive symbols. And he reiterated a point that had been made in Solicitor General Charles Fried's brief: the prohibitions of the Establishment Clause were confined either to "government coercion or adherence to particular religious beliefs or government use of public funds to establish and support a church." He added, "I think we have to recognize that we're on the periphery of what the framers sought to address in the Establishment Clause in the first place."

Roslyn M. Litman, who represented the American Civil Liberties Union in the *Allegheny* argument before the Court, challenged the picture that Buscemi had drawn of an inconspicuous, inoffensive nativity scene in the Allegheny County Courthouse. The crèche was placed in the most beautiful and most public area of the courthouse, she said, and it profoundly affected the feelings of non-Christians. Addressing a critical point that Justice O'Connor had made in her *Lynch* concurrence, Litman argued that Allegheny County's crèche sent the message to non-Christians that they were outsiders in the political community. If that were true, O'Connor's *Lynch* test would make it unconstitutional. Litman referred to a Jewish law clerk to a judge who had offices in the Allegheny County Courthouse. He had testified at the trial in *Allegheny* that he had to pass the nativity scene many times a day and "that looking at the scene evoked in him a memory of when his people in the middle ages were persecuted and forced to live in ghettos."

"The two displays [the crèche, and the Christmas tree and menorah] are somewhat different, aren't they, Mrs. Litman?" Justice Blackmun inquired.

They are different displays, Litman responded, but she said that the ACLU took the position that both were unconstitutional under the Establishment Clause.

"From your point of view," Blackmun said, "the county one [the crèche] is easier, isn't it?"

Litman conceded that the crèche "could be considered to be an easier one in one sense"—that the potency of the religious message, as attested to by the Jewish law clerk, was unmistakable.

"Mrs. Litman, does the government have a duty to accommodate religion?" Justice Kennedy asked.

"I believe that it does, Justice Kennedy," she replied. "But in this case one of the critical factors is that we don't have accommodation."

"Well, I understand," Kennedy said. "But at some point that certainly precludes the appearance of hostility to religion, does it not?"

"I think clearly that it does," Litman replied.

Kennedy pursued the point that the government risked showing hostility to religion if it were to "purge" religious symbols. "Suppose that government officials at the Inauguration left during the invocation that preceded the presidential inaugural," Kennedy offered. "Should government officials have left? Or perhaps sat down while everybody else was standing up?"

Litman conceded that in both of Kennedy's hypotheticals government officials, who also had free-exercise rights under the First Amendment, were not required to take such drastic action. But she distinguished Kennedy's hypothetical examples from the facts in *Allegheny*.

"What makes this case easy is that there is no tension between free exercise and establishment [under the First Amendment]. In this case, this is not accommodation. This is promotion. This is not neutrality. This is favoritism."

In preparation for the *Allegheny* case, Justice Brennan's law clerk wrote a two-page memorandum which supported Brennan's separationist position. The first task in order to achieve victory, Brennan's law clerk suggested, was to distinguish *Allegheny* from *Lynch v. Donnelly*, where the five-member Court majority had found the Pawtucket, Rhode Island, display of a crèche constitutional, and Brennan could only dissent. To this end, Brennan's clerk wrote in his memorandum that the crèche displayed in the Allegheny County Courthouse, unlike the one in Pawtucket, Rhode Island, was located in the most prominent place of the county government's main office building. The Pawtucket crèche was located in a private park in the city's commercial district. And the Allegheny County crèche was unadorned by holiday decorations and other nonreligious trappings, another factor distinguishing the case from *Lynch*. The message of the Allegheny County crèche "was unquestionably one of endorsement of a Christian religious celebration in its religious dimension by county government," the memorandum concluded.

The Christmas tree–menorah display was different but no less unconstitutional, the clerk's memorandum continued, because the two symbols, taken together, showed government's endorsement of Judeo-Christian beliefs. The easiest way to make the point was to ask if Allegheny County and the City of Pittsburgh, in celebrating the holiday season of all religions, would have honored a request for the city to mount eighteen-foot photos of the Ayatollah Khomeini and the Reverend Moon on the face of the seat of government. "My guess is that the city would call off the whole display so fast it would make your head spin," the memo suggested. "And why is that? It can only be because the city believes—and rightly so—that citizens will regard a display affixed to the government's main official building as an endorsement of the beliefs and values associated with that display."

Rehnquist opened the justices' conference on February 24, 1989, by strongly endorsing the position taken by Peter Buscemi and

Charles Fried. *Allegheny* gave the justices the opportunity to expand on the *Lynch* doctrine. "I follow *Lynch* that Christmas is a general, not a special Christian holiday," Rehnquist told his colleagues in conference. The First Amendment "was not offended" by the special attention given to Christmas by the holiday displays.

White agreed with the chief justice, and so did Scalia, saying that the First Amendment did not prohibit the state from celebrating Christmas. Kennedy, who had been active in oral argument in asserting an accommodationist position, expressed a conviction that government could not be hostile to religion. The government, Kennedy said, "surely can accommodate religious beliefs."

Both holiday displays, Brennan said, plainly violated the Establishment Clause. The crèche was located in the most prominent place in the county government's main office building; the message sent to non-Christians by the crèche was unequivocally one of endorsement of a Christian religious celebration. As to the Christmas tree and menorah displays, he contended that the tree and menorah standing together conveyed a clear religious message.

Justice Marshall's support of Brennan's view was never in doubt; he had always taken a position of absolute separation between church and state. Every Christmas season, Marshall reminded Chief Justice Rehnquist of that position by declining the chief's invitation to participate in a Court-sponsored Christmas party. "As usual, I will *not* attend the Christmas Party but I will pay my share of the bill," Marshall wrote Rehnquist in a typical annual note. "I still believe in the separation of church and state."

Justice John Paul Stevens gave Brennan a third vote in *Allegheny*. He, too, had long taken the position that the Establishment Clause prohibited any government-sponsored support for religion. In conference, Stevens admitted that *Lynch* (in which he dissented) was a hard case. The crèche, Stevens said, was different from other Christmas symbols: "It has a real religious message." The Court must exercise judgment on the basis of fact and with the crèche display, Stevens said, "the religious message is just too strong." He voted to affirm the appellate court's decision on both displays. As to the Christmas tree–menorah display, unlike the crèche, Stevens said that he would emphasize that the framers intended to prohibit support of "multiple establishments," i.e., more than one religion.

The *Allegheny* conference produced two surprise votes, one from the moderately conservative O'Connor, and the other from the usually liberal Blackmun. O'Connor, who had supported the Court's decision in *Lynch*, though not the broad endorsement of government's accommodation of religion in Chief Justice Burger's majority opinion, said that the crèche display in *Allegheny* should be distinguished from that in *Lynch*. The Pittsburgh nativity scene, unlike Pawtucket, Rhode Island's, O'Connor noted, was located in a government building where the public engaged in official business. That put it over the constitutional line, in her view. The Christmas tree–menorah display was "tougher," O'Connor said, but she voted to affirm the appellate court's decision in that case as well. That made four justices (Rehnquist, White, Scalia and Kennedy) in favor of upholding the constitutionality of both holiday displays and four (Brennan, Marshall, Stevens and O'Connor) who said that both were unconstitutional.

Justice Blackmun cast the pivotal votes in both cases—and split the difference between the contending Court factions. At conference, Blackmun accepted the Court's holding in *Lynch* (although he had been in dissent) on its narrow facts, i.e., that a crèche display surrounded by nonreligious symbols in a private park was constitutional. But, he added, "that doesn't mean that *Lynch* controls this case." Blackmun contended that *Lynch* relied on the overall "secular thrust" of the Pawtucket display (which included, besides a crèche, a Santa Claus, reindeer and a Christmas tree). In *Allegheny*, the crèche stood by itself and was not part of a larger holiday display. To Blackmun, that difference was critical, as he had suggested to the ACLU's Litman at the *Allegheny* oral argument. He would affirm the appellate court's judgment that the display of the nativity scene was unconstitutional. As to the exhibit of the Christmas tree and menorah, Blackmun regarded "the mixed display as saying 'believe as you will.'" He therefore voted to reverse the lower appellate court decision in the second case. Since he held the key vote in both cases, Blackmun was assigned to write the majority opinion.

· · ·

Three months later, Blackmun circulated a thirty-page first draft of his *Allegheny* opinion, with an apology for the large number of footnotes. "Usually, to quote W. Churchill," Blackmun wrote his colleagues wryly, "that many [footnotes] is something up with which I usually do not put." (Justice Stevens would respond in kind: "Assuming that severe criticism is something up with which you are able to put," Stevens wrote, "I offer you these comments.")

The Blackmun draft contained fifty-nine footnotes, and more than half (thirty-two) dealt with the history and symbols of the Christmas and Chanukah celebrations. Blackmun's extensive discussion of Christmas and Chanukah in both his narrative and footnotes was, it soon became apparent, more than a purely academic exercise. For in *Allegheny*, Blackmun considered the historical significance of the holidays and the context in which the holiday symbols were displayed essential to the Court's judgments.

Having laid the foundation for his constitutional analysis, Blackmun addressed the relevant principles of the First Amendment's Establishment Clause. He quoted Justice Hugo Black's "often-repeated summary" of modern Establishment Clause doctrine in the 1947 Court decision in *Everson v. Board of Education*. In *Everson*, Black had set out in broad, declarative sentences what the First Amendment's Establishment Clause demanded:

The "establishment of religion" clause of the First Amendment means at least this: Neither a state nor the Federal Government can set up a church. Neither can pass laws which aid one religion, aid all religions, or prefer one religion over another. Neither can force nor influence a person to go or to remain away from church against his will or force him to profess a belief or disbelief in any religion. No person can be punished for entertaining or professing religious beliefs or disbeliefs, for church attendance or non-attendance. No tax in any amount, large or small, can be levied to support any religious activities or institutions, whatever they may be called, or whatever form they may adopt to teach or practice religion. Neither a state nor the Federal Government can, openly or secretly, participate in the affairs of any religious organizations or groups and vice versa. In the words of Jefferson, the clause against establishment of

247

religion by law was intended to erect "a wall of separation between Church and State."

Blackmun also cited the Court's decision in *McCollum v. Board of Education*, decided a year after *Everson*. Black again wrote the majority opinion, which found unconstitutional a religious instruction program in Champaign, Illinois, conducted in public school buildings during regular school hours. Illinois had provided an invaluable aid to sectarian groups, Black wrote, by offering classes teaching religious doctrine in tax-supported school buildings during compulsory public school hours. "This is not separation of Church and State," Black concluded. Justice Felix Frankfurter, usually at odds with Black in First Amendment cases, concurred in *McCollum*, declaring that "[s]eparation means separation, not something less. Jefferson's metaphor in describing the relation between Church and State speaks of a 'wall of separation,' not of a fine line easily overstepped."

The Warren Court's controversial 1962 decision, *Engel v. Vitale*, which struck down New York's Regents' Prayer ("Almighty God, we acknowledge our dependence upon Thee, and we beg Thy blessings upon us, our parents, our teachers and our Country"), was also cited by Blackmun. In *Engel*, Black had written that the Establishment Clause's "most immediate purpose rested on the belief that a union of government and religion tends to destroy government and to degrade religion." Black, who had been a Baptist Sunday school teacher for many years, declared that religion was "too personal, too sacred, too holy to permit its unhallowed perversion by a civil magistrate."

In his *Allegheny* draft, Blackmun acknowledged the Burger Court's so-called *Lemon* test (announced in *Lemon v. Kurtzman*) providing that a law was constitutional if (1) its purpose is secular, (2) its primary effect is neither to advance nor inhibit religion, and (3) there is no excessive entanglement between government and religious institutions. But Blackmun wrote that the *Lemon* test had been refined by later decisions in which the Court had "paid particularly close attention to whether the challenged governmental practice either has the purpose or effect of 'endorsing' religion, a concern that has long had a place in our Establishment Clause jurisprudence."

Blackmun then confronted the Court's 1984 *Lynch* decision in which Chief Justice Burger's majority opinion had declared that the Establishment Clause "affirmatively mandates accommodation, not merely tolerance, of all religions." Burger's opinion had also dismissed Jefferson's metaphor of a wall of separation between church and state as "a useful figure of speech" but "not a wholly accurate description of the practical aspects of the relationship that, in fact, exists between church and state." Blackmun rejected Burger's analysis and charged that his majority opinion was confusing, and offered no guidelines for the Court to decide which displays were permissible and which were not. Nowhere in Burger's majority opinion, Blackmun observed, had the chief justice explained why the Pawtucket crèche display was of only "indirect, remote and incidental" benefit to religion.

Having discarded Burger's *Lynch* opinion, Blackmun supported what he considered the more persuasive concurrence written by Justice O'Connor, which had declared that government could not appear to endorse religion. Embracing O'Connor's endorsement standard, Blackmun wrote that the First Amendment prohibited "government from appearing to take a position on questions of religious belief, or [quoting O'Connor] 'making adherence to a religion relevant in any way to a person's standing in the political community.' "

Blackmun then buttressed his view that O'Connor's Lynch concurrence ought to serve as the Court's standard, noting approvingly that it "squarely rejects any notion that this Court will tolerate some Government endorsement of religion." O'Connor's opinion, not Burger's, Blackmun wrote, "articulates a method for determining whether the government's use of an object with religious meaning has the effect of endorsing religion."

Edging slowly closer to the *Allegheny* cases, Blackmun contended that the answer to the question of whether a holiday display was constitutional depended upon the message that the government's practice communicated. The critical question, for First Amendment purposes, Blackmun wrote, was how those who viewed the display would understand its purpose—and that, in turn, depended upon the context in which the display appeared.

At last, Blackmun applied his constitutional analysis to the facts of *Allegheny*. The Pittsburgh crèche display, unlike that in Pawtucket, Rhode Island, violated the First Amendment because the nativity scene was unadorned by secular symbols. No one could mistake the religious message conveyed in the Pittsburgh crèche display since, above the figures of Mary, Joseph and the baby Jesus, was written GLORY TO GOD IN THE HIGHEST (because of the birth of Jesus).

Applying O'Connor's standard to the menorah case, Blackmun arrived at a different conclusion. The display of the Chanukah menorah did not carry the same unadulterated religious message as the crèche. Placing the menorah in the overall context of the holiday display, Blackmun concluded that the Jewish symbol for the Festival of Lights could be fairly interpreted by onlookers as secular. He was reassured in this conclusion, Blackmun wrote, by the fact that a Christmas tree stood adjacent to the menorah. The Christmas tree, Blackmun wrote, was acknowledged by the Court as having a secular, as well as a religious, connotation. The mayor of Pittsburgh's holiday greeting, a salute to liberty, sealed Blackmun's conclusion that the three displays—the menorah, the Christmas tree and the mayor's salute to liberty—communicated a secular message.

In the covering memorandum that Blackmun circulated with this first draft on May 30, 1989, he attempted to lighten the mood with a reminder to his colleagues, "The holidays are less than seven months away!" That cheerful note did nothing to dissipate the anger of Justice Anthony Kennedy.

In his first full year on the Court, Tony Kennedy had proved a vocal exception to the unwritten rule that a junior justice approaches his new job with a quiet deference to his senior colleagues. The late Justice Potter Stewart once described the awe that he felt when he first worked with his new colleagues, Justices Black and Frankfurter. It was difficult to forget, said Stewart, that not so many years earlier, he had studied Black and Frankfurter opinions when he was a law student. But in 1958, the year Stewart was appointed to the Court at the age of forty-three, he was suddenly confronted with the disconcerting realization that these same justices were now his colleagues.

His first anxiety attacks, Stewart recalled, occurred at the early conferences. The modest Stewart could not force himself to extend a casual "Hello, Hugo" or "Hello, Felix" salutation; but he knew a "Justice Black" or "Justice Frankfurter" was now inappropriate. So what did he call Black and Frankfurter in his early days on the Court? "I didn't call them anything," Stewart recalled with a smile.

Tony Kennedy had no such freshman jitters. Warm and outwardly self-assured, Kennedy was quickly on a first-name basis with his senior colleagues. But beyond the informality of his collegial exchanges, Kennedy put the brethren on notice that he did not consider his junior status an impediment to speaking his mind—and crossing sharp verbal swords—when he deemed it necessary. Kennedy's exchanges with the Court's senior justice, William J. Brennan, Jr., in the racial harassment case *Patterson v. McLean Credit Union* had dispelled any doubts on that score.

Now, less than a month after he had challenged Brennan in *Patterson*, Kennedy announced his intention in the first draft of his *Allegheny* opinion to take on a second member of the Court's diminishing liberal wing, Justice Harry Blackmun. Kennedy had already expressed indignant displeasure with Blackmun's civil rights opinions in *Croson* and *Wards Cove*, which, Kennedy suggested in his unpublished *Patterson* footnote, had unfairly and self-righteously questioned the conservative majority's commitment to equal justice for blacks. In *Allegheny*, Kennedy prepared a second tongue-lashing for Blackmun.

In his twenty-four-page written response to Blackmun's first draft, which was circulated on June 16, Kennedy accused Blackmun of disregarding precedent and historical fact in an approach that "threatens to trivialize constitutional adjudication." According to Kennedy, Blackmun had misrepresented the Court's sound majority opinion in *Lynch*, and replaced it with a "jurisprudence of minutiae." While he admitted that his analysis of Blackmun's test might appear "uncharitable," Kennedy suggested that Blackmun's opinion left him little choice. Noting that Blackmun had distinguished *Lynch* from *Allegheny* by their factual settings, so that the constitutionality of a display would turn on the surroundings, Kennedy wrote in a sarcastic aside, "After

251

today's opinion, municipal greenery must be used with care."

What had really set Kennedy off was Blackmun's audacious discarding of Chief Justice Burger's majority opinion in *Lynch* as the Court's analytical framework in Establishment Clause cases, in favor of Justice O'Connor's concurrence. Both Kennedy and Blackmun knew that the effect of abandoning Burger's *Lynch* analysis was to weaken the conservatives' determinedly narrow view of what was prohibited government activity under the Establishment Clause. Since *Lynch* was a precedent that supported his own accommodation approach, Kennedy was not eager to give it up. "As a general rule, the principle of *stare decisis* directs us to adhere not only to the holdings of our prior cases," Kennedy lectured Blackmun, "but also to their explications of the governing rules of law." It was a lesson that the Court's conservatives did not always adhere to when liberal precedents were at risk, as their votes in abortion and death penalty cases had demonstrated. But in *Allegheny*, Kennedy, later joined by Rehnquist, Scalia and White, rebuked Blackmun for rejecting Burger's *Lynch* majority opinion. Kennedy also accused Blackmun in his opinion of showing "an unjustified hostility toward religion, a hostility inconsistent with both history and precedent."

But Kennedy's rendering of history and precedent exhibited a selective appreciation of both. His narrative did not contain a single reference to the constitutional history of the First Amendment's Establishment Clause. James Madison's writings were covered in one sentence (quoted from a secondary source, a 1961 Court opinion). Jefferson was accorded a footnote, and only to show him to be an exception to the rule that Kennedy wanted to emphasize: since George Washington, the nation's presidents have acknowledged in their Thanksgiving proclamations the important role that religion has played in American society. Kennedy's point was that the Court should be guided by traditional practices of the federal government in illuminating the meaning of the Establishment Clause. He referred to the practice of a chaplain reciting a prayer in Congress at the time the Bill of Rights was passed. He quoted from Washington's Thanksgiving Proclamation, Franklin Roosevelt's recommendation that there be a nationwide reading of the Holy Scriptures, and the Reverend Billy Graham's 1989 invocation at President George Bush's inauguration

("We acknowledge Thy divine help in the selection of our leadership each four years").

As to judicial precedents, Justice Kennedy put Chief Justice Burger's majority opinion in *Lynch v. Donnelly* at the top of his list; Burger's *Lynch* opinion was repeatedly cited. Indeed, the single greatest influence on the First Amendment's Establishment Clause jurisprudence emerging from Kennedy's opinion was not Madison or Jefferson, Black or Frankfurter, but former Chief Justice Warren Burger. Kennedy devoted more lines to quotations from Burger's Establishment Clause opinions than to any other justice in Court history. Besides quoting from Burger's *Lynch* opinion, Kennedy gave prominent notice to *Marsh v. Chambers*, the chief justice's 1983 majority opinion that sanctioned a chaplain's prayer in the Nebraska legislature. In contrast to the generous sprinkling of Burger quotations, Kennedy gave less than two full lines to *Everson* and none to the majority opinions in *McCollum* and *Engel v. Vitale*—the modern Court's three most explicit declarations that the justices were obligated to maintain a separation between church and state.

Kennedy concluded that the Court's duty in its interpretation of the Establishment Clause was to permit government "some latitude in recognizing and accommodating the central role religion plays in our society." Anything less, Kennedy declared, "would border on latent hostility toward religion, as it would require government in all its multifaceted roles to acknowledge only the secular, to the exclusion and so to the detriment of the religious."

Having framed the constitutional question favorably to government-sponsored holiday displays, Kennedy had no trouble in finding both the crèche and the menorah and Christmas tree displays in Pittsburgh well within acceptable constitutional boundaries. Applying the standard urged upon the Court by Allegheny County's attorney at oral argument, Kennedy wrote that "government may not *coerce* anyone to support or participate in any religion or its exercise."* He found no such coercion in either challenged display in *Allegheny*; after all, Kennedy observed, passersby were free to ignore the displays. "Ab-

---

* Kennedy posited a second standard—government could not give direct benefits to religion that established, or tended to establish, a state religion—and found no such violation in *Allegheny*.

sent coercion," Kennedy wrote, "the risk of infringement of religious liberty by passive or symbolic accommodation is minimal."

Justice Harry Blackmun had always been a loner and a bit of an enigma to his colleagues. One colleague privately noted with bemusement that Blackmun spent much of his time in the Court library doing his own detailed research. While other justices delegated that burdensome task to law clerks, Blackmun did not, even checking most legal citations himself. His chambers were among the quietest in the building, though the justice showed an endearing warmth to his clerks, with whom he ate breakfast every weekday morning in the Court cafeteria.

Among his colleagues, Blackmun could reveal a mischievous sense of humor. Once, when he realized that the chief justice and all of his colleagues who were senior to him were out of town, "Acting Chief Justice" Blackmun wrote a memorandum to the brethren announcing new Court policies which included "striking some [cases] as too difficult to decide, setting July and August argument sessions, closing the building now for a week or two, scheduling square dancing in the Great Hall (of the Court building), and obtaining a Court cat to chase down the mice and 'Boris' who, I am told, is the rat upstairs. . . ."

But for most of the long hours, seven days a week, that Harry Blackmun spent on his job, he was all business. And when his professional work product was denigrated, as Kennedy had done in his *Allegheny* draft, Blackmun fought back with a vengeance. "Tony's writing requires a response," Blackmun tersely wrote his colleagues on June 26, 1989, and "this is it." He attached a second draft of his *Allegheny* opinion, which had increased to more than forty pages.

"Although Justice Kennedy repeatedly accuses the Court of harboring a 'latent hostility' or 'callous indifference' toward religion," Blackmun wrote in his second draft, "nothing could be further from the truth, and the accusations could be said to be as offensive as they are absurd. Justice Kennedy apparently has misperceived a respect for religious pluralism, a respect commanded by the Constitution, as hostility or indifference to religion. No misperception could be more antithetical to the values embodied in the Establishment Clause."

Blackmun noted that Kennedy had written that there would be a First Amendment violation if a large Latin cross were erected permanently on the roof of city hall. By what criteria did Kennedy arrive at that conclusion? he asked. "If one wished to be 'uncharitable' to Justice Kennedy," Blackmun wrote, "one could say that his methodology requires counting the number of days during which the government displays Christian symbols and subtracting from this the number of days during which non-Christian symbols are displayed, divided by the number of different non-Christian religions represented in these displays, and then somehow factoring into this equation the prominence of the display's location and the degree to which each symbol possesses an inherently proselytizing quality." To Kennedy's charge that Blackmun had engaged in "an Orwellian rewriting of history," Blackmun replied that Kennedy was using "Orwellian newspeak."

Blackmun concluded that Kennedy's "proselytization" test was an ill-conceived attempt to lower the level of scrutiny that the Court was required to apply to government-sponsored religious displays.

The sparring between Blackmun and Kennedy continued through two more rounds of drafts but, finally, on July 3, Blackmun announced the *Allegheny* decision for a splintered Court.* Kennedy's unusually caustic opinion attacking Blackmun's Establishment Clause analysis was joined by Rehnquist, White and Scalia.

A split decision on the Court rarely satisfies anyone in the audience and *Allegheny* was no exception. For Michael Novak, director of social and political studies at the conservative American Enterprise Institute, the Court's "alienating" message was that the government of the United States was secular—"Jews and Christians stay home." A more liberal *Washington Post* editorial viewed the *Allegheny* decision nervously as an indication of another civil liberties area where the Court "seems to be embarked on a U-turn."

---

* Besides Blackmun's Court opinion and Kennedy's dissent (on the nativity scene display), Justice O'Connor wrote a concurrence (having changed her vote on the Christmas tree–menorah issue after Blackmun had circulated his opinion supporting her endorsement standard in *Lynch*), and Justices Brennan and Stevens wrote opinions that concurred on the nativity scene display but dissented on the Christmas tree–menorah display.

No one, least of all Kennedy, seemed to consider the Blackmun opinion in *Allegheny* to be the Court's final word on Establishment Clause doctrine. In his opinion, Kennedy suggested that a rematch might be imminent. "[S]ubstantial revision [in a future decision] of our Establishment Clause doctrine," he wrote, "may be in order."

CHAPTER 11

"AMERICA, THE RED, WHITE AND BLUE, WE SPIT ON YOU"

On March 21, 1989, one month after the justices heard oral arguments in *Allegheny*, they listened to arguments in a second difficult First Amendment case, *Texas v. Johnson*, in which they were asked whether there are limits to the First Amendment's speech protections when they collide with Americans' need to honor the flag. Like many earlier First Amendment challenges, this case had been provoked by a political radical, Gregory "Joey" Johnson.

In the summer of 1984, President Ronald Reagan and Maoist Joey Johnson both had dates in Dallas for the Republican National Convention, the president to accept his party's nomination for a second term, Johnson to lead a protest against the Reagan Administration. While the president was listening to encomiums to his conservative Administration, Joey Johnson and his small band of fellow revolutionaries rampaged through downtown Dallas, spray-painting obscenities before collapsing in a "die-in" heap. One of the demonstrators stole an American flag from the Mercantile Bank Building and handed it to Johnson, who doused it with lighter fluid and set it afire in front of the Dallas City Hall to the chant, "America, the red, white and blue, we spit on you."

Daniel Walker, a West Point graduate and Korean War veteran, fought back tears as he watched the flag burn. Afterward, Walker collected the ashes and returned to his home in Fort Worth, where he buried them in his backyard.

Dallas police arrested Johnson as the leader of the demonstration and charged him with violation of a Texas statute that made it illegal to desecrate the American flag. Johnson was convicted in a state court, fined $2,000, and sentenced to one year in prison, but worked in a Houston warehouse while his lawyer successfully appealed his conviction to the Texas Criminal Court of Appeals. In a 5-to-4 ruling, the Texas appellate court overturned the conviction, declaring that Johnson, in burning the American flag, had been exercising his First Amendment right to "symbolic speech." The State of Texas appealed the decision to the Supreme Court. In agreeing to hear arguments in *Texas v. Johnson*, the justices offered the nation the first opportunity to learn how the Rehnquist Court would define the limits of political dissent.

The most noteworthy quality of the legal brief written by attorney David Cole of New York's Center for Constitutional Rights on behalf of Joey Johnson was the lean, muscular narrative. There was no scent of rhetoric, no trace of ideology. Cole's understated tone was somewhat surprising, since his commitment to liberal causes was well documented in his work for the activist Center. He had, for example, successfully attacked U.S. Information Agency regulations as an unconstitutional burden on documentary filmmaking and had forced the U.S. Customs Service to cease intelligence-gathering operations against citizens returning from Nicaragua. But in his Supreme Court brief, Cole chose to record the facts surrounding Johnson's arrest on August 22, 1984, in Dallas without embellishment and guide the reader for thirty-four pages through an unemotional, detailed analysis of the Texas statute and U.S. constitutional law. Cole's analysis, naturally, led to the conclusion that the Texas statute under which Joey Johnson was convicted was a violation of his free-speech rights guaranteed by the First Amendment, applicable to the states through the Fourteenth Amendment.

At the outset, Cole wanted to establish that Johnson was engaged in political expression when he was arrested for burning the American flag. He emphasized that Johnson and his fellow demonstrators had carefully planned a political protest at the Republican Convention, and that the Dallas police had received advance notice of their intentions. The wild spree through corporate office buildings, the "die-in" and the burning of the American flag were all part of a political protest against the policies of the Republican Party and the U.S. government. Cole noted that the flag-burning was peaceful and led to no violence (an effort to undermine Texas's argument that its statute was justified as a measure to prevent breach of the peace).

After quoting from the decision of the Texas Criminal Court of Appeals ("Recognizing that the right to differ is the center-piece of our First Amendment freedoms, a government cannot mandate by fiat a feeling of unity in its citizens"), Cole raised the constitutional issue on his terms: "This case presents the question whether, consistent with the First and Fourteenth Amendments to the United States Constitution, a state can criminally convict a person of peacefully burning a flag in an overtly political demonstration under a statute that hinges punishment on the act's communicative effect on third persons 'likely to observe or discover' it." Having asked the question, Cole answered: the Texas statute was unconstitutional on its face and as it applied to Joey Johnson.

Cole conceded that desecration of the American flag "stirs strong emotions precisely because of the flag's unique symbolic power." But he reminded the justices that the Court in 1943 in *West Virginia Board of Education v. Barnette* had struck down a public school requirement that students salute the flag as a violation of the First Amendment. In the Court's *Barnette* opinion, Justice Robert Jackson wrote that the First Amendment had long stood for the proposition that "freedom to differ is not limited to things that do not matter much. . . . The test of its substance is the right to differ as to things that touch the heart of the existing order." The Texas statute, Cole asserted, collided with *Barnette*, since it was not directed at the physical protection of the American flag but the communicative effect of its burning. As evidence of the statute's intent, Cole wrote in his brief, only flag-burning that "seriously offends" was punished. But the Supreme Court, under *Barnette*, had insisted that government could not impose a particular point of view but, rather, must exhibit "viewpoint neutrality." In later cases, the Court had reinforced the First Amendment protection by rejecting the notion that there could be a "heckler's veto" of a speaker by an offended bystander.

For the Court's proponents of "original intent"—i.e., what was intended by the framers—Cole noted that flag-desecration statutes were unknown to the framers and that, prior to 1896, no state compelled respect for the American flag through legislation. For historians, Cole pointed out that the first American flag was designed "not as the quasi-sacred symbol of national unity that Texas describes," but merely as a protective signal that the four vessels of the infant American Navy were not pirate ships.

In *Barnette*, the Supreme Court had recognized that a primary purpose of the First Amendment's protection of speech was to prevent government from forcing respect for its authority by prohibiting dissent. A chilling example of governmental abuse when there were no civil liberties protections, Cole wrote in a footnote, was Germany's pre–World War II flag-desecration statutes, which were broadened under Hitler to punish by imprisonment anyone who profaned the German Nationalist Socialist Workers' Party, or its banners, insignias or decorations.

Cole considered the two justifications that Texas had put forward in defense of its desecration statute: preserving the flag as a symbol of national unity and preventing breaches of the peace. Preserving the flag as a symbol of nationhood had never been accepted as "compelling" (the highest standard of proof, since First Amendment rights were at stake) by the Supreme Court, Cole wrote. In addition to *Barnette*, he cited the 1969 decision *Street v. New York*. The Court in *Street* overturned on First Amendment free-speech grounds the conviction of Sidney Street, a black man who, while publicly burning an American flag after hearing a radio report that civil rights leader James Meredith had been shot, said, "If they let that happen to Meredith, we don't need an American flag."

But even if Texas could show that preservation of the flag as a symbol of national unity was a compelling interest, Cole argued that the state had not demonstrated that that interest was endangered by the flag-burning in Dallas. "People choose to burn the flag to express dissent precisely because it is such a powerful symbol," Cole wrote. The physical burning of the flag could not make its symbolic value disappear.

As to the second stated justification for the Texas statute, preventing breaches of the peace, Cole argued that the Texas law was not carefully drafted for that purpose. It was, first of all, too vague—how could the state determine what was "seriously offensive" as opposed, say, to merely "offensive"? Cole also contended that the statute was too broad. The statute prohibited "all physical mistreatment" of the flag, Cole noted. If the rules for proper treatment of the flag under the U.S. Code were fully enforced, Texas would be obligated to prosecute anyone who displayed the flag in inclement weather, hoisted it slowly rather than "briskly" or placed the flag to the right of a public speaker.

Cole did not end his brief, as he might have, with a stirring quotation from a judicial opinion of Justices Holmes, Brandeis or Black, exalting the high place that free speech commands in a free society. Instead, Cole's last paragraph was written in the same methodical tone as the first thirty-three pages of the brief and, he hoped, would lead the Court to his conclusion: under a long line of Supreme Court precedents, Joey Johnson's conviction for flag-burning must be overturned and the Texas statute be declared unconstitutional.

Attorney William M. Kunstler, who, like David Cole, was also affiliated with the Center for Constitutional Rights, had accepted Joey Johnson's invitation to argue his case before the Rehnquist Court. At the age of seventy, Bill Kunstler was still the nation's premier "movement" lawyer, eager to defend radical cause or client, the more despicable in the public's eye, the better. A graduate of Yale College and the Columbia Law School, Kunstler had abandoned a conventional law practice in New York City in the early 1960s to defend black civil rights leaders, not just the revered Reverend Martin Luther King, but young militants like H. Rap Brown and Stokely Carmichael. When the protests turned from civil rights to Vietnam and became increasingly ugly and violent, Kunstler was still at the ramparts. After the tumultuous 1968 Democratic National Convention in Chicago, Kunstler defended the so-called Chicago Seven (which included a wide range of political dissidents, from the yippie Abbie Hoffman to Black Panther Bobby Seale to old-time pacifist David Dellinger), who were charged with conspiracy to overthrow the government. By the 1980s, Kunstler had replaced his past civil rights clients with a different kind of defendant, mostly young blacks accused of serious crimes.

Joey Johnson had told Kunstler that he did not want him to take the venerated libertarian position, what Kunstler termed "the stinking fish" approach to the First Amendment—"I may detest what you say, but I will defend to the death your right to say it." Johnson insisted that Kunstler promise to defend his radical cause not just in the Supreme Court, but also at political rallies that Johnson had lined up before the oral argument.

As promised, Kunstler accompanied Joey Johnson to a rally at a small park across the street from the Supreme Court Building on March 21, 1989, the day that Kunstler was later scheduled to argue *Texas v. Johnson*. Joey harangued the crowd about the corruption of American society, and Kunstler's longtime colleague Professor Arthur Kinoy of the Rutgers Law School spoke of the importance of dissent in the United States. When it was his turn to speak, Kunstler unleashed a broad attack on what he termed "the Gang of Five" on the Supreme Court, the emerging five-member conservative majority (Rehnquist, Scalia, O'Connor, Kennedy and White) that he accused of ignoring basic civil liberties.

Despite his angry denunciation of the Court's conservatives, Kunstler was convinced that he would win his case by a comfortable margin in the Supreme Court. His prediction: "Nine–nothing: win." The reason for his extreme confidence, he later suggested, was that the Court precedents blew only in his direction.

Had Kunstler been more attentive to the nuances in some of the Court's past decisions, he might not have felt so confident. In the Court's 1969 decision, *Street v. New York*, for example, the Court majority had ruled on extremely narrow grounds—that it was impossible to know if Sidney Street had been arrested for the words he expressed while burning the American flag, or for the burning alone. The majority clearly stated that Street's words—"If they let that happen to Meredith, we don't need an American flag"—were protected under the First Amendment. But that same majority was silent on the issue of whether flag-burning alone was protected, and it was that issue that was presented in *Texas v. Johnson.*

Kunstler might also have worried that three members of the Supreme Court had dissented in *Spence v. Washington,* a 1974 decision in which the majority held that a student at the University of Washington could not be convicted of improperly using the American flag after he taped a peace symbol on a flag that he had hung from his apartment window. Two of the *Spence* dissenters were still on the Court in 1989 and one of them had been elevated to chief justice. In his dissenting opinion in *Spence,* Rehnquist, supported by Justice Byron White, had written: "The Court [majority] demonstrates a total misunderstanding of the state's interest in the integrity of the American flag. . . . The true nature of the state's interest in this case is not only one of preserving 'the physical integrity of the flag' but also one of preserving the flag as 'an important symbol of nationhood and unity.' "

Even the vote of Justice John Paul Stevens, increasingly recorded on the liberal side of the Court in civil liberties matters, could not be taken for granted. Like Rehnquist and White, Stevens was a World War II veteran whose feelings for his country and its national symbol, the American flag, were deep. Did preservation of the American flag present an exception to the First Amendment's protection of political expression by dissidents such as Joey Johnson? Texas's argument would not be lightly dismissed by a majority on the Rehnquist Court, certainly not without a closer constitutional analysis than Bill Kunstler thought necessary.

After lunch on March 21, Kathi Alyce Drew, the assistant district attorney for Dallas County, Texas, rose to address the Court in *Texas v. Johnson.* Before her dialogue with the justices began, Drew made a surprising concession to her adversary. "For purposes of this argument today and with the Court's indulgence," Drew said, "the state will assume the symbolic speech standard and proceed directly to the question of Texas's compelling interest in regulating this type of conduct."

Drew's concession was an unexpected gift to Kunstler. He had been prepared to devote a considerable amount of his time at oral argument, as David Cole had done in his brief, to establishing the fact that Joey Johnson's flag-burning was political expression protected by the First Amendment. Once Johnson's flag-burning was accepted as political expression, the government would have to meet the highest constitutional standard of justification for its statute: that its interest was "compelling."

Drew told the justices that Texas's statute was justified in the interests of preventing the breach of the peace and preserving the American flag as a symbol of nationhood and national unity. She began with the second justification. "We feel very certain that Congress has the power to both adopt a national symbol and to take steps to prevent the destruction of that symbol," Drew said.

Justice Scalia immediately interrupted. "Now why did the defendant's actions here destroy the symbol?" Scalia asked. "His actions would have been useless unless the flag was a very good symbol for what he intended to show contempt for. His action does not make it any less a symbol."

"Your honor," Drew replied, "we believe that if a symbol over a period of time is ignored or abused that it can, in fact, lose its symbolic effect."

"I think not at all," Scalia retorted. "I think when somebody does that to the flag, the flag becomes even more a symbol of the country."

And then Scalia indulged his habit, often to the intense displeasure of his colleagues, of taking over the oral argument. "I mean, it seems to me you're running quite a different argument, not that he's destroying its symbolic character, but that he is showing disrespect for it, that you do not just want a symbol, but you want a venerated symbol, and you don't make that argument because then you're getting into a sort of content preference. But I don't see how you can argue that he's making it any less of a symbol than it was."

Scalia had leaped several furlongs ahead of Drew's argument and, in the process, decimated, at least in his view, her first contention— that the flag-burning destroyed the national symbol. Before he was finished, Scalia had also considered a second argument, and rejected it—that the statute's purpose was to preserve respect for the flag— even before the Dallas assistant district attorney had had the chance to catch her breath.

Finally, Scalia allowed Drew to reply, and she did so cautiously but in the only way that she could. "Your Honor," she said to Scalia, "I'm forced to disagree with you. . . ."

"All right," said Scalia.

"Because," continued Drew, "I believe that every desecration of the flag carried out in the manner that he [Johnson] did here—and certainly I don't think there can be any question that Mr. Johnson is a hard-core violator of this statute—if his actions in this case under the facts of this case do not constitute flag desecration, then I really am not quite certain what would constitute flag desecration."

Scalia pressed his original point. "They desecrate the flag, indeed, but do they destroy the symbol?" he asked. "Do they make it any less symbolic of the country? That's the argument I thought you were running, that we have a right to have a national symbol. And if you let the people desecrate the flag, you don't have a national symbol. I don't see how that follows."

With characteristic ebullience, and confidence, Scalia jumped to a second argument that Drew might make—before she could open her mouth. "We may not have a respected national symbol, but that's a different argument. Now if you want to run that argument, that we have the right to insist upon respect for the flag, that's a different argument."

"Texas is not suggesting that we can insist on respect," Drew responded. "We are suggesting that we have the right to preserve the physical integrity of the flag so that it may serve as a symbol, because its symbolic effect is diluted by certain flagrant public acts of flag desecration."

Chief Justice Rehnquist rescued Drew by suggesting to the Texas attorney, as well as to his colleagues, a more persuasive response to

Scalia's attack. "Well, in a sense you're arguing a minimal form of re-spect for the flag, aren't you," Rehnquist said, offering Drew a more defensible position for her constitutional argument than she had put forward. "Not that you have to take your hat off or salute when it goes by. Now, the state can't require that of you—but at least can it insist that you not destroy it?"

Just as Justice Scalia seemed to bound ahead of Ms. Drew, so, too, did Rehnquist, but in a different direction. The chief justice had al-ready anticipated the effect that the Court's *Barnette* decision, which struck down a public school's compulsory flag-salute requirement, would have on his colleagues' thinking. For Rehnquist, there was a vast difference, and a constitutional distinction to be made, between a government's forcing a citizen to actively show obeisance to a national symbol (ruled out in *Barnette*) and requiring restraint from doing something, like burning the American flag.

Drew eagerly pursued the chief justice's line of thought: "Yes, Your Honor. To the extent that we are asking for any respect for the flag, we are asking for respect for its physical integrity. Certainly we do not demand that any individual view it with any discernible emotion whatsoever, only that its physical integrity be respected. And I think that that is a very minimal basis to ask from any individual."

But unfortunately for Drew, Justices Kennedy and O'Connor did not pick up on the chief justice's argument as readily as they did on Justice Scalia's. Justice Kennedy suggested that other respected sym-bols, such as the Latin cross, survived without legislation. Although he conceded the distinction between the cross, a religious symbol, and the American flag, Kennedy made the point that "it may be that you can protect symbols by public respect and by measures other than the imposition of the criminal law."

Justice O'Connor also confronted Drew with a hypothetical that suggested that she was skeptical of Texas's argument. Could Texas prohibit the burning of a copy of the Constitution? O'Connor asked Drew. No, replied Drew, but she distinguished Constitution-burning from flag-burning without explaining the reason for the distinction.

Virtually all of Drew's time was devoted to her argument, and the justices' questions, on the government's authority to preserve the integrity of the American flag as a symbol of nationhood.

"What is the juridical category you're asking us to adopt in order to say we can punish this kind of speech?" Kennedy asked. Just an exception for flags? Is there a flag exception to the First Amendment?

When Kathi Drew sat down, it looked as if Bill Kunstler could rest his case without uttering a word. He could reasonably assume that the most liberal members of the Court—Justices Brennan, Blackmun, Marshall and, possibly, Stevens—would support his argument. And on the basis of the justices' questioning of Drew, it also seemed reasonable to anticipate the support of at least one, and perhaps as many as three, of President Reagan's appointees—Scalia, O'Connor and Kennedy.

Kunstler's manner contrasted sharply with that of Kathi Drew, who had appeared nervous and defensive throughout her presentation. Kunstler greeted the justices with outward confidence and the relaxed informality of an attorney who had argued more than his share of celebrated lawsuits. But soon enough, he was put on notice that several members of the Court, beginning with the chief justice, were not prepared to concede his case.

With David Cole's brief serving as the foundation for his argument, Kunstler invoked the authority of *Barnette* for the constitutional proposition that the government could not coerce patriotism.

The chief justice interrupted. "Well, the facts of *West Virginia v. Barnette* were quite different," Rehnquist said. "There the students were required to salute the flag."

"And here, Chief Justice," Kunstler replied, "people are required not to do something."

"Yes," Rehnquist said, expectantly.

"And I think that's a comparable situation," Kunstler continued. "We can't order you to salute the flag. . . . Can we order you not to do something about the flag?"

Kunstler had asked the question as if his answer—that the two were comparable—was obvious. But the chief justice did not agree. "Well, to me, they're quite different," said Rehnquist. "You could say that if you can't do one, you can't do the other. But it seems to me one could quite easily say you can't do one, but you can do the other."

Kunstler attempted to bolster his argument, as Cole had done in the brief, by citing *Street v. New York.* Kunstler suggested that *Barnette*, in which students were required to salute the flag, and *Street*, where the petitioner had burned the flag, were analogous. "I think they're the same, in all due deference," Kunstler said to the chief justice. But when prompted by the chief, the attorney admitted that the precise holding in *Street* could be distinguished from *Barnette.* Still, he held to the analogy. "I don't know if I've convinced you," Kunstler added lightheartedly.

Rehnquist was satisfied that his point had been made. "Well, you may have convinced others," he said, provoking laughter throughout the courtroom.

The chief continued his Socratic dialogue with Kunstler as if they were in a law school classroom. Did Kunstler remember the Court's decision in a case challenging the requirement that residents of New Hampshire display the words LIVE FREE OR DIE on their license plates?

Kunstler recalled the decision.

In that decision, the chief justice reminded the attorney, the Court held that New Hampshire could not require a resident to display LIVE FREE OR DIE on the license plate. But certainly, the chief said, New Hampshire could have prevented a resident from making statements on his license plate. The ruling in the New Hampshire case, the chief justice argued, was consistent with *Barnette.* "The reasoning of the Court [in *Wooley v. Maynard*, the New Hampshire decision] was that you can't require someone to make an affirmation," Rehnquist said. "To me, that's *West Virginia v. Barnette.* But if someone applied for a New Hampshire license plate that has a lot of foul language on it, very likely that limited thing can be proscribed."

Kunstler responded by arguing that the petitioners who had painted out LIVE FREE OR DIE on their New Hampshire license plates were in the analogous position of Joey Johnson. "They burned the flag, in essence."

A skeptical chief justice peered down at Kunstler, who said, jokingly, "I don't think we're going to see eye-to-eye on this."

Joking aside, the chief justice had suggested a constitutional interpretation that could lead his colleagues away from *Barnette* and the powerful argument that First Amendment considerations trump the government's authority to insist on protection of the American flag. Typically, Rehnquist had made his point, as he often did in conference, on technical judicial grounds. There was no hint of his earlier stated aversion to radical dissenters. (In the late 1960s, for example, Rehnquist characterized dissenters on college campuses as "the new barbarians.")

Before he finished his questioning of Kunstler, Rehnquist had raised another constitutional issue—the Court's recognition of an exception to the First Amendment's speech protection, known as the "fighting words" doctrine.* If flag-burning was the equivalent of "fighting words," police were justified in arresting the person whose expression could have made the crowd uncontrollable. Kunstler later said in an interview that he thought the chief's point was "esoteric."

After his dialogue with the chief justice, Kunstler was challenged from an unexpected source. Stevens wanted to know if it was ever appropriate for the government to regulate the display of the American flag in public places. Kunstler's response was first to distinguish ordinary regulations from those, like Texas's, that carried criminal sanctions. Then he offered a casual aside to show the transitory nature of flag regulations. "It used to be you couldn't fly the flag at night," he said. "Now you can fly it if it's illuminated, and so on."

Kunstler's digression made Stevens impatient. "Do you think the federal government has any power at all to regulate how this flag is displayed in public places?" he asked.

"I don't think so," Kunstler replied.

"There's no state interest whatsoever?" Stevens pressed.

"I don't see any state interest whatsoever."

"I feel quite differently," said Stevens.

At that moment, Kunstler knew "that [he] didn't have Stevens." But he still thought it was going to be 6 to 3 or 7 to 2.

• • •

---

* The Court in a 1942 decision, *Chaplinsky v. New Hampshire*, defined "fighting words" as "those which by their very utterance inflict injury or tend to incite an immediate breach of the peace."

Three days after the oral argument, the justices met in judicial conference to discuss the case. The chief justice spoke first and said that he still held to the position that he had taken in his dissenting opinion in *Spence v. Washington*: the Texas statute should be declared constitutional. "Flag-burning and fighting words may be punished constitutionally," he concluded.

Brennan disagreed, saying that he would vote to affirm the Texas Criminal Court of Appeals decision that had ruled the Texas statute unconstitutional. *Texas v. Johnson* was a classic case of political speech being punished solely because it might bring offense to third parties. At bottom, Brennan believed that Texas's argument rested on the idea that the government may punish those who show disrespect for the flag and who might offend others by doing so. But the Court had repeatedly declared that speech could not be restricted solely because of its communicative impact.

White supported the chief justice. "To affirm [the Texas Criminal Court of Appeals decision] runs the First Amendment into the ground," White said.

Marshall agreed with Brennan and voted to affirm the Texas appeals court decision.

This was an "emotional case," Justice Blackmun remarked. But Johnson's flag-burning was "expressive conduct," protected by the First Amendment, he said, and argued that the Court's *Spence* decision (which struck down the conviction of the student who had superimposed a taped peace symbol on the flag) "governs here." Even apart from *Spence*, Blackmun maintained that "First Amendment law requires affirmance" (of the Texas Court of Appeals decision).

Stevens had not wanted the Court to take the case in the first place, and had earlier voted to deny review. The Court's First Amendment jurisprudence was better left undisturbed by a case like *Texas v. Johnson*, which provoked such strong feelings, he believed. At the conference, Stevens was uncharacteristically tentative: he wanted to pass without registering a formal vote. If he had to take a position at conference on the merits, Stevens said, he would prefer to overturn the Texas statute on grounds of "vagueness." He contended that Johnson was not being punished for his message but rather his manner of communicating it. Still, he did not record a formal vote at conference.

O'Connor appeared to be firmly in the Brennan camp. She said, according to one set of notes taken at the conference, "Even though our cases require affirming the lower court decision, the state says to carve out an exception." She concluded, "This is core speech for political purposes." Despite her strong words in support of Johnson's argument, O'Connor told her colleagues that her vote to affirm the Texas Criminal Court of Appeals decision was still tentative. She would make a final decision after reading the circulated opinions.

Both Justices Scalia and Kennedy said that they agreed with the free-speech position that Justice O'Connor had stated, and would affirm the lower court ruling declaring the Texas statute unconstitutional.

It seemed, therefore, that Kunstler would win the case, possibly by the comfortable margin of 7 to 2, assuming Stevens would strike the Texas statute on "vagueness" grounds.

Given the Court's current unsettled atmosphere, with justices switching votes in several fields, and its complicated history in cases involving the clash between civil liberties and patriotism, Justice Brennan approached his task of writing the majority opinion in *Texas v. Johnson* cautiously. He could anticipate an unflinching opinion from the chief justice defending the government's right to protect the American flag. Justice White had made it clear that he would support the chief. Both O'Connor and Stevens had appeared to lean Brennan's way at conference, but none too confidently; Brennan could not depend on their votes.

Without a doubt, Marshall's vote was secure. But a second usually reliable liberal justice, Blackmun, voiced uneasiness about the case in a note to Brennan. "I struggled with this difficult and distasteful little (big?) case," he wrote Brennan three months after the justices' conference. Still, he held to the position he had taken in conference.

Justice Scalia was never cursed by Blackmun's doubts. He had conducted a dialogue with himself at the oral argument, and resolved the issue to his complete satisfaction. In his conservative jurisprudential universe, he simply could not find a principled basis for supporting the government.

Brennan needed the vote of one more justice to assure his victory: Tony Kennedy, who had infuriated Brennan by abandoning him in *Patterson v. McLean* earlier that term. In *Patterson*, Kennedy had switched his vote several months after contributing the fifth vote to Brennan's majority in conference, depriving Brennan of a major triumph in the civil rights field. If Kennedy changed his vote again, he might deliver a second devastating defeat to Brennan in the equally critical area of free expression.

Brennan had good reason, then, to draft a narrow opinion, sticking closely to the facts and the favorable constitutional precedents. In his first *Johnson* draft, which he circulated on June 4, 1989, he recited the facts and the holding of the Texas Criminal Court of Appeals decision with great care. Joey Johnson, alone among the demonstrators in Dallas, had been arrested for burning the American flag. The highest criminal court in the state of Texas had concluded that Johnson's flag-burning was political expression. The Supreme Court of the United States had decided in *West Virginia Board of Education v. Barnette* (relied on by the Texas appellate court) that such political expression was constitutionally protected, even when it was directed at a venerable national symbol.

Once he established that Johnson's act was political expression, Brennan focused on the Texas statute, which, he maintained, was designed to curb such content-based expression. That contention allowed Brennan to insist that Texas meet the highest constitutional test—that the government's objective must be "compelling" and its regulations necessary to achieve its goal—to justify its statute. Brennan first considered the state's argument that the statute's objective to prevent a breach of the peace was a compelling interest. Pointing out that the peace had not been disturbed by Johnson's act, Brennan declared that the state could not arrest someone for merely offending a bystander, as the Texas statute permitted. It was true, as Rehnquist had stated in judicial conference, that the Court had made a constitutional exception for "fighting words." But here Johnson's expression of political protest was not "a direct personal insult or an invitation to exchange fisticuffs." More generally, this was not expression likely to incite "imminent lawless action," the standard that the modern

Supreme Court in a 1969 decision, *Brandenburg v. Ohio*, had required for government to suppress speech.

The second defense by the State of Texas, and the one that Brennan knew would be more difficult to overcome among his colleagues, was that the American flag was a unique symbol of nationhood. In a word, the flag was different from all else (including a copy of the Constitution) and deserved special consideration. The flag was a unique symbol for the nation, it was argued, and its protection superseded any First Amendment prohibitions.

But the flag as a symbol was not destroyed, Brennan wrote, even if it was burned. He built on the point made by David Cole in his brief, as well as by Justice Scalia at oral argument, but went further: "We are tempted to say, in fact, that the flag's deservedly cherished place in our community will be strengthened, not weakened, by our holding today. Our decision is a reaffirmation of the principles of freedom and inclusiveness that the flag best reflects, and of the conviction that our toleration of criticism such as Johnson's is a sign and source of our strength."

Only in a single paragraph toward the end of his draft opinion did Brennan engage in a little patriotic flag-waving of his own. "We can imagine no more appropriate response to burning a flag than waving one's own, no better way to counter a flag-burner's message than by saluting the flag that burns, no surer means of preserving the dignity even of the flag that burned than by—as one witness here did—according its remains a respectful burial. We do not consecrate the flag by punishing its desecration, for in doing so we dilute the freedom that this cherished emblem represents."

On June 5, the day after Brennan circulated his first draft, Justice Anthony Kennedy formally endorsed it. For Kennedy, *Texas v. Johnson* contained a bald challenge to free expression guaranteed by the First Amendment. It was, therefore, unlike the task of interpreting a congressional statute, such as the Civil Rights Act of 1866, that had caused him to change his mind in *Patterson v. McLean*. In *Johnson*, there was not the problem of deciphering the intentions of the legislature. Here the justices were charged with interpreting the meaning of the First Amendment, and for that task they alone were held constitutionally responsible. Blackmun, Marshall and Scalia also formally joined Brennan's opinion, giving him the necessary five votes for a majority. He needed every vote, since both O'Connor and Stevens ultimately joined the original dissenters, Rehnquist and White, in concluding that the Texas statute was constitutional.

Kennedy spent a weekend drafting a concurrence in which he reaffirmed, in even more dramatic language than Brennan's, the five-member Court majority's conclusion:

> Though symbols often are what we ourselves make of them, the flag is constant in expressing beliefs that Americans share, beliefs in law and peace and that freedom which sustains the human spirit. The case here today forces recognition of the costs to which those beliefs commit us. It is poignant but fundamental that the flag protects those who hold it in contempt.
>
> For all the record shows, this respondent was not a philosopher and perhaps did not even possess the ability to comprehend how repellent his statements must be to the Republic itself. But whether or not he could appreciate the enormity of the offense he gave, the fact remains that his acts were speech, in both the technical and the fundamental meaning of the Constitution. So I agree with the Court that he must go free.

The chief justice bristled at what he termed the "patronizing civics lecture" in Brennan's majority opinion but then, in his dissent, he offered one of his own, filled with literary references to Old Glory. He began with Ralph Waldo Emerson's "Concord Hymn" ("By the rude bridge that arched the flood / Their flag to April's breeze unfurled / Here once the embattled farmers stood / And fired the shot heard round the world"). He also recited "The Star-Spangled Banner" in its entirety, and he quoted verbatim John Greenleaf Whittier's sixty-line Civil War poem, "Barbara Frietchie" (which included the line, " 'Shoot if you must, This old grey head, But spare your country's flag,' she said"). He recalled the brave Continental Army near Boston in 1776 and the bloody horrors of the Civil War; he mourned the tragedies and celebrated the glories of Americans in twentieth-century conflicts from World War I to Vietnam.

Besides offering an emotional defense of patriotism, Rehnquist provided an elaborate technical argument: the Court was justified in suspending the protections of the First Amendment when the American flag was burned. He ignored *Barnette*, but distinguished other unfavorable precedents, including *Street* (the Court, he noted, did not decide the flag-burning issue) and *Spence v. Washington* ("Unlike the instant case, there was no risk of a breach of the peace, no one other than the arresting officers saw the flag, and the defendant owned the flag in question"). He also cited approvingly Chief Justice Earl Warren's dissent in *Street* (Warren had declared that the government had the right to protect the American flag "from acts of desecration and disgrace").

For Rehnquist, it was inconceivable that "the government may conscript men into the Armed Forces where they must fight and perhaps die for the flag, but the government may not prohibit the public burning of the banner under which they fight."

Rehnquist lost the judicial battle, 5 to 4. But in the summer of 1989, it looked as if Rehnquist's words might well inspire victory in a larger political war. By a vote of 97 to 3, the U.S. Senate passed a resolution expressing "profound disappointment" with the Court's ruling in *Texas v. Johnson*. One of the three senators to question the majority was Republican Gordon J. Humphrey of New Hampshire, who called the vote "an exercise in silliness [and] hypocrisy." Members of the House offered a flurry of patriotic speeches and denunciations of the Court's decision. Invoking the memory of the six Marines who raised the American flag on Iwo Jima, Montana Republican Representative Ron Marlenee said, "Yesterday these six brave soldiers were symbolically shot in the back by five men in black robes."

At the White House, President Bush was asked about the Court's decision. "I have to give you my personal emotional response," Bush said. "Flag burning is wrong, dead wrong." A day later, in a hastily planned ceremony at the foot of the Iwo Jima Marine Monument, the president announced his support for a constitutional amendment that would outlaw flag-burning, and reverse the Court's decision in *Texas v. Johnson*.

CHAPTER TWELVE

HISTORY LESSONS

President George Bush's call for a constitutional amendment to override the Supreme Court's decision in *Texas v. Johnson* brought constitutional scholars from both sides of the ideological aisle to Capitol Hill to testify before the Senate Judiciary Committee on the wisdom of the president's proposal and an alternative proposal for a federal flag-desecration statute.

At the invitation of the committee, Robert Bork, the judge who had failed to win confirmation for the Supreme Court two years earlier, warned the Senate against half measures. Noting the two solutions that had been proposed to reverse *Texas v. Johnson*—one the proposed constitutional amendment, the other a congressional statute— Bork endorsed the constitutional amendment. "If anything at all is to be accomplished, it must be by amendment," he testified. "No statute will accomplish anything other than delay."

Bork told the committee that the Court's decision in *Texas v. Johnson* was wrong and then put forward the opinion that "probably no other Supreme Court in our history would have reached [the *Johnson* decision]." Bork told the senators not to worry about "tampering" with the Constitution. A constitutional amendment would not under-mine the Constitution, but would only reverse a bad Court decision "that a switch in just one vote would have caused to go the other way." Bork did not need to complete the thought out loud: if the Senate had confirmed Judge Robert Bork for a seat on the Supreme Court, the *Johnson* decision would have been 5 to 4 in favor of upholding the Texas flag-desecration statute, and there would have been no need for his testimony in the summer of 1989.

Prominent liberal constitutional scholars like Harvard Law Profes-sor Laurence Tribe and Professor Walter Dellinger of the Duke Law School, who testified before the Senate committee, opposed the con-stitutional amendment as a dangerous threat to the First Amendment. But they suggested that a carefully drafted, content-neutral statute might be constitutional. Legislation might be drafted, Dellinger testi-fied, that could eliminate the constitutional problem that the Court majority uncovered in *Johnson* if the statute did not punish the ex-pression of even a "contemptuous" idea, but simply protected all flags against destruction without regard to any idea that might be communicated.

It was left to President Reagan's former solicitor general, Harvard Law Professor Charles Fried, to tell the Judiciary Committee that it must rise above politics and reject both the proposal for a constitu-tional amendment and the proposed federal statute. "Gregory Lee Johnson's burning of the American flag was a vile and distressing act," Fried said. "I do not like coming here to urge you to leave alone the laws and Constitution that say he may not be punished for that act." But Fried told the Senators that he spoke from the special per-spective of an immigrant from Czechoslovakia who had watched the Nazis and, later, the Soviets destroy what had been a deep and hu-mane tradition of democratic values.

"So America, its traditions and values, and its flag are important to me," Fried testified. "Foremost among those values is the principle that no one shall be punished for his political expressions, no matter how offensive or bizarre. That commitment to liberty is our first and greatest contribution to the history of mankind. I would not tamper with it. Though I do not often agree with Justice Brennan, I agree with

him entirely that our disdainful tolerance of the likes of Gregory Johnson only honors the flag he sought so ineffectively to dishonor."

The Senate ignored both Fried's and Bork's advice, and attempted
to punish flag-burning by federal statute. The Flag Protection Act of
1989 was passed by both houses of Congress and prohibited the
physical destruction of the American flag, except when it was "worn
or soiled."

President Bush stood by his proposal for a constitutional amendment and made a conspicuous display of his displeasure with the
statute by refusing to sign it (allowing the bill to become law without
his endorsement). He continued to lobby for the amendment.

Outside of a U.S. post office near downtown Seattle on October 28, 1989, the day that the Flag Protection Act of 1989 took effect,
protesters burned hundreds of tiny paper U.S. flags, then pulled down
the flag from atop the post office and sent it back up the flagpole in
flames. Four Seattle demonstrators were later arrested for violating
the new federal statute. The defendants' legal challenge drew the support of the nation's most famous flag-burner, Gregory "Joey" Johnson,
who said that he was "happy to be linking up with these righteous defendants who are protesting the fascist flag protection act of '89."

William Kunstler, who represented the Seattle defendants, held a
news conference outside the Seattle courtroom where he had appeared on the defendants' behalf. He said that the congressional
drafters of the new legislation had asked Americans to forget that the
flag flew over massacres of American Indians and over villagers in
My Lai, Vietnam. "It's not a religious symbol," Kunstler said. "It is a
symbol of good and it is a symbol of bad, and people ought to be able
to use it to protest the bad."

On May 15, 1990, two groups of demonstrators faced each other
outside the Supreme Court Building. One group burned tiny American
flags, and the other shouted, "Commies, go home!" Inside, Kunstler
was making his second appearance before the Court in little more than
a year to defend flag-burning protesters. Since the Court's regular argument schedule had been completed, the chief justice had convened
a special one-hour session (the first since 1981) to hear argument in

United States v. Eichman, representing appeals from two lower court decisions that had held the Flag Protection Act of 1989 unconstitutional. Both lower court decisions, one from Seattle, the other from the District of Columbia, had been based on *Texas v. Johnson*.

Although President Bush had called the Flag Protection Act inadequate, his solicitor general, Kenneth Starr, urged the justices at the May oral argument in *Eichman* to uphold it as constitutional. "As long as Congress has the power to create the flag," Starr argued, "it has the power to protect the flag." The statute was carefully drawn to guard the flag without curtailing free speech, Starr said. He argued, further, that Congress had the power to protect national symbols such as the flag, and that it was in the national interest to do so.

Kunstler countered that "respect for the flag must be voluntary. Once people are compelled to respect a political symbol, they are no longer free and the respect for it is diluted." Attacking the specific language of the statute, Kunstler contended that the burning of the flag could never be a "content-neutral" form of expression. "The burning of the flag, by itself, even with no message, conveys a message," he argued.

There had been speculation that the justices would completely change sides for this second constitutional challenge to a flag-desecration statute. According to the theory, those who had voted to support Joey Johnson's First Amendment rights would uphold the new statute, for fear that striking it down would provoke the far more drastic solution of a constitutional amendment. Under the same reasoning, the Court's anti-*Johnson* conservatives would vote to strike down the statute in the hope that a more far-reaching constitutional amendment would result.

The logic of that prediction was quickly put to rest during the justices' questioning at oral argument in *Eichman*. Justice Kennedy, the most likely member of the *Johnson* majority to change course, appeared even more committed to the libertarian position that he had taken in *Johnson*. Citing the recent demonstrations for democracy in Eastern Europe, Kennedy asked the solicitor general if it were not true that flag-burning "was recognized as a form of protest internationally."

• • •

The justices' alignment on the challenge to the 1989 Flag Protection Act did not, in fact, differ from the positions taken a year earlier in *Texas v. Johnson*. Justice Brennan again assigned himself the majority opinion for the same five members who had declared the Texas flag-desecration statute unconstitutional, and now were prepared to throw out Congress's attempt to punish flag-burning.

The only behind-the-scenes palpitations occurred in Brennan's chambers after Brennan's clerk-intelligence network picked up signals that Justice Kennedy might be persuaded by his conservative clerks to break ranks. It turned out to be a false alarm. After receiving Brennan's draft opinion, which affirmed the principles he had announced in *Johnson*, Kennedy suggested only two minor changes "of the footnote variety," which Brennan happily accommodated, in footnotes.

By its statutory terms, Brennan wrote in his opinion for the five-member majority, the Flag Protection Act was unconstitutional. It punished disrespectful treatment of the flag (but permitted destruction of "worn or soiled" flags), underscoring Congress's interest in the expressive content of flag-burning. Brennan quoted from his *Johnson* opinion: "If there is a bedrock principle underlying the First Amendment, it is that the Government may not prohibit the expression of an idea simply because society finds the idea itself offensive or disagreeable." And, he concluded, "Punishing desecration of the flag dilutes the very freedom that makes this emblem so revered, and worth revering."

Rehnquist drafted a short dissent. But after he read Justice Stevens's dissenting opinion—which defended the government's authority to protect the flag without, in Stevens's view, undercutting free speech—the chief justice chose to let Stevens speak for both of them.

After the Court's decision was announced in late June, there were more threats among irate members of Congress to pass a constitutional amendment. President Bush, fighting to capture the flag to the end, expressed his disappointment in the latest Court decision. In a ceremony and photo-opportunity session in the White House Rose

Garden, the president received a replica of the Iwo Jima Marine Memorial from the sculptor and renewed his pledge to campaign for a constitutional amendment, because "[f]lag-burning endangers the fabric of our country." But political energy for the constitutional amendment eventually dissipated and the Court's *Johnson* and *Eichman* decisions appeared secure in the constitutional law textbooks.

While President Bush had lost his fight to punish flag-burning, attorneys in his Justice Department were at work developing another First Amendment challenge, focusing on the Establishment Clause. They had been encouraged by the narrow conservative defeat in the 1989 *Allegheny* Establishment Clause decision to search for another opportunity to change the Court's church-state doctrine. It came in the case of *Lee v. Weisman*, argued before the Court on November 6, 1991. *Weisman* seemed well suited to fulfill the ambitions of Justice Kennedy and the other *Allegheny* dissenters to revise the modern Supreme Court's Establishment Clause jurisprudence, perhaps once and for all. It involved the church-state issue that had mired the Court in controversy for three decades: government-sponsored prayer.

Vivian and Daniel Weisman, like other parents attending Nathan Bishop Middle School's 1986 graduation ceremonies in Providence, Rhode Island, had watched proudly as the achievements of their older daughter and her classmates were celebrated. But their happiness turned to chagrin when the Baptist minister who delivered the benediction asked the audience to stand for a moment of silence to give thanks to Jesus Christ. The Weismans, who are Jewish, were humiliated and angered. "As a Jew," recalled Daniel Weisman, "it was terribly uncomfortable and inappropriate . . . to have an activity sponsored by the state attack me on the basis of my religion."

Weisman, a professor of social work at Rhode Island College, complained by letter to Bishop Middle School officials. When he received no reply, he put the matter out of his mind. Three years later, however, when the Weismans' younger daughter, Deborah, was scheduled to graduate from the same middle school, Daniel Weisman renewed his complaint about prayer at the public school graduation ceremonies.

He was told by the school's principal that this time his daughter would hear an invocation and benediction given by a clergyman of the Weismans' faith. But Daniel Weisman was just as offended. All that he wanted was a nonreligious graduation ceremony; a prayer by a rabbi could, he contended, be just as offensive to non-Jewish students and their parents as the Baptist minister's benediction had been to the Weismans three years earlier. He threatened legal action if the school proceeded with its plan to have Providence Rabbi Leslie Gutterman deliver the invocation and benediction.

Daniel Weisman went to the federal district court in Providence on behalf of himself and his daughter to stop Rabbi Gutterman from participating in the graduation ceremony. After District Court Judge Francis Boyle refused to grant the temporary restraining order that Weisman sought, Rabbi Gutterman opened and closed the Bishop Middle School's 1989 graduation ceremonies. Both his invocation and benediction, unlike the Baptist minister's in 1986, were nondenominational. "O God, we are grateful for the learning which we have celebrated on this joyous commencement," the rabbi said in his benediction. "We give thanks to you, Lord, for keeping us alive, sustaining us and allowing us to reach this special, happy occasion."

Despite the rabbi's nondenominational prayer, Weisman persisted with his lawsuit and was represented in the legal action by the American Civil Liberties Union. Weisman prevailed in the federal district court, where Judge Boyle decided that Rabbi Gutterman's invocation and benediction had violated the First Amendment's Establishment Clause; specifically, Judge Boyle said the rabbi's prayers were disqualified by the second prong of the Court's *Lemon* test, which prohibited the state from either advancing or inhibiting religion. "In this case," wrote Judge Boyle, "the benediction and invocation advance religion by creating an identification of school with a deity, and therefore religion." In a brief order, the federal appeals court affirmed Judge Boyle's decision.

After Providence public school officials appealed, one member of the school board complained that the appeal was an expensive waste of time (the appeal's estimated cost to the city was between $25,000 and $50,000). But by then, powerful advocates from the former Reagan Administration and the current Bush Administration had joined the fight on the side of Providence school officials. Washington attorney Charles Cooper, a former law clerk to Chief Justice Rehnquist and a former assistant attorney general in the Reagan Administration, represented the school officials at the oral argument before the Court. Cooper was joined at oral argument by Solicitor General Kenneth Starr.

In their legal briefs, Cooper and Starr had urged the Court to reverse the lower federal court decisions and rule that the commencement prayer was constitutional. In argument, Cooper and Starr explicitly asked the Court to lower the traditional barrier between church and state. They recommended that the Court adopt the "coercion" test—i.e., a government act supporting religion was unconstitutional only if it forced participation, a standard advocated by Justice Kennedy in his *Allegheny* dissent.

Cooper and Starr had strong reasons to press their case in *Lee v. Weisman* for a revision of the Court's Establishment Clause doctrine. The justices joining Kennedy's *Allegheny* opinion (Rehnquist, Scalia and White) had expressed strong support for an approach to the Establishment Clause that would allow much greater accommodation of government toward religion than several important modern Court precedents had suggested was constitutionally permissible. A fifth member of the Court, Justice O'Connor, while more cautious than the three justices joining Kennedy's *Allegheny* opinion, had nonetheless shown in her concurrences in the 1984 *Lynch* decision as well as in *Allegheny* that she was not committed to a rigid doctrine of separation of church and state. More important for Cooper and Starr's purposes, two Bush appointees, Justices Souter and Thomas, had replaced the Court's most ardent separationists, Justices Brennan and Marshall.

Both Souter and Thomas had, understandably, been cautious in their responses to questions from Senate Judiciary Committee members about their views of the First Amendment's religion clauses. One obvious reason was that they wanted to maintain their impartiality on church-state issues they would likely confront on the Court if they were confirmed. There was also a pragmatic reason for their caution: church-state issues transmitted highly charged political currents, and clearly expressed views could jeopardize chances for confirmation.

At his confirmation hearings in September 1990, Souter had been asked about his views on the Court's approach to church-state issues and had shown that he was well aware of the ongoing debate on the Court. He acknowledged the criticism of the Court's *Lemon* test, which had attempted to establish basic guidelines for the Court to determine if there had been a violation of the Establishment Clause, and suggested that the Court might review its *Lemon* test and possibly engage in a deeper reexamination about the very concept behind the Establishment Clause. At his confirmation hearings, Souter satisfied committee members by assuring them that he had no fixed position on the doctrine. "[I]f I were to go to the Court," Souter told the committee, "I would not go with a personal agenda to foster that [i.e., a deeper reexamination]; neither would I go in ignorance of the difficulty which has arisen in the administration of *Kurtzman.*"

When Judge Clarence Thomas appeared before the Senate Judiciary Committee a year after Souter, he faced much more aggressive questioning. Unlike Souter, who had been a quiet, cerebral state court judge for much of his career, Judge Thomas had built his reputation as an outspoken conservative in the Reagan Administration with controversial views on a broad spectrum of political topics. Judiciary Committee members, particularly liberal Democrats, felt justified, therefore, in attempting to probe Thomas's specific positions on volatile constitutional issues, such as the constitutional boundary between church and state.

But on this topic, as on virtually every other, Thomas was unwilling to discuss his own views, while disowning any notion that his positions were radical, or even noticeably conservative. "I have an open mind with respect to the debate over the application of the *Lemon v. Kurtzman* test," Thomas testified. "And I recognize that the Court has applied it with some degree of difficulty. But, at the same time, I'm sensitive to our desire in this country to keep government and religion separated—flawed as it may be—by that Jeffersonian wall of separation."

• • •

Only minutes into the oral argument in *Lee v. Weisman,* the confident air of Charles Cooper, who represented Providence school officials, was shattered by an unlikely antagonist. After the attorney had advocated that the Court adopt the "coercion" test, O'Connor asked Cooper if, under his test, there was any constitutional difference between a state's choosing an official religion and choosing "the bolo tie as the state necktie"? Neither, said O'Connor, involved "coercion."

Cooper replied that the Constitution would permit a state to designate an official religion, so long as no one was forced to practice the designated faith. Unless there was a finding of "coercion," Cooper asserted, there was no violation of the Constitution.

"Well, that certainly has not been our case holdings over a substantial period of time," replied O'Connor sharply.

"[W]e are quite frank in our request," Cooper said, reminding O'Connor and the other justices that he had asked them to reexamine the Establishment Clause precedents.

Cooper's argument was too extreme, even for Justice Scalia, who had long been critical of modern Supreme Court precedents on church-state issues. "You are trying to say that the only test is coercion," Scalia said, "but I don't think that comports with our tradition. [W]e don't say, 'Jesus Christ save the United States and this honorable Court' . . . or 'In Jesus Christ We Trust' on the coins," although, Scalia said, the use of the name Jesus Christ would not be more coercive than the nonsectarian invocation of God.

Refusing to retreat, Cooper replied that the name of Jesus Christ could not be used on the government's coins or by the marshal in opening the Supreme Court sessions because "at this stage, that would not be politically possible."

"If we could get the votes for it," a skeptical Scalia asked, "we could do it under the Constitution? Is that what you think?"

"It would not violate the First Amendment's Establishment Clause," replied Cooper, "any more than a congressional resolution declaring the Year of the Bible (which was passed in 1983)."

Justice Kennedy was less assertive in his questioning of Cooper than Scalia, but no less skeptical of his argument—even though

Cooper was advocating the "coercion" test that Kennedy had supported in his *Allegheny* opinion. Kennedy was troubled by Cooper's contention that a public school graduation ceremony was not coercive, since, Cooper argued, attendance was voluntary. "In our culture," said Kennedy, "a graduation is a key event in a young person's life. The family comes, aunts, uncles, brothers, sisters. And I think it is a very, very substantial burden on the person to say that he or she can elect not to go."

Solicitor General Starr, who spoke after Cooper, attempted to soften the edge of the government's position, assuring the justices that a holding in his and Cooper's favor would not necessarily doom modern Court precedents such as *Engel v. Vitale*, which had declared that New York's Regents' Prayer recited in its public schools violated the Establishment Clause. Even if a child were free not to join in a classroom prayer, Starr said, there is "a powerful, subtle, indirect pressure on the child in the classroom" that would make organized prayer in that setting unconstitutional. Starr argued that the commencement prayer in *Weisman* was more like the prayer at a presidential inauguration (which the *Allegheny* dissenters were on record as supporting) than that in a public school classroom.

Justice Souter was not persuaded. The Court was obligated to reconcile two traditions, Souter suggested to Starr, one permitting religious expression on public occasions and the other prohibiting it in public school classrooms (as the Court had declared in *Engel v. Vitale*). "If *Engel* is good law," said Souter, "we've got to choose which tradition it is going to be."

"I don't think the *Engel* tradition is implicated outside the classroom," Starr insisted.

"Isn't the analogy a lot closer here [to *Engel*]," Souter suggested, "than it is to a presidential inauguration?"

Sandra Blanding, the ACLU attorney representing the Weisman family, enthusiastically seized upon Souter's point when it was her turn at the lectern. "This case is essentially a school prayer case, and it must be looked at in that context," she told the justices. If the Court accepted the government's "coercion" standard, Blanding argued, *Engel* and its progeny would inevitably have to be overruled.

• • •

The Court's decision in *Lee v. Weisman* proved once again how wrong the most firmly held assumptions about the philosophies, and votes, of individual justices can be. Justice Anthony Kennedy, defying all predictions, ultimately refused the Bush Administration's invitation to join the Court's most conservative members in rewriting much of the modern Supreme Court's Establishment Clause doctrine.

After oral argument in *Weisman*, Kennedy had considered upholding the commencement prayer as a purely ceremonial invocation, akin constitutionally to the prayer recited at the presidential inauguration. But he remained troubled by the coercion factor—that junior high school students felt enormous pressure to attend their commencement ceremonies, a pressure that was missing among adults voluntarily attending a presidential inauguration or, in Kennedy's view, those who observed the holiday displays in downtown Pittsburgh at issue in *Allegheny*.

Kennedy had to make the choice that Souter, at oral argument, had suggested was necessary: either accept the commencement prayer as comparable to the invocation at a presidential inauguration and decide that it does not violate the Establishment Clause, or see it as similar to New York's Regents' Prayer that was declared unconstitutional in *Engel v. Vitale*. In the end, Kennedy made the second choice and wrote the opinion for a five-member majority (Kennedy, Blackmun, O'Connor, Souter and Stevens) holding that the commencement prayer violated the Establishment Clause.

In his opinion, Kennedy first established that the state had endorsed the prayer, pointing out that the middle-school principal had invited Rabbi Gutterman to give the prayer and had sent written guidelines on the appropriate content of prayers for civic ceremonies such as the school's graduation. Citing *Engel*, Kennedy wrote: "It is a cornerstone principle that 'it is no part of the business of government to compose official prayers for any group of the American people to recite as a part of a religious program carried on by the government,' *Engel*, and that is what the school officials attempted to do." Kennedy also rejected the government's contention that there was no coercion involved, writing that primary- and secondary-school-age students were vulnerable to subtle pressures to conform, and those pressures included attendance at public ceremonies such as commencement.

"The lessons of the First Amendment are as urgent in the modern world as in the 18th Century when it was written," Kennedy declared. "One timeless lesson," he continued, "is that if citizens are subjected to state-sponsored religious exercises, the State disavows its own duty to guard and respect that sphere of inviolable conscience and belief which is a mark of a free people."

Nowhere in Kennedy's opinion were the billowing phrases of accommodation that had pervaded his *Allegheny* opinion. In their place was Kennedy's clear reaffirmation of the Warren Court's controversial separationist decision, *Engel v. Vitale*, which struck down New York's Regents' Prayer.

Another addition to Kennedy's opinion in *Weisman*, which distinguished it from his *Allegheny* dissent, was the prominent references to the writings of James Madison. Kennedy introduced Madison as "the principal author of the Bill of Rights," noting that Madison did not rest his opposition to the government's support of religion only on his concern for its effect on a minority. In addition, Kennedy wrote, Madison had expressed his belief that the separation of church from state was the best guarantee of preserving the integrity of religion: "[E]xperience witnesseth that ecclesiastical establishments, instead of maintaining the unity and efficacy of Religion," wrote Madison (quoted by Justice Kennedy), "have had a contrary operation."

In contrast to his *Allegheny* opinion, which exhibited an eagerness to take on broad doctrinal issues, Kennedy's *Weisman* opinion was striking in its cautious tone and determination to confine the Court's holding to the school prayer context and the facts in the Providence case.

There were many theories, both in and outside the Supreme Court Building, about Justice Kennedy's change of direction in *Weisman*. One had it that Kennedy was obviously afflicted with the rare but fatal "third choice" disease. Like Justice Harry Blackmun, Kennedy was also the third presidential choice for a Court appointment (after the failed nominations of Judges Robert Bork and Douglas Ginsburg) and had fallen victim to creeping liberalism.

A more serious assessment was offered by Kennedy's friend and former law clerk Judge Alex Kozinski, who had served with him on the U.S. Court of Appeals for the Ninth Circuit. "He listens," said Judge Kozinski, "and he's still evolving in his thinking."

A close look at the substance and timing of Kennedy's *Weisman* opinion offers a further explanation. Confronted with the choice of participating in a radical shift in the Court's constitutional direction, Kennedy chose, instead, to emphasize the continuity between his position in *Weisman* and the Court's school prayer precedents. He had acted in a similar manner in the Court's abortion decision *Planned Parenthood of Southeastern Pennsylvania v. Casey*, announced the same day as *Weisman*. Three years earlier, Kennedy had revealed in his comments at the justices' private conference in *Webster*, and in his support for the chief justice's plurality opinion, that he was a committed critic of *Roe v. Wade*. But when Kennedy had the opportunity to act on that criticism in *Casey* by casting the decisive fifth vote to abandon *Roe*, he balked. His criticism of *Roe* remained intact, but his institutional concern, that the Court preserve its authority through a traceable continuity in its decisions, prevailed.

In *Weisman*, Kennedy again resisted pressure from the Court's ardent conservatives—Rehnquist, White and Scalia, and now Thomas—to ignore established precedents in pursuit of a different constitutional vision. Whatever Kennedy may have thought of the merits of the Court's previous Establishment Clause decisions, he was unwilling to forsake them in favor of a shiny new conservative perspective.

Justice Scalia's roiling *Weisman* dissent accused Kennedy of rank judicial treachery. How could Kennedy, the author of the *Allegheny* opinion that Scalia had joined, possibly have written the *Weisman* opinion for the Court? Since Scalia was confident that Kennedy had it right the first time (in his *Allegheny* opinion), he could only wonder why Kennedy had gone astray. He ridiculed Kennedy's "psycho-journey" in *Weisman* that concluded that Bishop Middle School graduates could be coerced by Rabbi Gutterman's commencement prayer. This was, Scalia wrote, "psychology practiced by amateurs." Emphasizing that such commencement prayers were part of a laudable tradition, Scalia proclaimed that the rabbi's prayers "are so characteristically American they could have come from the pen of George Washington or Abraham Lincoln himself."

The task of challenging Scalia's and Rehnquist's narrow reading of the Establishment Clause prohibitions was assumed by Justice David Souter, who, in only his second term, had become an influential centrist on the Court.

In his *Weisman* concurrence, Souter explored the history of the religion clauses of the First Amendment and included a discussion of the debates of the First Congress. He concluded that he could not agree with the chief justice's interpretation in his 1985 *Wallace v. Jaffree* dissent, in which the majority struck down Alabama's public school requirement of a moment of silence for meditation or voluntary prayer. In his dissent, Rehnquist attacked the entire separation doctrine: "It is impossible to build sound constitutional doctrine upon a mistaken understanding of constitutional history, but unfortunately the Establishment Clause has been expressly freighted with Jefferson's misleading [wall of separation] metaphor for nearly 40 years." According to Rehnquist, the First Congress's purpose in drafting the Establishment Clause was only to prohibit a national church and the preference of one religious sect over another. Nor did Souter accept Scalia's comparably narrow interpretation of the Establishment Clause's prohibitions expressed in his dissent in *Lee v. Weisman*, which applauded the celebration of religious traditions in public ceremonies.

In fact, Souter's opinion assumed a subtle separationist tone. A state "may not favor or endorse either religion generally over nonreligion or one religion over others," Souter maintained. "Our aspiration to religious liberty embodied in the First Amendment," he wrote, "permits no other standard."

Two years after the *Weisman* decision, the Court (with Justice Ruth Bader Ginsburg having replaced Byron White) accepted another invitation to elaborate on its evolving Establishment Clause doctrine. In 1994, the justices agreed to review legislation passed by the New York legislature that created a school district to accommodate the special education needs of the children of residents of Kiryas Joel, an ultra-Orthodox Jewish community. The justices were asked to decide whether the New York law violated the First Amendment's Establishment Clause.

The school district of Kiryas Joel in Orange County, New York, located fifty miles northwest of New York City, consisted of a single building in which the handicapped children of the Satmar Hasidic residents of the village of Kiryas Joel were educated. The state legislature, responding to a request from village residents, had created the special school district for the specific purpose of providing the disabled children with an education that was insulated from the surrounding community. Without the special school district, the Satmar Hasidic parents feared that their children would be harmed by the stress and possible ridicule from the outside world. But once the special school district was established, Louis Grumet, executive director of the New York State School Boards Association, successfully challenged the law in the New York courts. The New York legislature, in accommodating the needs of the handicapped children of Kiryas Joel, had violated the separation between church (or, in this case, synagogue) and state demanded by the Establishment Clause.

On March 30, 1994, at the oral argument in the Kiryas Joel case, Justices Kennedy, O'Connor and Souter, who had comprised three-fifths of the majority in *Lee v. Weisman*, closely questioned Nathan Lewin, the attorney for the Hasidic school district. Lewin contended that the New York law did not favor religion.

But wasn't it fair to say, Kennedy asserted, that the state's government power was transferred to the school district of Kiryas Joel based on the religious beliefs of its residents? Lewin insisted that the village of Kiryas Joel, which benefited from the school district, functioned as a normal government with secular concerns. The attorney held up a thick book containing the legal code of the village to emphasize the secular regulations of the residents. Would it be unconstitutional for the villagers to refuse to collect their garbage on the Sabbath? Lewin asked.

No, it would not, Justice O'Connor responded, so long as there was a general, neutral law permitting people of the village of Kiryas Joel—as well as other villages—to collect the garbage themselves on another day. The problem with the Kiryas Joel *school district*, O'Connor suggested, was that it was not set up under generally applicable legislation (as the village of Kiryas Joel was) but under a special law that dealt only with the special education needs of the Orthodox Jewish community.

From the bench, Justice Scalia questioned the relevance of Kennedy's and O'Connor's questions. This was not a case of a state legislature favoring a religious community, Scalia said, but of a good-faith effort by New York legislators to accommodate the cultural preferences of the villagers living in Kiryas Joel. "Their customs spring out of their religion," Scalia said, but the state was accommodating their customs. He distinguished the state's response to the villagers' cultural needs from the notion that New York was accommodating any religious beliefs.

After the oral argument, the justices split 6 to 3, with the five members of the *Weisman* majority (Kennedy, Souter, Blackmun, O'Connor and Stevens) and the newest member of the Court, Justice Ruth Bader Ginsburg, voting to strike down the New York law as a violation of the Establishment Clause. The Court's most conservative members, Rehnquist, Scalia and Thomas, dissented. Blackmun, as the senior justice in the majority, assigned the Court's opinion to Souter.

In his opinion for the Court, Souter focused on the unusual facts of the case ("exceptional to the point of singularity") and on the intense religiosity of the Satmar Hasidic sect that established the village of Kiryas Joel. "The residents of Kiryas Joel are a vigorously religious people," Souter wrote, "who make few concessions to the modern world and go to great lengths to avoid assimilation in it." He noted that they interpreted the Torah strictly, segregated the sexes outside the home and spoke Yiddish as their primary language.

While there could be accommodation under the Establishment Clause to alleviate special burdens of religious groups, Souter conceded, "accommodation is not a principle without limits, and what petitioners seek is an adjustment to the Satmars' religiously grounded preferences that our cases do not countenance." Reiterating a point that he had made two years earlier in his *Lee v. Weisman* concurrence, Souter emphasized "a principle at the heart of the Establishment

Clause, that government should not prefer one religion to another, or religion to irreligion."

Justice Scalia responded to the first draft of Souter's opinion with a characteristic no-holds-barred dissent that accused Souter of taking "to new extremes a recent tendency in the opinions of this Court to turn the Establishment Clause into a repealer of our nation's tradition of religious toleration." And with hyperbolic flourish, Scalia mocked Souter's conclusion that the special school district violated the Establishment Clause. "The Court today finds that the Powers that Be, up in Albany, have conspired to effect an establishment of the Satmar Hasidim," Scalia wrote derisively.

Souter did not turn the other cheek, as Kennedy had done after Scalia's attack on Kennedy's *Weisman* opinion. Instead, Souter added a two-page rebuttal in a revision of his opinion that addressed Scalia by name. "Justice Cardozo once cast the dissenter as 'the gladiator making a last stand against the lions,' " Souter wrote. "Justice Scalia's dissent is certainly the work of a gladiator, but he thrusts at lions of his own imagining." Souter responded directly to Scalia's charge that he had confused religious toleration with the establishment of religion. "The license he [Scalia] takes in suggesting that the Court holds the Satmar sect to be New York's established church is only one symptom of his inability to accept the fact that this Court has long held that the First Amendment reaches more than classic 18th century establishments." While conceding that Scalia's approach would succeed in reducing the Court's work to a few simple rules, such an approach, Souter asserted, "would be as blind to history as to precedent."

The conservatives' constitutional history seminars of the 1980s on the meaning of the Establishment Clause had been led by Rehnquist, enthusiastically joined by Scalia and actively encouraged by the Reagan and Bush administrations. But by the early 1990s the seminars had taken an unexpectedly moderate tone, largely because of Kennedy, O'Connor and Souter—the same three justices whose joint opinion in *Casey* had frustrated the ambitions of Rehnquist, Scalia and the Reagan and Bush administrations to destroy *Roe v. Wade.*

The conservatives' spirited efforts to change the direction of Establishment Clause jurisprudence—so promising only a few years earlier—appeared by the mid-1990s to have failed. The political agendas of the Reagan and Bush administrations had indeed been translated into constitutional arguments—but not into constitutional law.

EPILOGUE

CHAPTER THIRTEEN

BEYOND THE
REHNQUIST COURT

Judge Ruth Bader Ginsburg of the U.S. Court of Appeals for the District of Columbia dressed immaculately for the formal occasion of her Senate Judiciary Committee hearings in July 1993, wearing a bright blue suit and an elegant brooch and earrings. As a woman nominated to the Court to succeed retiring Justice Byron White, Ginsburg was still something of a novelty, since only once before in the Court's 203-year history had a president appointed a member of her sex. But the more significant fact about the nomination was that Ginsburg, a former Columbia Law School professor and pioneering women's rights advocate, was the first Supreme Court nominee appointed by a Democratic president in a generation; it had been twenty-six years since President Johnson had nominated Thurgood Marshall.

The Ginsburg nomination interrupted the steady succession of appointments by four Republican presidents, from Richard Nixon's appointment of Chief Justice Warren Burger in 1969 to George Bush's nomination of Clarence Thomas twenty-two years later. More important, the Ginsburg appointment promised to contain the most serious threats to civil rights and liberties by the conservatives on the Rehnquist Court.

Comparing Judge Ginsburg to Justice Sandra Day O'Connor, the first woman to serve on the Court, was natural, but the more relevant professional comparison was to the last Democratic nominee, Thurgood Marshall. Ginsburg and Marshall were linked by their unique accomplishments as lawyers: Marshall would always be remembered as the great advocate of the civil rights movement, and Judge Ginsburg was justifiably admired as the lawyer who used the courts to force recognition of women's constitutional rights under the Equal Protection Clause.

After President Bill Clinton had stumbled through an awkward weekend of indecision in mid-June 1993, his nomination of Ginsburg allowed the entire nation to heave a collective sigh of relief. Ginsburg possessed the attributes of an excellent Court nominee—penetrating intellect, broad experience in the law, a calm, deliberate judicial temperament—and none of the prickly ideological thorns that had often transformed the Senate Caucus Room, where recent confirmation hearings had been held, into a political briar patch.

One political cartoon depicting the Ginsburg hearings had balloons floating festively above the senators, who sported conical party hats and displayed a large welcome sign: CONGRATULATIONS RUTH GINSBURG! And, indeed, the committee members, Republicans as well as Democrats, greeted the nominee with celebratory enthusiasm. The expanded committee* of eighteen senators practically fell over one another in their rush to praise Judge Ginsburg; their laudatory prepared statements alone consumed a full two hours.

When she finally was allowed to read her own prepared statement, Judge Ginsburg, a small, sixty-year-old woman, who wore oversized glasses and her hair tightly brushed back in a bun, delivered the Brooklyn version of Clarence Thomas's Pin Point Remembrances— an affecting, personal trip backward in time to thank those who had helped her along the way to professional achievement. "Neither of my parents had the means to attend college, but both taught me to love

---

* Since the Clarence Thomas–Anita Hill debacle, the committee had added four new members, including two women, California's Dianne Feinstein and Illinois's Carol Moseley-Braun.

learning, to care about people, and to work hard for whatever I wanted or believed in," Judge Ginsburg told the committee members. "Their parents had the foresight to leave the old country when Jewish ancestry and faith meant exposure to pogroms and denigration of one's human worth. What has become of me could happen only in America. . . ."

In her statement, Judge Ginsburg selected her judicial heroes carefully, quoting Judge Learned Hand, as well as Justices Holmes and Cardozo. All three practiced, and counseled their colleagues to exercise, judicial restraint. "Justice is not to be taken by storm," Judge Ginsburg said, quoting Cardozo. "She is to be wooed by slow advances." The nominee made the theme of judicial caution her own. "My approach, I believe, is neither liberal nor conservative," Ginsburg told the committee. "Rather, it is rooted in the place of the judiciary in our democratic society. The Constitution's preamble speaks first of 'we the people' and then of their elected representatives. The judiciary is third in line, and it is placed apart from the political fray so that its members can judge fairly, impartially, in accordance with the law and without fear about the animosity of any appreciate group."

At the end of her opening statement, Ginsburg invited the committee members to judge her on the basis of her professional record of thirty-four years—briefs, lectures, articles and opinions—an invitation, in fact and spirit, that contrasted starkly with the previous Court nominee, Judge Clarence Thomas. Thomas did not encourage the Judiciary Committee to judge him on his written record; indeed, he disavowed much of it. There was a second, equally instructive, difference between the confirmation hearings of Ginsburg and Thomas. Judge Ginsburg built her answers to committee members' questions organically, from basic premises to general conclusions— in contrast to Judge Thomas, whose prepackaged responses seemed calculated to pass the committee's examination with the minimum amount of intellectual effort.

In the electronic age of punchy soundbites, Judge Ginsburg preferred serious discourse. Her answers were punctuated with long pauses, not, it was immediately obvious, because she could not think of an appropriate response, but because she could—and for this she demanded time to carefully organize her thoughts before she spoke.

Ginsburg was the first Court nominee, for example, to provide the Senate Judiciary Committee with a comprehensive analysis of her views on *Roe v. Wade*. She had ruminated publicly about an alternative to the *Roe* analysis, suggesting that both the Court and the nation might have been better served by a more cautious ruling. Ginsburg nonetheless gave her firm endorsement to a woman's constitutional right to an abortion, rooted either in the Due Process Clause or Equal Protection Clause of the Fourteenth Amendment (both of which she happily analyzed for the senators).

By the end of her three days of testimony, Ginsburg had provided the committee and the full Senate with a sound framework by which to evaluate her judicial qualifications and approach to the Court's work. Judge Ginsburg received 99 Senate votes for confirmation, 47 more than the previous nominee, Clarence Thomas. Ginsburg's lopsided Senate vote and her overwhelmingly positive public approval ratings suggested that her appointment traversed the nation's political spectrum.

Almost exactly a year after the Ginsburg confirmation hearings, President Clinton's second nominee to the Court, Chief Judge Stephen Breyer of the U.S. Court of Appeals for the First Circuit, sat at the same witness table before the Senate Judiciary Committee. Breyer, who had been nominated to replace the retiring Justice Harry Blackmun, had come tantalizingly close to making his appearance before the committee a year earlier. President Clinton, in a widely publicized invitation, had asked Breyer at that time to come to the White House to be interviewed as a possible successor to Justice Byron White. At the last moment, however, Clinton chose Judge Ruth Bader Ginsburg, not Breyer.

When Breyer finally faced the committee in July 1994, he appeared eager to demonstrate that the president had chosen well in nominating him. Breyer's gaunt, ascetic appearance concealed a warm and ingratiating personality. He spoke proudly of his maternal grandparents' immigration to the United States from Eastern Europe. And he credited his mother for profoundly influencing his values and aspi-

rations. "She was the one who made absolutely clear to me in no uncertain terms that whatever intellectual ability I might have means
nothing and won't mean anything unless I can work with other people
and use whatever talents I have to help them," he told the committee.
Breyer's mother had advised him not to spend too much time with
books, and the nominee conceded that she was right. "I mean, my
ideas about people do not come from libraries," he said.

Breyer could afford to emphasize his interpersonal skills since his
outstanding academic record and professional accomplishments
needed little elaboration. An honors graduate of the Harvard Law
School, Breyer had clerked for Supreme Court Justice Arthur Goldberg, taught law at Harvard and served as chief counsel for the Senate Judiciary Committee before his appointment to the federal
appeals court. His reputation on the U.S. Court of Appeals for the
First Circuit was that of a lucid thinker and writer whose philosophy
was not easily categorized—though he tended to lean slightly to the
liberal side of center, a description that also fit Ruth Bader Ginsburg. And like Ginsburg, Breyer also reveled in the judge's craft, analyzing a legal problem exhaustively to arrive at what he considered
to be a fair solution.

At his confirmation hearings, Breyer exhibited a child's enthusiasm in explaining the technical aspects of a judicial decision; he rap-
turously recited the details, for example, of a seventy-two-year-old
property rights decision by Justice Oliver Wendell Holmes, Jr. He
also quoted Holmes's famous aphorism that law reflects not so much
logic as history and experience. The law, Breyer said, had a single basic purpose: to help Americans "live together productively, harmo-
niously and in freedom."

The nominee carefully sidestepped a discussion of specific constitutional issues that might come before the Court. Breyer nonetheless
affirmed that a woman's right to an abortion was the law (but would
not speculate on what state regulations of abortion would be constitutional). He also spoke openly about the wall of separation between
church and state, Jefferson's metaphor that had been attacked by
Rehnquist Court conservatives.

And though he rarely missed an opportunity to please his interrogators, Breyer was not always easily led by a senator's suggested conclusion. The ranking Republican member of the committee, Senator Orrin Hatch, invited the nominee to agree with him that a judge's role was limited to applying the law. "Of course, that is true," Breyer replied, but it wasn't always so clear what the law is in the "vast, open areas" in which the Supreme Court was required to judge. Since there were usually good arguments on both sides of important policy issues, the Court's job, Breyer suggested, was "to find the correct solution, the helpful solution consistent with the underlying human purpose." By implication, Breyer signaled that he would not bring to the Court an overarching ideology with ready answers to the most protracted constitutional problems.

Breyer's testimony satisfied Senator Hatch and an overwhelming majority of his colleagues, who confirmed the nominee for a seat on the Supreme Court.

If Ginsburg's and Breyer's extensive records on the federal appeals courts are a reliable guide to their future Court performances, there will be no special pleadings to their colleagues. Rather, Justices Ginsburg and Breyer will put forward their positions with fastidious regard for the legal contours of their arguments and arrive at narrow results that will reflect their own judicial caution. In that approach, they closely resemble another centrist on the Court, Justice David Souter.

At their confirmation hearings, all three—Souter, Ginsburg and Breyer—spoke admiringly of Justices Holmes; they admitted that their judicial model reflected their own interest in the labor-intensive craft of judging. Souter, Ginsburg and Breyer pride themselves on their technical abilities to break down a constitutional problem into its smallest component parts. They honor the Court's precedents, not in the abstract, but as a basis for building continuity into the law. And yet they are willing to act, however cautiously, in response to the changing demands of law in a dynamic society.

Justices Ginsburg and Breyer, like Souter, approach the writing of their opinions as an artist constructs a collage—with careful regard for the materials at hand but also with a desire to bring their unique experience and sensibilities to the project. As no two artists will produce the same collage, Souter, Ginsburg and Breyer will not always agree on the correct constitutional perspective. Souter's constitutional values are essentially conservative. Ginsburg and Breyer bring libertarian instincts to the Court—they have viewed the law from an outsider's perspective, Ginsburg as a woman and both Ginsburg and Breyer as Jews.

The final word on the Court of the 1990s has not, of course, been written. We know that either President Clinton or his successor in office will round out the Court appointments for this century, and, further, that no one can accurately predict where any single case will lead any of the sitting or future justices. But even if we accept these qualifications, there remains the unmistakable conclusion that the Ginsburg and Breyer appointments mark a critical turning point for the Rehnquist Court. Justices Ginsburg and Breyer have solidified the moderate center of this Court, and neither pressure from the right wing—Rehnquist, Scalia and Thomas—nor any later appointments are likely to undercut the prevailing judicial ethos of moderation.

By design, the Rehnquist Court has heard progressively fewer cases, and in many of their recent decisions the language of the Court majorities has tended to be more technical and less sweeping than in the past. But even if future Court majorities harbor less aggressive ambitions than the liberal activists on the Warren Court of the 1960s or the conservative activists on the Rehnquist Court, the results will be historic. For the centrists will reaffirm, in their restrained fashion, Madison's belief that an independent judiciary should stand as "an impenetrable bulwark" of liberty and strike down as unconstitutional any acts by the legislative and executive branches that violate the Bill of Rights. If that seems to be a tepid result, consider the alternative.

Had George Bush been reelected president in 1992, he would have had the opportunity to replace Justices White and Blackmun on the Court. If he modeled his second-term appointments on his last nominee, Clarence Thomas, Bush would have been able to accomplish what Chief Justice Rehnquist and his fellow conservative activists on the Court almost succeeded in doing without the help of a second

Bush Administration: a wholesale reordering of the Court's constitutional priorities.

For those who value the civil rights and liberties protections guaranteed by the decisions of the modern Supreme Court spanning more than three decades, it was a very close call.

SOURCE NOTES

The source notes are, for the most part, self-explanatory. I have used acronyms to identify frequently used sources after the initial entry. Justice Thurgood Marshall's papers at the Library of Congress become TMP. Supreme Court decisions and law-review articles follow legal methods of citation: *Patterson v. McLean Credit Union*, 491 U.S. 164 (1989), means that the Supreme Court decided the case in 1989 and that the opinions begin at page 164 of *United States Reports*, the official volumes of the Court's decisions. A law-review article cited as 82 *Yale L.J.* 920 (1973) means that the article was published in 1973 and can be found at page 920 of volume 82 of the *Yale Law Journal*. Whenever possible, I have identified written sources as well as persons interviewed. Because of the sensitive nature of the materials and interviews, however, many sources must remain confidential and are identified in the notes as confidential sources (CS).

PREFACE
15 "[Justice] Black was . . . ": W. Rehnquist, *The Supreme Court: How It Was, How It Is* (1987), p. 33.

PART ONE: RACE
17 Epigraph: *Patterson* draft dissent of Justice William J. Brennan, Jr. (WJB), 6-12-89, Thurgood Marshall Papers (TMP), Library of Congress, Washington, D.C.

CHAPTER ONE: A DREAM DESTROYED
19 *Patterson v. McLean Credit Union*: 491 U.S. 164 (1976).
20 *Runyon v. McCrary*: 427 U.S. 160 (1989).
22 "It was a": *Patterson* trial transcript.
   "was going to": *ibid*.
23 "blacks are known": *ibid*.
   "She felt humiliated": *ibid*.
   "Well, is this": *ibid*.
24 *Patterson* appellate decision: U.S. Court of Appeals, Fourth Circuit, 805 F. 2d 1143 (1986).
   "Mr. Chief Justice": transcript of *Patterson* oral argument before the Supreme Court, U.S. Supreme Court Library (SCL), Washington, D.C.
27 Clerk's memorandum: confidential sources (CS).
   Jones v. Mayer: 392 U.S. 409 (1986).
28 Justices' *Patterson* conference: TMP, CS.
30 "accords with the": *Runyon, op. cit.*
31 Background on Rehnquist: R. Mersky and J. Jacobstein, eds., *The Supreme Court of the United States: Hearings and Reports on Successful and Unsuccessful*

Nominations of Supreme Court Justices by the Senate Judiciary Committee, vols. 8, 12 and 12A; Robert H. Jackson Papers (RHJP), Oct. 1952 Court term, Library of Congress, Washington, D.C.; S. Davis, *Justice Rehnquist and the Constitution* (1989); W. Rehnquist, *op. cit.*; D. Savage, *Turning Right: The Making of the Rehnquist Court* (1992), pp. 32–47; J. Simon, *In His Own Image: The Supreme Court in Richard Nixon's America* (1973), pp. 229–241; W. Weaver, "Mr. Justice Rehnquist, Dissenting," *New York Times Magazine*, 10-13-74; CS. "I'm going to": *Washington Post*, 7-6-86.
"We learned early": *ibid.*

32   F. Hayek, *The Road to Serfdom* (1944).
"Harvard liberalism": *Washington Post*, 7-6-86.
"Bill was so": *New York Times Magazine*, 10-13-74.
"He could give": D. Savage, *op. cit.*, p 34.
Terry v. Adams: 345 U.S. 461 (1953).

33   "I have a": William H. Rehnquist (WHR) to Justice Robert H. Jackson (RHJ), Oct. 1952 term, undated, RHJP.
"It is about": *ibid.*

34   "To the argument": *ibid.*
"The particular memorandum": *New York Times*, 12-9-71.

35   "Justice Jackson did": *New York Times*, 8-11-86.
"absurd": *Time*, 6-30-86.
Jackson unpublished *Brown* memorandum: 3-15-54, RHJP.
"a perfectly reasonable": D. Savage, *op. cit.*, p. 38.

36   "left-wing": *Washington Post*, 7-7-86.
"extreme solicitude for": *U.S. News*, 12-13-57.
"unwanted customer": D. Savage, *op. cit.*, p. 32.

37   "with a motive": *Los Angeles Times*, 9-7-86.
"an insult to": *Washington Post*, 7-7-86.
"may accept you": *ibid.*
Rehnquist's civil rights voting record: Report of the NAACP Legal Defense and Educational Fund, Inc., Sept. 1986.
Segregated-school tax decision: *Bob Jones University v. U.S.*, 461 U.S. 617 (1983).

38   Blackmun reaction: author's interview (AI) with Justice Harry A. Blackmun (HAB), 5-7-91, Washington, D.C.
"some neglected subtlety": *Patterson v. McLean Credit Union*, 485 U.S. 617 (1988).

39   "If the Court": *ibid.*
"One might think": *ibid.*

40   "I am in": Justice Anthony M. Kennedy (AMK) to WHR, 4-8-88, CS.
Regents of University of California v. Bakke: 438 U.S. 265 (1978).
Historians' amicus brief: *Patterson* briefs, SCL.

42   Congressional amicus brief: *ibid.*
State attorneys general amicus brief: *ibid.*

CHAPTER TWO: "FIVE VOTES CAN DO ANYTHING AROUND HERE"

43   "Brenda had a": AI with Julius L. Chambers (JLC), 2-3-92, New York City.

44   "And as we": transcript of *Patterson* oral argument, SCL.

45   Clerk's memorandum: CS.

46   Justices' *Patterson* conference: TMP, CS.

49   Background on Brennan: R. Mersky and J. Jacobstein, eds., *op. cit.*, vol. 6; K. Eisler, *A Justice for All: William J. Brennan, Jr., and the Decisions That Transformed America* (1993); R. Goldman with D. Gallen, *Justice William J. Brennan, Jr.: Freedom First* (1994); N. Hentoff, "Profile: The Constitutionalist," *New Yorker*, 3-12-90; J. Leeds, "A Life on the Court," *New York Times Magazine*, 10-5-86; CS.
      "I don't expect": *New Yorker*, 3-12-90.
      "What got me": *ibid.*
50   "Did you see": *ibid.*
      "the friendly Irish": *New York Times*, 9-30-56.
51   "all the ins": *ibid.*
      "is also proof": *ibid.*
52   *Brown v. Board of Education*: 347 U.S. 483 (1954).
      Cooper v. Aaron: 358 U.S. 1 (1958).
      "We knew the": AI with Justice William J. Brennan, Jr., 11-17-87.
      "which promise realistically": *Green v. County School Board*, 391 U.S. 430 (1986).
53   *Swann v. Charlotte-Mecklenburg Bd. of Education*: 402 U.S. 1 (1970).
      Brennan's memorandum in *Swann*: 12-30-70, Justice William J. Brennan, Jr., Papers (WJBP), Library of Congress.
      "[C]ommon sense": *Keyes v. School District No. 1, Denver, Colo.*, 413 U.S. 189 (1973).
      Title VII decision: *United Steel Workers v. Weber*, 443 U.S. 193 (1979).
54   "Five votes": *New Yorker, op. cit.*
      Internal Court materials on *Patterson*: Oct.–Dec. 1988, CS.
61   Brennan's draft opinion: 12-3-88, TMP.

CHAPTER THREE: FINE PHRASES

62   White's draft dissent: 1-12-89, TMP.
      City of Richmond v. J. A. Croson Co.: 388 U.S. 469 (1989).
63   Kennedy's draft opinion: 4-27-89, TMP.
64   Internal Court materials on *Patterson*: April, May, 1989, CS.
65   Brennan's draft opinion: 5-2-89, TMP.
66   Kennedy's draft opinion: 5-16-89, *ibid.*
      White's draft opinion, 5-17-89, *ibid.*
67   Background on Kennedy: R. Mersky and J. Jacobstein, eds., *op. cit.*, vols. 15 and 15A; D. Savage, *op. cit.*, pp. 169–182; CS.
70   "an unconstitutional decision": E. Bonner, *Battle for Justice: How the Bork Nomination Shocked America* (1989), p. 92.
      "In Robert Bork's": R. Mersky and J. Jacobstein, eds., *op. cit.*, vol. 14.
      "[you] did not have": *ibid.*, vol. 15.
71   "I do not": *ibid.*
      Kennedy's draft opinion: 5-22-89, TMP.
74   *Griggs v. Duke Power*: 401 U.S. 424 (1971).
      Wards Cove Packing Co. v. Atonio: 490 U.S. 642 (1989).
      Martin v. Wilks: 490 U.S. 755 (1989).
75   Brennan's draft opinion: 6-8-89, TMP.
76   Kennedy's draft opinion: 6-11-89, *ibid.*
      Brennan's draft opinion: 6-12-89, *ibid.*
77   Kennedy's footnote: 6-13-89, *ibid.*

78   Internal Court materials: 6-13-89, CS.
79   Brennan's draft opinion: 6-13-89, TMP.
      Kennedy's final draft: 6-14-89, *ibid.*
      "a field goal": *New York Times*, 6-16-89.
      "a disaster for": *ibid.*
80   "a victory in": *ibid.*
81   Civil Rights Act of 1991: P.L. 102–166, 105 Stat. 1071.

PART TWO: ABORTION

83   Epigraph: *Webster* draft dissent of HAB, 6-21-89, TMP.

CHAPTER FOUR: A BULL BY THE TAIL
86   "It was a": AI with HAB, 5-7-91.
87   "I did exactly": S. Weddington, *A Question of Choice* (1992), p. 14.
88   "Go get 'em": *ibid.*, p. 110.
89   Transcript of *Roe* oral argument: SCL.
      "The truth was": S. Weddington, *op. cit.*, p. 117.
90   Blackmun's concerns: AI with HAB, 5-7-91.
      "we had a": *ibid.*
      Justices' *Roe* conference: TMP, WJBP, Justice William O. Douglas Papers (WODP), Library of Congress.
      Background on *Roe*: D. Garrow, *Liberty and Sexuality: The Right to Privacy and the Making of Roe v. Wade* (1994); D. O'Brien, *Storm Center: The Supreme Court in American Politics* (1986); B. Schwartz, *The Ascent of Pragmatism* (1990) and *The Unpublished Opinions of the Burger Court* (1988); B. Woodward and S. Armstrong, *The Brethren* (1979).
93   Blackmun's recollection of conference vote: AI with HAB, 5-7-91.
      "to sustain the": Justice William O. Douglas (WOD) to Chief Justice Warren E. Burger (WEB), 12-18-71, WODP.
      "At the close": WEB to WOD, 12-20-71, *ibid.*
      "The confusion surrounding": AI with HAB, 5-7-91.
95   "The right to": WOD draft, 12-22-71, WODP.
      Griswold v. Connecticut: 381 U.S. 479 (1965).
      Brennan's critique: 12-30-71, WODP.
96   "I nominate for": HAB to WEB, 1-18-72, *ibid.*
      Blackmun's first draft in *Roe*: 5-18-72, WODP.
97   "Dear Harry": WJB to HAB, 5-18-72, WJBP.
      "[W]e should meet": WOD to HAB, 5-19-72, WODP.
      Blackmun's first draft in *Doe*: 5-25-72, *ibid.*
98   Douglas's support for Blackmun's drafts: WOD to HAB, 5-25-72, WODP.
99   "these cases": Burger memorandum, 5-31-72, WODP.
      Blackmun's response: 5-31-72, *ibid.*
      "fine job": WOD to HAB, 5-31-72, *ibid.*
      Powell's and Rehnquist's meeting with Blackmun: AI with Justice Lewis F. Powell, Jr. (LFP), 9-25-90, Washington, D.C.
      "from a purely": Powell memorandum, 6-1-72, WODP.
100 "telling what is": WOD to WEB, 6-1-72, *ibid.*
      Background on Douglas: W. Douglas, *Go East, Young Man* (1974) and *The*

Court Years (1980); J. Simon, *Independent Journey: The Life of William O. Douglas* (1980).

"All your anxiety": W. Douglas, *Go East*, p. i.

"the outstanding professor": J. Simon, *op. cit.*, p. 109.

101   Douglas's procreation opinion: *Skinner v. Oklahoma*, 316 U.S. 535 (1942).

Douglas's opinion on right to be left alone: *Public Utilities Commission v. Pollak*, 343 U.S. (1952).

"I have only": J. Simon, *op. cit.*, p. 250.

"Bill Douglas is": AI with Justice Potter Stewart (PS), 12-7-78, Washington, D.C.

102   "We must realize": W. Douglas, *Points of Rebellion* (1970), p. 95.

"inflammatory volume": J. Simon, *op. cit.*, p. 405.

Douglas draft dissent: 6-2-72, WODP.

103   "Dear Bill": WJB to WOD, 6-3-72, *ibid.*

"high-handed way": WJB to WOD, undated, WODP.

104   Douglas's sixth draft: 6-13-72, *ibid.*

"Douglas literally exploded": AI with HAB, 11-16-92, Washington, D.C.

Blackmun's reassurances to Douglas: *ibid.*

105   "I am upset": WOD to WEB, 7-4-72, WODP.

"simply to keep": WEB to WOD, 7-27-72, *ibid.*

106   "that chapter in": WOD to WEB, 8-7-72, *ibid.*

Blackmun's research: AI with HAB, 5-7-91.

Justices' *Roe* conference: WJBP; WODP; TMP.

107   Blackmun's first draft: 11-21-72, WODP.

108   Background on Blackmun: R. Mersky and J. Jacobstein, eds., *op. cit.* vol. 8; D. Savage, *op. cit.*, pp. 233–238; J. Simon, *In His Own Image*, pp. 141–148; J. Jenkins, "A Candid Talk with Justice Blackmun," *New York Times Magazine*, 2-20-83; AI with HAB, 5-7-91; CS.

"Felix would get": AI with HAB, 11-16-92.

109   Blackmun confirmation hearings: R. Mersky and J. Jacobstein, eds., *op. cit.*, vol. 8.

110   Blackmun opinion in welfare mother case: *Wyman v. James*, 400 U.S. 309 (1971).

Blackmun opinion in Jackson swimming pool case: *Palmer v. Thompson*, 403 U.S. 217 (1971).

111   "White Anglo-Saxon": *New York Times Magazine*, 12-6-70.

113   Marshall's letter: TM to HAB, 12-12-72, TMP.

114   "One of my": PS to HAB, 12-14-72, WODP.

Rehnquist's draft dissent: 1-11-73, *ibid.*

Blackmun's statement: 1-16-73, *ibid.*

CHAPTER FIVE: ANYONE WHO CAN COUNT

116   Court's first post-*Roe* directive: *Planned Parenthood v. Danforth*, 428 U.S. 52 (1976).

117   "work for the": T. White, *America in Search of Itself* (1978), p. 319.

Lee's amicus brief: SCL.

Akron decision: *Akron v. Akron Center for Reproductive Health*, 462 U.S. 416 (1983).

Maher v. Roe: 432 U.S. 464 (1977).

118 *Akron* oral argument: transcript, *ibid.*
119 O'Connor's draft dissent: 5-10-83, TMP.
     Background on O'Connor: R. Mersky and J. Jacobstein, eds., *op. cit.*, 1983 supp.; D. Savage, *op. cit.*, pp. 111–116; CS.
122 "You have intelligence": *Washington Post*, 7-12-81.
123 "a disaster": D. Savage, *op. cit.*, p. 114.
124 "The *Roe* framework": A. Cox, *The Role of the Supreme Court in American Government* (1976).
     Fried's brief: *Thornburgh v. American College of Obstetricians and Gynecologists* (1986), SCL.
125 "a very amazing": L. Caplan, *The Tenth Justice: The Solicitor General and the Rule of Law* (1987), p. 143.
     Thornburgh decision: 476 U.S. 747 (1986).
128 *Times* poll: *New York Times*, 4-26-89.
     "With only four": L. Tribe, *Abortion: The Clash of Absolutes* (1990), p. 20.
129 Transcript of *Webster* oral argument: SCL.
130 "Clearly the threat": *New York Times*, 4-27-89.
132 Justices' *Webster* conference: TMP, CS.
134 Rehnquist's first draft: 5-25-89, TMP.
135 "Dear Chief": JPS to WHR, 5-30-89, *ibid.*
136 Blackmun's first draft dissent: 6-21-89, *ibid.*
137 O'Connor's draft opinion: 6-23-89, *ibid.*
     Scalia's opinion: *Webster v. Reproductive Health Services*, 492 U.S. 490 (1989).
138 Background on Scalia: R. Mersky and J. Jacobstein, eds., *op. cit.*, vol. 13; D. Savage, *op. cit.*, pp. 23, 24; CS.
     "People just competed": *Washington Post*, 6-22-86.
139 "It never bothered": *Los Angeles Times*, 7-6-86.
     "have found rights": *Washington Post*, 6-22-86.
140 "Not only had": *Washington University Law Quarterly*, 147 (1979).
141 "understands the doctrine": *ibid.*
     "he'll plant his": *Washington Post*, 6-18-86.

CHAPTER SIX: A NEUTRON BOMB

144 Minnesota and Ohio cases: *Hodgson v. Minnesota* and *Minnesota v. Hodgson*, 487 U.S. 417 (1990), and *Ohio v. Akron Center for Reproductive Health*, 497 U.S. 502 (1990).
145 Judge Alsop's decision: petitioner's *Hodgson* brief, SCL.
     Transcript of *Hodgson* oral argument: *ibid.*
146 Justices' *Hodgson* conference: TMP, CS.
147 O'Connor's clarification: 12-4-89, TMP.
     Stevens's memorandum: 12-7-89, *ibid.*
148 Rehnquist's assignment: 12-8-89, *ibid.*
     "John's views": Justice Sandra D. O'Connor (SDO) to WHR, 12-8-89, *ibid.*
     "As matters now": WHR to the Conference, 12-8-89, *ibid.*
149 "[at] the end": SDO to the Conference, 6-11-90, *ibid.*
     "two unfortunate consequences": JPS to the Conference, 6-15-90, *ibid.*
     Stevens's opinion: 6-15-90, *ibid.*
150 "join as much": HAB to WJB, TM and JPS, 6-18-90, *ibid.*
     "I am in": WJB to HAB, 6-18-90, *ibid.*
     Scalia's opinion: 6-20-90, *ibid.*

151 Transcript of *Rust* oral argument: SCL.
Rust v. Sullivan: 500 U.S. 173 (1991).
153 Souter's recommendations: DHS to WHR, 4-25-91, TMP.
"The votes are": AI with HAB, 5-7-91.
154 Court's 1986 decision *Thornburgh v. American Coll. of Obst. and Gyn.*: 476 U.S. 747 (1986).
155 Transcript of *Casey* oral argument: SCL.
156 *Casey* story: CS.
158 "Have I ever": *New York Times*, 7-21-90.
Background on Souter: R. Mersky and J. Jacobstein, eds., *op. cit.*, vol. 16; D. Savage, *op. cit.*, pp. 352–358; D. Garrow, "Justice Souter: A Surprising Kind of Conservative," *New York Times Magazine*, 9-25-94; CS.
159 "about 135 pounds": *New York Times*, 7-24-90.
"the single most": *ibid*.
161 "keen intellect as": *ibid*.
162 "his own best": *New York Times*, 9-27-90.
"After days of": *ibid*.
"putting a lot": *Washington Post*, 7-24-90.
165 "was as if": CS.
Casey decision: 112 Sup. Ct. 2791 (1992).
167 "Daddy, are you": AI with HAB, 11-16-92.

PART THREE: CRIME AND PUNISHMENT

169 Epigraph: Marshall memorandum to the Conference in *McCleskey v. Bowers*, 9-24-91, TMP.

CHAPTER SEVEN: A FATAL MISTAKE

171 Stewart's observations: AI with PS, 12-7-78.
172 Greenhouse's observations: *New York Times Magazine*, 3-7-93.
173 Boger's expectations and strategy: author's telephone interview with John C. Boger (JCB), 4-28-93.
Background on *McCleskey* case: briefs, SCL.
174 *Furman v. Georgia*: 408 U.S. 238 (1972).
Gregg v. Georgia: 428 U.S. 153 (1976).
Batson v. Kentucky: 476 U.S. 79 (1986).
175 "To proceed when": transcript of *McCleskey* oral argument, SCL.
178 "They were all": AI with JCB, 4-28-93.
179 White memorandum: 10-16-86, TMP.
Justices' *McCleskey* conference: TMP, CS.
181 Background on Powell: R. Mersky and J. Jacobstein, eds., *op. cit.*, vol. 8; J. Jeffries, *Justice Lewis F. Powell, Jr.* (1994); J. Simon, *In His Own Image*, pp. 243–249; AI with LFP, 9-25-90; CS.
183 "was not only": AI with LFP, 9-25-90.
McCleskey v. Kemp: 481 U.S. 279 (1987).
"I was unhappy": AI with LFP, 9-25-90.
184 "We are the": *ibid*.
Powell's views on *McCleskey* and the death penalty: see generally J. Jeffries, *op. cit.*, pp. 434–454.
"at his last": AI with JCB, 4-28-93.

"We had always": *ibid.*
185   "The only way": *ibid.*
     Massiah v. U.S.: 377 U.S. 201 (1964).
186   "police officers had": *McCleskey* transcript, SCL.
     Appeals court decision: 890 F. 2d 342 (1989).
     Boger's expectations: AI with JCB, 4-28-93.
187   "This is a": transcript of *McCleskey* oral argument, SCL.

CHAPTER EIGHT: "GUILTY AS SIN"

190   Background on *Fulminante* case: briefs, SCL.
191   "He would have": respondent's brief in *Fulminante, ibid.*
192   Arizona Sup. Ct. decision: *State v. Fulminante*, 778 p. 2d 602 (1988).
     "had absolutely no": transcript of *Fulminante* oral argument, SCL.
193   Justices' *Fulminante* conference: TMP, CS.
     "guilty as sin": WHR to RHJ, Oct. 1952 term, undated memorandum for *Stein v. New York*, 346 U.S. 156 (1953), RHJP.
194   Background on White: R. Mersky and J. Jacobstein, eds., *op. cit.*, vol. 6; D. Savage, *op. cit.*, pp. 88–94; J. Simon, *In His Own Image*, pp. 168–174; CS.
197   "to genuinely coerced": SDO to BRW, 11-29-90, TMP.
     "I think that": WHR draft, 11-29-90, *ibid.*
198   "As Byron's opinion": AMK to WHR and BRW, 12-9-90, *ibid.*
     "I realize now": DHS to WHR and BRW, 12-21-90, *ibid.*
     "a limited category": AS to WHR, 1-15-91, *ibid.*
199   "At Conference I": SDO to WHR, 1-9-91, *ibid.*
     "I think the": WHR draft, 1-11-91, *ibid.*
     "I have spoken": WHR to the Conference, 1-15-91, *ibid.*
200   "In the interest": AS to BRW, 1-17-91, *ibid.*
     "the Court properly": WHR draft, 3-18-91, *ibid.*
     "apart, perhaps, from": AMK concurrence, *Arizona v. Fulminante*, 111 Sup. Ct. 1246 (1991).
201   "HABEAS CORPUS, THEN": WHR to RHJ, Oct. 1952 term, undated, RHJP.
     "verges on the": *New York Times*, 5-16-90.
202   Kennedy opinion: *McCleskey v. Zant*, 111 Sup. Ct. 1454 (1991).
203   "shocked at the": AI with JCB, 4-28-93.
     "lawless": Marshall draft, 4-3-91, TMP.
     Stevens's memorandum: JPS to TM, 4-3-91, *ibid.*
204   "They did the": Marshall interview, Columbia University Oral History Collection (COHC), New York City.
     Background on Marshall: R. Mersky and J. Jacobstein, eds., *op. cit.*, vol. 7; TMP; Marshall interview, COHC; NAACP Papers (NAACPP), Library of Congress; R. Goldman and D. Gallen, *Thurgood Marshall: Justice for All* (1992); C. Rowan, *Dream Makers, Dream Breaker: The World of Thurgood Marshall* (1993); M. Tushnet, *Making Civil Rights Law: Thurgood Marshall and the Supreme Court, 1936–1961* (1994); CS.
     "ruined": Marshall interview, COHC.
     "He never told": *ibid.*
205   "Ironpants": *ibid.*
     "drive home to": *ibid.*
     Missouri segregation decision: *Missouri ex rel Gaines v. Canada*, 305 U.S. 337 (1938).

"I intend to": R. Goldman and D. Gallen, *op. cit.*, p. 26.

206 "the powers": TM memorandum to NAACP New York office, 11-17-41, NAACPP.

Background on *Lyons* case: *ibid.*

"nigger lawyer from": TM to Walter White (WW), 2-2-41, *ibid.*

"Imagine it": TM to WW, 1-29-41, *ibid.*

207 "you'll be the": *Daily Oklahoman*, 1-29-41.

"the defendant may": *ibid.*

"You know": TM to WW, 2-2-41, NAACPP.

Supreme Court decision: *Lyons v. Oklahoma*, 322 U.S. 596 (1943).

"Many Negroes guilty": Marshall report, NAACPP.

208 "[T]he mob got": Marshall interview, COHC.

White primary decision, *Smith v. Allright*, 321 U.S. 649 (1944).

Morgan v. Virginia: 328 U.S. 373 (1946).

Shelley v. Kraemer: 334 U.S. 1 (1948).

"Separate educational facilities": *Brown, op. cit.*

209 "Lawyer, don't let": Marshall interview, COHC.

Coleman v. Thompson: 111 Sup. Ct. 2546 (1991).

Death penalty decisions: *Penry v. Lynaugh*, 492 U.S. 302 (1991); *Wilkins v. Missouri*, 109 Sup. Ct. 2969 (1991).

Harmelin decision: *Harmelin v. Michigan*, 111 Sup. Ct. 2680 (1991).

Police investigation decisions: *California v. Acevedo*, 111 Sup. Ct. 1982 (1991); *County of Riverside v. McLaughlin*, 111 Sup. Ct. 1661 (1991).

210 Bus search decision: *Florida v. Bostick*, 111 Sup. Ct. 2382.

"a loyal foot soldier": *California v. Acevedo, op. cit.*

Payne v. Tennessee: 111 Sup. Ct. 1661 (1991).

Overturned precedents: *Booth v. Maryland*, 482 U.S. 496 (1987); *South Carolina v. Gathers*, 490 U.S. 805 (1989).

CHAPTER NINE: DEPRECIATING LIBERTY

213 "Only in America": *New York Times*, 7-2-91.

Background on Thomas: Senate Judiciary Committee hearings, *New York Times*, Sept. 11–17, 1991; T. Phelps and H. Winternitz, *Capitol Games: The Inside Story of Clarence Thomas, Anita Hill and a Supreme Court Nomination* (1992), pp. 31–60; D. Savage, *op. cit.*, pp. 423–437; J. Williams, "A Question of Fairness," *Atlantic Monthly*, Feb. 1987; CS.

"It was hard": *New York Times*, 9-11-91.

"Old man Can't": T. Phelps and H. Winternitz, *op. cit.*, p. 38.

"Boy, you are": *ibid.*, p. 37.

214 "Smile, Clarence, so": *Atlantic Monthly, op. cit.*

"Good, I hope": *ibid.*

"Turn 20 summer": T. Phelps and H. Winternitz, *op. cit.*, p. 46.

215 "You had to": *ibid.*, pp. 49, 50.

216 "I am unalterably": quoted in *Time*, 7-15-91.

217 "I'll put the": *ibid.*

"The most compassionate": *ibid.*

"were unyielding in": *New York Times*, 7-2-91.

219 "Senator": *New York Times*, 9-12-91.

"My motto is": T. Phelps and H. Winternitz, *op. cit.*, p. 178.

220 "I believe if": *New York Times*, 9-24-91.

"an outrage": *ibid.*

"We had a": *ibid.*

221 "there is no": AMK to the Conference, *McCleskey v. Bowers*, 9-24-91, TMP.

Marshall memorandum: TM to the Conference, *ibid.*

222 "the ugly issue": *New York Times*, 10-8-91.

"I have never": *New York Times*, 10-12-91.

223 Hill charges: *ibid.*

"This is a": *ibid.*

224 Recent publications on Thomas–Hill hearings: D. Brock, *The Real Anita Hill: The Untold Story* (1993); J. Danforth, *Resurrection: The Confirmation of Clarence Thomas* (1994); J. Mayer and J. Abramson, *Strange Justice: The Selling of Clarence Thomas* (1994).

225 "unabashed judicial activism": Stevens's dissent in *California v. Acevedo, op. cit.*

"A word": Stevens's address, "The Bill of Rights: A Century of Progress," University of Chicago Law School, 10-25-91.

227 Background on Stevens: R. Mersky and J. Jacobstein, eds., *op. cit.*, vol. 8A; S. Taylor, Jr., "The Last Moderate," *American Lawyer*, June 1990; CS.

"ivory tower jurisprudence": WHR to RHJ, undated, RHJP.

228 "This case brings": *New York Times*, 11-29-75.

229 1987 decision: *Johnson v. Transportation Agency*, 480 U.S. 616 (1987).

230 "What matters most": *New York Times*, 7-28-91.

"I would like": *New York Times*, 9-12-91.

"I could not": L. Higginbotham, Jr., "An Open Letter to Justice Clarence Thomas from a Federal Judicial Colleague," 140 U. of Pa. L.R. 1005 (1992).

231 Hudson decision: *Hudson v. McMillian*, 112 Sup. Ct. 995 (1992).

232 "overriding justification": *Riggins v. Nevada*, 112 Sup. Ct. 1810 (1992).

"may make eminent": *Foucha v. Louisiana*, 112 Sup. Ct. 1780 (1992).

Texas death penalty decision: *Graham v. Collins*, 113 Sup. Ct. 89 (1993).

PART FOUR: THE FIRST AMENDMENT

235 Epigraphs: *Allegheny* draft opinion of AMK, 6-16-89, TMP; *Allegheny* draft opinion of HAB, 6-26-89, TMP.

CHAPTER TEN: JEFFERSON'S WALL

238 "Rambo-mania": *Los Angeles Times*, 3-13-89.

misleading: *Wallace v. Jaffree*, 472 U.S. 38 (1985).

239 *Texas v. Johnson*: 491 U.S. 397 (1989).

Allegheny County (Pa.) v. Greater Pittsburgh Chapter of the American Civil Liberties Union: 492 U.S. 573 (1989).

240 Fried's *Allegheny* brief: SCL.

243 Transcript of *Allegheny* oral argument: *ibid.*

244 Clerk's memorandum: CS.

Lynch v. Donnelly: 465 U.S. 668 (1984).

Justices' *Allegheny* conference: TMP, CS.

245 "As usual, I": TM to WHR, 11-1-90, TMP.

247 Blackmun draft: 5-30-89, *ibid.*

"Usually, to quote": HAB to the Conference, 5-30-89, *ibid.*

"Assuming that severe": JPS to HAB, 5-31-89, *ibid.*

Everson v. Bd. of Education: 330 U.S. 1 (1947).

248 *McCollum v. Bd. of Education*: 333 U.S. 203 (1948).
Engel v. Vitale: 370 U.S. 421 (1962).
Lemon v. Kurtzman: 403 U.S. 602 (1971).

250 "The holidays are": HAB to the Conference, 5-30-89, TMP.
Stewart's recollections: AI with PS, 12-7-78.

251 Kennedy draft: 6-16-89, TMP.

253 *Marsh v. Chambers*: 463 U.S. 783 (1983).

254 "Acting Chief Justice": HAB to the Conference, 2-9-90, TMP.
"Tony's writing requires": HAB to the Conference, 6-26-89, *ibid*.
Blackmun draft: *ibid*.

255 "alienating": *Washington Post*, 7-4-89.
"seems to be": *ibid*.

CHAPTER ELEVEN: "AMERICA, THE RED, WHITE AND BLUE, WE SPIT ON YOU"

257 "America, the red": *Los Angeles Times*, 3-13-89.

258 Cole's *Johnson* brief: SCL.

259 *West Virginia Bd. of Education v. Barnette*: 319 U.S. 624 (1943).

260 *Street v. New York*: 394 U.S. 576 (1969).

262 Johnson's instruction to Kunstler: AI with William M. Kunstler (WMK), 6-25-91, New York City.
"the Gang of": *ibid*.
Kunstler's prediction: *ibid*.

263 *Spence v. Washington*: 418 U.S. 405 (1974).
Transcript of *Johnson* oral argument: SCL.

268 New Hampshire decision: *Wooley v. Maynard*, 430 U.S. 705 (1977).

269 "the new barbarians": S. Davis, *op. cit.*, p. 6.
Chaplinsky v. New Hampshire: 315 U.S. 568 (1942).

270 Justices' *Johnson* conference: TMP, CS.

271 "I struggled with": HAB to WJB, 6-19-89, TMP.

272 Brennan draft: 6-4-89, *ibid*.

273 *Brandenburg v. Ohio*: 395 U.S. 444 (1969).

274 Kennedy draft: 6-18-89, TMP.
Rehnquist draft: 6-14-89, *ibid*.

275 "profound disappointment": *New York Times*, 6-23-89.
"an exercise in": *ibid*.
"Yesterday these six": *Washington Post*, 6-23-89.
"I have to": *ibid*.

CHAPTER TWELVE: HISTORY LESSONS

276 Scholars' testimony: J. Swanson and C. Castle, eds., *1990 First Amendment Handbook* (1990).

278 "happy to be": United Press International, 2-14-90.
"It's not a": *ibid*.
"Commies, go home": *New York Times*, 5-16-90.

279 Transcript of *Eichman* oral argument: SCL.

280 Brennan draft: 5-19-90, TMP.

281 "[f]lag-burning endangers": *Washington Post*, 6-14-90.
Lee v. Weisman: 112 Sup. Ct. 2649 (1992).

"As a Jew": *American Bar Association Journal*, Feb. 1992.
282 "In this case": respondent's *Weisman* brief, SCL.
284 "[I]f I were": R. Mersky and J. Jacobstein, eds., *op. cit.*, vol. 16.
    "I have an": *New York Times*, 9-13-91.
285 Transcript of *Weisman* oral argument: SCL.
289 "He listens": *Legal Times*, 7-6-92.
291 *Bd. of Education of Kiryas Joel Village School Dist. v. Grumet*: 114 Sup. Ct. 2481 (1994).
    Kiryas Joel oral argument: *New York Times*, 3-31-94.

EPILOGUE

CHAPTER THIRTEEN: BEYOND THE REHNQUIST COURT

298 "CONGRATULATIONS RUTH GINSBURG": *New York Times*, 7-25-93.
299 Ginsburg statement: *New York Times*, 7-21-93.
301 "She was the": *New York Times*, 7-13-94.
302 "Of course, that": *ibid.*
303 "an impenetrable bulwark": I. Glaser, *Visions of Liberty: The Bill of Rights for All Americans* (1991), p. 47.

ACKNOWLEDGMENTS

Many people helped make this project a completed book: Esther Newberg, my literary agent, whose advice was always on the mark; Alice Mayhew and Eric Steel at Simon & Schuster, whose expert editing gave the final manuscript shape and focus; my sources, many of whom spoke to me in confidence, for their time and invaluable insights; Chairman Bernard H. Mendik and the other members of the New York Law School Board of Trustees, who granted me a sabbatical to work on the book; Dean Harry H. Wellington and Professor Nadine Strossen of New York Law School, who read an early draft of the manuscript and made important suggestions for its improvement; Professor Randy Hertz of New York University Law School, who reviewed an early draft of chapters in Part Three; Steven R. Shapiro, legal director of the American Civil Liberties Union, who read and critiqued an early draft of chapters on the First Amendment; David Wigdor, assistant chief of the Manuscript Division of the Library of Congress, and the fine staff in the Manuscript Division, who made my research both pleasant and productive; the staff at the U.S. Supreme Court Library, who was always helpful; William Mills, associate librarian at New York Law School, who guided me to many important references; Oliver Aga, a student at New York Law School, who provided able research assistance; Maria Del Bagno and Debbie Denhart, who worked tirelessly and with meticulous care to produce the manuscript; and my wife, Marcia, who, as always, offered both sensitive support and superb editorial judgment.

INDEX

ABOUT THE AUTHOR

James F. Simon received a Bachelor of Arts degree from Yale College and a law degree from the Yale Law School. He has served as correspondent and contributing editor of *Time* magazine, specializing in legal affairs. He is the author of *The Judge; In His Own Image: The Supreme Court in Richard Nixon's America; Independent Journey: The Life of William O. Douglas;* and *The Antagonists: Hugo Black, Felix Frankfurter and Civil Liberties in Modern America. In His Own Image* won the American Bar Association's Silver Gavel Award in 1974. *Independent Journey* won the Scribes Award of the American Society of Writers on Legal Subjects in 1981. *The Antagonists* was awarded a Certificate of Merit by the American Bar Association in 1990. Simon has been a visiting lecturer in American studies at Yale University and a Harvard Fellow in law and humanities at Harvard University. He is the former Dean, and now Martin Professor of Law, at New York Law School.